DELEGATION AND ACCOUNTABILITY IN
EUROPEAN INTEGRATION

THE LIBRARY OF LEGISLATIVE STUDIES

General Editor
Philip Norton

ISSN 1460-9649

A series of new and recent books exploring the role of legislature in contemporary political systems. The volumes typically draw together a team of country specialist to provide in-depth analysis.

Parliaments in Contemporary Western Europe
edited by Philip Norton

Volume 1: *Parliaments and Governments in Western Europe*
Volume 2: *Parliaments and Pressure Groups in Western Europe*
Volume 3: *Parliaments and Citizens in Western Europe*

The Uneasy Relationships between Parliamentary Members and Leaders
edited by Lawrence D. Longley and Reuven Y. Hazan

Parliaments in Asia
edited by Philip Norton and Nizam Ahmed

Conscience and Parliament
edited by Philip Cowley

The New Roles of Parliamentary Committees
edited by Lawrence D. Longley and Roger H. Davidson

Members of Parliament in Western Europe
Roles and Behaviour
edited by Wolfgang C. Müller and Thomas Saalfeld

Parliaments in Western Europe
edited by Philip Norton

The New Parliaments of Central and Eastern Europe
edited by David M. Olson and Philip Norton

National Parliaments and the European Union
edited by Philip Norton

Delegation and Accountability in European Integration

THE NORDIC PARLIAMENTARY DEMOCRACIES AND THE EUROPEAN UNION

Editors

TORBJÖRN BERGMAN
ERIK DAMGAARD

FRANK CASS

LONDON • PORTLAND, OR

First published in 2000 in Great Britain by
FRANK CASS AND COMPANY LIMITED
Newbury House, 900 Eastern Avenue, London IG2 7HH, England

and in the United States of America by
FRANK CASS
International Specialized Book Services, Inc.
5804 N.E. Hassalo Street, Portland, Oregon 97213-3644

Website: www.frankcass.com

British Library Cataloguing in Publication Data

Delegation and accountability in European integration : the
Nordic parliamentary democracies. – (The library of legislative
studies)
1. European Union – Scandinavia 2. Representative government
and representation – Scandinavia 3. Scandinavia – Foreign
relations – European Union countries 4. Scandinavia – Politics
and government
I. Bergman, Torbjörn II. Damgaard, E. (Erik)
320.9'48

ISBN 0 7146 5066 8 (hb)
ISBN 0 7146 8115 6 (pb)

Library of Congress Cataloging-in-Publication Data

Delegation and accountability in European integration: the Nordic parliamentary
democracies and the European Union / editors, Torbjörn Bergman, Erik Damgaard.
    p. cm. – (The library of legislative studies, ISSN 1460-9649)
"This group of studies first appeared in a special issue of Journal of legislative studies
... vol. 6, no. 1" – T.p. verso.
ISBN 0-7146-5066-8 – ISBN 0-7146-8115-6 (pbk.)
    1. Scandinavia – Politics and government – 1945– 2. Delegation of powers –
Scandinavia. 3. Responsibility – Scandinavia. 4. European Union – Scandinavia.
I. Bergman, Torbjörn. II. Damgaard, Erik. II. Series.

JN7011 .D46 2000
328.48'0749 – dc21   00-020072

This group of studies first appeared in a Special Issue of *Journal of Legislative Studies* (ISSN
    1357-2334), Vol.6, No.1 (Spring 2000), [Delegation and Accountability in European
    Integration].

Printed in Great Britain by Antony Rowe, Chippenham, Wilts.

Contents

Introduction:
Delegation and Accountability in
European Integration

TORBJÖRN BERGMAN

The overall question of this volume is how the European Union (EU) effects national decision making in the Member States. This question has to do with both change 'in progress' and with the future of democracy in these countries. Our approach to studying how democratic decision making is changing involves three very important choices. One is that rather than studying bits and pieces of EU impact, we examine the whole chain of national democracy from voters to civil servants. Second, we study this chain from a particular theoretical perspective – a principal–agent-based delegation and accountability perspective. Third, we focus on a particular set of countries, the Nordic parliamentary democracies.

One aspect of EU membership is that domestic decision makers interact with their European counterparts and make binding decisions in supranational (as opposed to international) institutions.[1] Analyses of the effects of this process have often concluded that national-level democracy is becoming increasingly more complex and diffuse. Albert Weale has very aptly summarised the main argument: there has been 'a reduction of the degree of policy control by individuals within member states; an intrusion of the EU into functions that were previously performed by the nation state; a weakening of legislative control over the executives within nation states; and an overall lack of democratic accountability and transparency'.[2] These

Torbjörn Bergman is a post-doctoral research fellow in the Department of Political Science at Umeå University, Sweden

The contributors to this volume gratefully acknowledge the Bank of Sweden Tercentenary Foundation's support to Torbjörn Bergman and the research programme on 'Constitutional Change and Parliamentary Democracy' (1996:0801). Torbjörn Bergman, Wolfgang C. Müller, University of Vienna, and Kaare Strøm, University of California, San Diego, head the programme.

Bergman would like to thank the other contributors to this volume for their help with both the introduction and the volume. He would also like to thank Magnus Blomgren and Thomas Larue for research assistance and Cynthia Kite for help with language editing. As agents, they all prove the high value of careful ex ante screening.

findings pinpoint important aspects of the impact of EU membership on national democracy. However, this volume is not about gloom and doom with regard to the consequences of the EU for national democracy. Instead, our main working hypothesis is that the transfer of power from the national level to the supranational does not necessarily mean that delegation fails or that there is a reduction in accountability at the national level. While it is true that membership transfers significant authority to EU institutions, the precise impact is multifaceted and open-ended and should be assessed through empirical studies. In some instances, supranational integration might actually reduce the agency loss that can potentially arise in all relationships between (domestic) principals and agents. With this rather open point of departure, our approach leads us to undertake a careful assessment of the pros and cons of the EU impact.

Rather than claiming that we present the final verdict about the EU's impact on national-level democracy, we want to stress that our answers are preliminary and exploratory. Having said this, however, it is also important to point out that the contributors provide state-of-the-art accounts of the consequences for the Nordic parliamentary democracies. The contributors share a clear focus, a common starting point and a coherent conceptual apparatus. It should also be noted that we are interested in domestic adaptation and institutional innovation rather than in a notion of change rooted in mechanical and/or deterministic causality. It is for this reason that we adopt a principal–agent perspective and focus specifically on matters concerning delegation and accountability.

DELEGATION AND ACCOUNTABILITY

Delegation occurs when a principal (for example, a parliament) delegates to an agent (for example, a cabinet) the authority to act on his (or its) behalf under a particular set of rules by which the agent can be held accountable.[3] As Arthur Lupia points out in the article following this introduction, we have good theoretical reasons for focusing on principal–agent relationships when studying the effects that political integration can have on national democracy.[4]

The single most defining characteristic of the parliamentary form of representative democracy is that the prime minister and the cabinet are accountable to the parliament and can be voted out of office by it. This means that the ideal-type chain is singular and unitary.[5] Voters elect a parliament; the parliament must tolerate the cabinet; the cabinet can delegate authority to individual ministers; civil servants implement decisions that are a result of this chain of delegation.[6]

Of course, we do not expect the idealised chain to be perfectly reflected in existing parliamentary democracies. Instead we use it as a common starting point precisely because we want to study both similarities and differences between the ideal-type and the way in which the process actually works in practice. This focuses attention on delegation and accountability problems and on how the EU shapes agency problems. Agency problems exist when principals and agents do not have identical interests or preferences and when an agent is able to behave in ways which are difficult for the principal to monitor (hidden action) and/or when an agent has access to more and better information than does the principal (hidden information). In such cases, principals may put into place certain safeguards that come into play before authority is delegated to an agent (*ex ante*), or afterwards (*ex post*).

As Lupia also points out, accountability can have two meanings. On the one hand, accountability refers to the *process* by which principals supervise and control agents. This directs our attention to the various institutional mechanisms that govern the relationship between principals and agents in each step of the chain. These mechanisms can be based on constitutional documents, laws, statutes and strong conventions. Accountability in this sense is the main focus of the country studies, which emphasise the impact of the EU on established rules and procedures. We also investigate institutional reforms that have been implemented and others that are currently being undertaken at the national level.

The other aspect of accountability is whether or not the Agent's actions lead to the Principal's desired result. In this case, accountability refers to the *outcome* of the whole chain and the entire process. This can apply to a particular principal–agent relationship, but also to the result produced by a whole chain of such relationships. If a principal (for example, the electorate) clearly prefers a particular policy and the interaction between principals and agents further down the chain ultimately produces this policy, then – for the electorate – one can speak about accountability in terms of outcome. When accountability is examined from this perspective, a particular step in the chain might suffer from certain institutional weaknesses, but that does not have to mean that the entire chain fails.

In the country studies, the contributors have been given the difficult task of considering both aspects of accountability. The dual notion of accountability makes the analysis both more complicated and more interesting. While our analyses of accountability as outcome can only be preliminary and suggestive, we include this aspect because we believe that the perspective has much to offer – not least for future studies of particular principal–agent relationships in the EU context. In the work presented here, each contributor draws general conclusions about the overall relationship between process and outcome as well as about the effects that recent developments can have on the legitimacy of constitutional and institutional arrangements in their country.

The next section discusses the normative underpinnings of our analytical starting point. The following section goes on to explain our choice of countries. The section after that presents a basic introduction to some common EU concepts and acronyms. The last section gives an outline of the basic structure of the five country studies.

REPRESENTATION FROM BELOW?

The answer to the general question of the impact of the EU on national-level democracy is likely to vary depending on what definition of democracy is used. For example, the classical view of democracy as direct rule by the people has roots going back to the city-state of Athens and to Rousseau. Given this definition of democracy, neither national nor EU institutions can be considered democratic. In contrast, today democracy is built on the notion of representation.[7]

For national-level representative democracy, different schools of thought offer different answers to the question of what 'proper' representative democracy involves.[8] One school, *participatory democracy*, highlights the participatory and discursive aspects and is critical of many other aspects of representation as currently practised, not least because of the emphasis put on decision making and leadership.[9] A contrasting notion of representation, *competitive elitism*, emphasises the free choice of voters among competing elites. Voters choose their leaders from a group of politicians, and parties compete with each other to win voter support. A central virtue highlighted by those sympathetic to this notion of representation is that the existence of competing elites allows voters to remove unwanted political leaders from their positions of power.[10] Between these rather different views of representative democracy is a third school. It does not emphasise either participation or the selection and removal of leaders as the core value of democracy. For this school, representative democracy is as much about how those who are represented can monitor their representatives as it is about participation or leadership selection. Delegation problems always exist, and the accountability of democratically elected leaders is therefore always a concern. Moreover, selection and control problems exist at every stage of representative democracy, not only at the top leadership level. This picture of representative democracy is sometimes referred to as a Jeffersonian view of democracy (after Thomas Jefferson).[11]

In existing democracies, we can identify elements from each of these schools of thought. For example, the regular selection and removal of leaders is a major event in any democratic country. The elections of political leaders are, unquestionably, the focal point of representative democracy. In fact, the role of political leaders and leadership is so important that political scientists have written about 'representation from above'.[12] In doing so, they refer to the notion that elected representatives do not, and probably should not, simply follow the wishes of their voters. Political leaders also educate, shape and sometimes even create public opinion in favour of issues and standpoints that they want to promote. Despite these observations, however, a central aspect of representative democracy is how well the chain of delegation and accountability from voters to elected representatives to policy implementers actually works. As is common in the principal–agent literature, the articles in this issue all take the third (Jeffersonian) school of thought as their point of departure; that is, we start from a perspective that emphasises 'delegation from below'.[13]

However, it should be noted that there is no necessary connection between any of the schools on democratic thinking and the principal–agent schema for analysis of delegation and accountability. The use of referenda raises many delegation and accountability issues about the relationship between principals and agents, not least when referenda are held in the context of a representative democracy. The notion of representation from above could also be analysed as a principal–agent relationship, perhaps as a problem of how an agent can influence a principal to change his preferences. Given that principal–agent analysis can thus be linked to various understandings of democracy, our connecting of the conceptual apparatus of principals and agents to democracy from below should be seen as a deliberate choice rather than as a given.

Starting from 'below' – that is, with voters – we focus on the institutional mechanisms whereby each principal can hold accountable the next step in the parliamentary chain. Doing so makes clear the importance of constitutional design for democracy. There has been a growing concern about constitutions and democracy in the comparative literature.[14] With respect to the EU and democracy, there are a number of interesting studies devoted to examining constitutional matters, parliaments and political parties.[15] Because we address the impact on the whole chain from voters to civil servants and because we draw conclusions about the comparative impact of the EU and its treaty-based constitutional arrangements, we hope that our efforts will help give the principal–agent analysis of democracy a central place within a body of literature that combines what now are two largely separate research traditions.

THE NORDIC PARLIAMENTARY DEMOCRACIES AND EUROPEAN INTEGRATION

One way to shed light on the impact of the EU and its institutions on national democracy is to study and compare a set of countries. For comparative purposes, the countries should differ from one another in some respects. However, to make sure that observed variation with regard to EU impact is not due to the simple fact that the countries under study are very different from one another to begin with, it is also preferable to hold some national-level characteristics 'constant'. The countries should share important constitutional traits and, preferably, have similar historical and cultural backgrounds.

With this in mind, in our study of the impact of the EU we focus on the five Nordic countries.[16] The Nordic EU Member States of Denmark, Finland and Sweden form a relatively coherent cultural group and their institutions of representative government and party systems are similar. Relative to most other EU states, each of the three has a sizeable group of EU opponents and a national parliament that is actively involved in EU affairs. In addition, all three are quite effective implementers of EU directives.[17]

At the same time, the three Nordic Member States differ in interesting ways. Denmark has been a member of the EU (and its predecessors) longer than Finland and Sweden. The Finnish presidency and the fairly high degree of autonomy enjoyed by Swedish executive agencies and civil servants are other examples of interesting variation. However, the most important advantage of studying the effects of the EU on the Nordic countries is that while three of them are EU members, two of them, Iceland and Norway, remain outside the formal structure of the EU. The latter two are part of the European Economic Area (EEA). The EEA agreement requires non-EU countries to follow EU rules for the internal market for goods, services, labour and capital. Thus, by studying the five Nordic countries, we capture three countries that are members and two that share with them a cultural and geographic region as well as many features of parliamentary government, but who differ with regard to their relations to the EU. This means that we can begin to distinguish the direct impact of membership in EU institutions from changes that might occur for other reasons.

For readers not familiar with the EU and the EEA, the next section outlines the basic structures and the most important institutions as well as acronyms commonly used in the country studies. This is followed by a discussion of the organisation of the country studies.

EU AND THE EEA

Since the mid-1980s, the powers of EU institutions have increased and the scope of the EU has expanded into new policy areas.[18] With the entering into force of the Single European Act on 1 July 1987, and the Treaty on European Union (TEU) – commonly known as the Maastricht Treaty – on 1 November 1993, an increase in the use of majority voting transferred political authority from the Member States to the Council of Ministers as a collective. The transfer of authority went further in 1999 when Economic and Monetary Union (EMU) permanently fixed the exchange rates for 11 Member States[19] on 1 January and when the Amsterdam Treaty (AMT) came into force on 1 May. The Amsterdam Treaty gives the European Parliament a substantially stronger role within the EU. The power of the supranational parliament increased with regard to both its role in the decision-making process and its control functions *vis-à-vis* the European Commission. The European Commission prepares and proposes EU decisions and oversees how decisions are implemented. Together with the Court (the European Court of Justice) it is charged with promoting integration in accordance with the treaties. On the basis of a series of treaties negotiated by EU Member States and subsequently ratified by the national parliaments, these four institutions decide and implement the EUs' community law, the *acquis communautaire*.

The Member States are represented primarily through the European Council, which are the summits involving prime ministers and presidents, and through the Council of Ministers. The authority of the Council of Ministers is increasingly challenged by the other EU institutions and by a strong opinion in favour of a more federal structure for the EU. One of the commons criticisms is that the EU suffers from a 'democratic deficit'. Proponents of a more federal Europe argue that the EU's fundamental problem is the relatively weak position of the European Parliament at the EU level.[20] For others, often those who favour an EU based primarily on member state co-operation (intergovernmentalism), the democratic deficit has more to do with the weak role of the national parliaments in the EU's decision-making process.[21]

In the EU established by the Maastricht and Amsterdam treaties, the Council of Ministers has been and continues to be the most important actor in the EU's legislative process. In what is known as the first pillar, which covers the internal market and the Common Agricultural Policy (CAP), a qualified majority in the Council now makes most of the decisions. In the other two pillars, Common Foreign and Security Foreign Policy (second pillar) and Justice and Home Affairs (third pillar), decisions are only taken by consensus (that is, unanimity). In contrast to decisions on first-pillar issues, these decisions have to be ratified by all 15 national parliaments before they enter into force.

The members of the Council of Ministers are the ministers from the governments (cabinets) of the Member States. There can be several Council meetings going on simultaneously. For example, the Foreign Ministers meet in the General Affairs Council, while the Ministers of Finance meet in the so-called ECOFIN. Council decisions are prepared by the permanent representatives of the Member States, the so-called COREPER. Representatives from the Member States also participate in the hundreds of Commission and Council groups and committees that prepare proposals and oversee the implementation of EU decisions. The committees responsible for overseeing implementation are sometimes referred to as the 'comitology' of the EU.[22]

Efforts have been made to co-ordinate the views of the national parliaments in the EU's legislative process.[23] A conference of parliamentary presidents (or speakers) meets regularly. There are also joint meetings of the representatives of the EU Affairs Committees of the Member States. These meetings are known as COSAC – a French acronym that stands for the conference of bodies specialising in EU affairs. However, these are rather informal fora for exchange of courtesies and information, and they have not played a decisive role in European co-operation. More important for the EU's legislative process are the European Affairs bodies that exist in all 15 national parliaments. Through these EU Affairs Committees – as they are also known – national parliaments, in varying degrees, try to influence and scrutinise the cabinet ministers that represent their country in decision-making in the Council of Ministers.

The parliaments in the EEA Member States (Iceland, Liechtenstein and Norway) do not have the option of holding EU decision makers accountable for their actions. This is because their governments do not formally take part in EU decisions. The EEA free trade agreement between the EU and the Member States of the European Free Trade Association (EFTA) came into force on 1 January 1994. Of the EFTA members, Austria, Sweden and Finland soon switched sides and joined the EU on 1 January 1995. The EEA treaty is meant to ensure that the EU's internal market for the free movement of people, goods, services and capital also applies to these states.[24] In addition, EEA Member States co-operate with the EU on the environment, social policy, education, and so on. Formally, the parliaments in the EEA states can refuse to ratify new EU legislation. In practice, however, the EEA treaty binds these countries to follow EU decisions or to jeopardise the entire EEA agreement. Their real option is to try to influence the EU by participating in the preparation of EU policy. The EEA treaty created institutions for the process of mutual exchange of information, which provides EEA states with a forum through which they can seek to exercise such influence.

The EEA Council consists of cabinet members from the Member States and the European Commission. This Council discusses the principles and guidelines of the agreement. Amendments to the agreement are decided by the EEA Joint Committee, which is composed of appointed representatives from the European Commission and each of the three EEA countries mentioned above. The decision rule is unanimity. The Commission and the EFTA Surveillance Authority (ESA) monitor implementation. Judicial control is carried out by the ECJ when an EU Member State is involved and by the EFTA Court if no EU country is involved. In addition, there is an EEA Joint Parliamentary Committee, in which are held consultative meetings between members of the national parliaments (MPs) from the three EEA states and Members of the European Parliament (MEPs).

THE COUNTRY STUDIES

In the next article, Arthur Lupia provides the formal-logical basis for our empirical inquiry into delegation and accountability problems in the five Nordic countries. In particular, he provides the logical basis for our hypothesis that the effects of integration are not one-sided. He also directs the attention to the importance of any principal's ability to have access to credible information. Lupia should be read because he introduces fundamental concepts and because of the logic and clarity of his argument. However, the country-based articles are not a full test of his propositions. With regard to theoretical concepts such as 'reversion points' and accountability in terms of 'outcome', the country articles provide only a first taste of the fruitfulness of the formal logic as a guide for empirical study. The theoretical arguments and our empirical work set the stage both for other comparative studies of integration and for more in-depth case studies of particular principal–agent relationships as they relate to outcomes.

We now turn to a discussion of the organisation of the country studies. For each step in the chain of delegation and accountability we outline the issues that the country studies address.

Voters as Principals and MPs as Agents

In this section the empirical chapters discuss the importance of the EU and EEA debate in national politics, in particular the role it has played in referenda, electoral politics and re-shaping the national party system. To what extent have referenda been used to resolve the issue of membership? Have direct elections to the European Parliament (or, in the case of Iceland and Norway, the absence of such elections) been important? Have there been major differences between regular national elections and the elections to the European Parliament? If so, what are these differences? Another important question is whether individual parties have benefited or been hurt by their positions on European integration issues? All country studies also provide an account of how voters are divided on EU membership, and, for Norway and Iceland, how public opinion perceives membership in the EU vis-à-vis membership in the EEA.

Parliament as Principal and Cabinet as Agent

In this section of the empirical studies we contrast (a) the traditional and general organisation and role of the parliament with (b) changes that have occurred because of the EU. As part of this, the nature of the delegation and accountability relations between the parliament and the prime minister (PM) and the cabinet as a whole are discussed. Has the way in which the parliament organises its work changed because of EU membership? Have parliament–cabinet relations changed because of the EU? If so, how, why and in what way? Have new mechanisms to ensure accountability been introduced? In the three EU Member States, considerable attention is given to the institutional innovation of European Affairs Committees that are supposed to monitor and scrutinise how cabinet ministers behave in the EU Council of Ministers. To what extent do they succeed? What are the main problems? Are there policy areas in which it is possible to say that the influence and importance of the parliament has actually increased relative to the cabinet and individual ministers?

Cabinet as a Principal and Individual Ministers as Agents

In the country chapters this section begins with a brief survey of the traditional division of labour between the cabinet and individual ministers. The opportunity that the parliament has traditionally had to monitor individual ministers is also discussed. What decisions are delegated to individual ministers? Cabinet decision rules, including the Prime Minister's authority to hire and fire ministers, are presented. We also review changes that have occurred in these areas as a result of either EU or EEA membership. The way in which the cabinet organises its representation in decision-making bodies such as the Council of Ministers, including the COREPER or the EEA (when applicable), is explained.

Cabinet/Ministers as Principals and Civil Servants as Agents

Some of the monitoring of individual ministers is done by the PM and other cabinet ministers. However, the parliament might also be able to hold individual ministers and ministries accountable. In this section we discuss both of these aspects. Other questions of interest include: how has the government administration been organised to deal with EU/EEA issues and procedures? How are national representatives to EU-level committees charged with preparing Commission and Council of Europe decisions chosen? How are they monitored?

Conclusion

In the conclusion of each study we discuss how the EU impacts on the national chain of parliamentary democracy. We focus on the *process* of delegation and accountability and discuss matters such as how authority is delegated, existing agency problems and *ex ante* and *ex post* mechanisms of accountability. We also provide a general assessment of the whole chain of delegation and accountability in terms of *outcome*. Are the policy preferences of voters far removed from the policies that are produced by EU institutions and by national institutions that are influenced by decision making at the European level? To what extent is it possible to talk about delegation success and delegation failure? How does this affect the legitimacy of representative democracy?

The country studies are presented in the following order. We begin with the EU members. Within this group, we begin with Denmark, the first of the Nordic states to join the supranational integration process. After we have presented the EU newcomers, Finland and Sweden, we present the two states that belong to the EEA rather than the EU, namely Iceland and Norway.

In the concluding contribution, Erik Damgaard presents a comparative analysis of the five countries. Starting from our common perspective, he identifies similarities and differences among the Nordic states. Some differences, such as the EU and EEA membership divide, have obvious and important consequences. Others, such as subtle differences in organisation and the flow of information, have less obvious but still very important consequences for the whole chain of principal–agent relationships in parliamentary democracies.

NOTES

1. While this is not explicitly studied in this volume, I would like to add that we study representative democracy at the national level not only because the EU affects that level, but also because national-level developments are important at the EU level. The heads of state and prime ministers that meet in the European Council and the cabinet ministers that meet in the dominant law-making body, the Council of Ministers, are replaced through democratic arrangements at the national level and not by any act of the European Parliament. Because of this, many of the EU's policy choices are linked to national politics.
2. A. Weale, 'Democratic Theory and the Constitutional Politics of the European Union', *Journal of European Public Policy*, Vol.4, No.4 (1997), pp.665–9, at p.667. His comments are made in the context of a review of J. Hayward's (ed.) *The Crisis of Representation in Europe* (London and Portland, OR: Frank Cass, 1995). For another example of a critical evaluation, see V. Schmidt, 'European Integration and Democracy: The Differences among Member States', *Journal of European Public Policy*, Vol.4, No.1 (1997), pp.128–45.
3. See also T. Moe, 'The New Economics of Organization', *American Journal of Political Science*, Vol.28, No.4 (1984); R. Kiewet and M. McCubbins, *The Logic of Delegation. Congressional Parties and the Appropriations Process* (Chicago, IL: The University of Chicago Press, 1991); A. Lupia and M. McCubbins, *The Democratic Dilemma. Can Citizens Learn What They Need To Know?* (Cambridge: Cambridge University Press, 1998); D. Epstein and S. O'Halloran, *Delegating Powers: A Transaction Cost Politics Approach to Policy Making Under Separate Powers* (Cambridge: Cambridge University Press, 1999); L. Martin, *Democratic Commitments: Legislatures and International Cooperation* (Princeton, NJ: Princeton University Press, forthcoming 2000).
4. A. Lupia, 'The EU, the EEA, and Domestic Accountability: How Outside Forces Affect Delegation within Member States' (this volume).
5. Depending on the constitutional framework, the ideal-typical chain of delegation can vary considerably. In a presidential system like that of the United States (USA), there is a dual chain of representation because voters elect the legislature and the executive separately. For a much more detailed and elaborate discussion of parliamentary democracy and the ideal-type which is our point of departure, see K. Strøm, 'Delegation and Accountability in Parliamentary Democracies', *European Journal of Political Research* (Special Issue edited by T. Bergman, W. Müller and K. Strøm, forthcoming 2000).
6. Most of the contributors to this volume are also contributors in a forthcoming volume by K. Strøm, W.C. Müller and T. Bergman (eds.), *Delegation and Accountability in Parliamentary Democracies* (Oxford: Oxford University Press, forthcoming). This book will provide a detailed account of the delegation and accountability aspects of parliamentary democracy in all 15 EU Member States as well as in Iceland and Norway.
7. H.F. Pitkin, *The Concept of Representation* (Berkeley, CA: University of California Press, 1967).
8. As Held points out, while these are central schools of thought on democracy, they are far from the only models of representative democracy that exist. D. Held, *Models of Democracy* (Stanford, CA: Stanford University Press, 2nd edn. 1996).
9. A modern classic in this tradition is C. Pateman, *Participation and Democratic Theory* (Cambridge: Cambridge University Press, 1970).

10. Schumpeter is a leading thinker in this tradition. J. Schumpeter, *Capitalism, Socialism and Democracy* (New York: Harper and Row, 1942).
11. R. Kiewet and M. McCubbins, *The Logic of Delegation*. This model of democracy also has roots back to the 'protective democracy' of Madison, Bentham and Mill. On protective democracy, see Held, *Models of Democracy*, pp.89–100.
12. P. Esaiasson and S. Holmberg, *Representation from Above: Members of Parliament and Representative Democracy in Sweden* (Aldershot: Dartmouth, 1996).
13. The best discussion of how the principal–agent approach is linked to a Jeffersonian notion of delegation from below is perhaps R. Kiewet and M. McCubbins, *The Logic of Delegation*.
14. A few noteworthy examples are K.G. Banting and R. Simeon (eds.), *The Politics of Constitutional Change in Industrial Nations* (London: Macmillan, 1985); V. Bogdanor (ed.), *Constitutions in Democratic Politics* (Aldershot: Gower, 1988); J. Elster and R. Slagstad (eds.), *Constitutionalism and Democracy* (Cambridge: Cambridge University Press, 1988); S.E. Finer, *Comparing Constitutions* (Oxford: Oxford University Press, 1995, rev. edn., ed. by Vernon Bogdanor); and G. Sartori, *Comparative Constitutional Engineering* (London: Macmillan, 1994).
15. See, for example, S. Andersen and K. Eliassen, *The European Union: How Democratic Is It?* (London: SAGE Publications, 1996); T. Bergman, 'National Parliaments and EU Affairs Committees: Notes on Empirical Variation and Competing Explanations', *Journal of European Public Policy*, Vol.4, No.3 (1997); T. Bergman, 'Utrikes inrikespolitik: riksdagen och EU-nämnden i EU', in I. Mattson and L. Wängnerud (eds.), *Riksdagen på nära håll* (Stockholm: SNS Förlag, 1997); K. Heidar and L. Svåsand, *Partier uten grenser?* (Tane Aschehoug, 1997); L. Miles (ed.), *The European Union and the Nordic Countries* (London: Routledge, 1996); P. Norton (ed.), *National Parliaments and the European Union* (London and Portland, OR: Frank Cass, 1996); T. Raunio, 'Always One Step Behind? National Legislatures and the European Union', *Government and Opposition*, Vol.34, No.2 (1999), pp.180–202; E. Smith, *National Parliaments as Cornerstones of European Integration* (London: Kluwer, 1996); M. Wiberg (ed.), *Trying to Make Democracy Work: The Nordic Parliaments and the European Union* (Stockholm: Gidlunds förlag, 1997)
16. Lee Miles further develops the argument about similarities and differences between the Nordic countries in L. Miles (ed.), *The European Union and the Nordic Countries* (London: Routledge, 1996), 'Introduction', pp.3–12.
17. T. Bergman, 'The European Union as the Next Step in the Delegation Process', *European Journal of Political Research* (Special Issue edited by T. Bergman, W. Müller and K. Strøm, forthcoming 2000).
18. Except where otherwise noted, this brief presentation of EU developments and institutions draws upon D. Chryssochoou, *Democracy in the European Union* (London: Tauris Academic Studies, 1998), J. McCormick, *Understanding the European Union: A Concise Introduction* (London: Macmillan, 1999) and M. Westlake, *The Council of the European Union* (London: Cartermill, 1995).
19. Of the 15 Member States, Denmark, Great Britain, Greece and Sweden have not joined the EMU and therefore have not permanently fixed their exchange rates *vis-à-vis* other EU members' currencies.
20. There exists additional, complementary definitions of the deficit. This one is what Chryssochoou, *Democracy in the European Union*, p.31, refers to as the 'orthodox view' of the EU democratic deficit.
21. For example, this is the position of the former British Prime Minister John Major, see p.178 in M. Shackelton's chapter, 'Interparliamentary Cooperation and the 1996 Intergovernmental Conference', pp.165–82, in F. Laursen and S. Pappas (eds.), *The Changing Role of Parliaments in the European Union* (Maastricht: European Institute of Public Administration, 1995).
22. See, for example, T. Christiansen, 'Tensions of European Governance: Politicized Bureaucracy and Multiple Accountability in the European Commission', *Journal of*

European Public Policy, Vol.4, No.1 (1997), pp.73–90, and W. Wessels, 'Comitology: Fusion in Action. Politico-Administrative Trends in the EU System', *Journal of European Public Policy*, Vol.5, No.2 (1998), pp.209–34.

23. Bergman 'National Parliaments and EU Affairs Committees'.
24. For an institutional description of the EEA agreement and how it has been implemented in one of the EEA member states, see U. Sverdrup, 'Norway: An Adaptive Non-Member', in K. Hanf and B. Soetendorp (eds.), *Adapting to European Integration. Small States and the European Union* (London: Longman, 1998), pp.149–66.

The EU, the EEA and Domestic Accountability: How Outside Forces Affect Delegation within Member States

ARTHUR LUPIA

The Nordic countries face a common challenge. The challenge is how to govern themselves given the emergence of powerful outside forces such as the European Union (EU) and the European Economic Area (EEA). Many people believe that the emergence of these powerful outside forces renders national governments less effective. Is this true? How do the EU and the EEA affect the ability of Member States to govern themselves?

Considerable scholarly effort has been directed towards explaining how international organisations such as the EU and the EEA affect domestic decision making. An emerging theme in this research is that national-level actors retain some power over decision making in the EU Council of Ministers and in the implementation of EU directives.[1] Nations often have the ability to delay implementation and they can stubbornly hold out for conditions favourable to them. Moreover, if the choices presented to sovereign nations are sufficiently bad, they can choose to be uncooperative on unrelated issues. So while the transfers of power inherent in the EU and EEA charters may weaken national governments in some respects, the magnitude of these changes is moderated because nations retain some discretion over how EU policies and the EEA treaty are implemented within their borders.

Research that focuses on the extent to which Member States abide by international agreements is necessary to determine how the EU and the EEA affect Member States. However, such research is not sufficient because the transfers of power that allow the EU and the EEA to impose rules on Member States may also affect relations *within Member States*. This article focuses on these domestic effects; clarifying whether and how the

Arthur Lupia is Professor in the Department of Political Science, University of California, San Diego, La Jolla.

The author wishes to thank Torbjörn Bergman, James Druckman, Elisabeth Gerber, Svanjur Kristjánnson, David Lake, Lisa Martin, Mathew D. McCubbins, Tapio Raunio and Kaare Strøm for helpful comments.

emergence of outside forces weakens the ability of Member States to accomplish important domestic objectives.

In what follows a theoretical framework is presented for understanding how the EU and the EEA affect *delegation and accountability within Member States*. This framework is used to argue that the EU and EEA can affect the relationship between a nation's voters, its members of parliament, its government and its civil service. Consistent with the belief that the EU and EEA weaken national governments, conditions are identified under which outside forces make governments less accountable to citizens and render civil servants less accountable to governments and ministers. However, also identified are conditions under which the EU and EEA make certain domestic governance arrangements easier to enforce. When these latter conditions hold, the EU and EEA increase domestic accountability and make it possible for governments to enact a different set of policies than they could in the absence of these outside forces.

Two sets of ideas are used to build this theoretical framework. The first set emanates from previous work conducted by this volume's research group.[2] This set of ideas begins with the premise that *representative democracy requires delegation*. An act of *delegation* occurs when one person or group, a *principal*, selects another person or group, an *agent*, to act on the principal's behalf. In an election, for example, citizens are *principals* who elect representatives to serve as their *agents* in parliament. All representative democracies rely on other delegations as well. For example, when civil servants implement legislation, they do so as the agents of the cabinet ministers or other officials who selected them.

This first set of ideas continues with the premise that a *chain of delegation* is the backbone for every modern parliamentary government. The typical chain includes a link that attaches voters to their agents (the members of parliament) a link that attaches members of parliament to their agent (the government) a link that attaches the government to their agents (individual ministers) and a link that attaches ministers to their agents (civil servants). So at one end of the typical delegation chain are citizens. At the other end of the chain are the civil servants that are charged with implementing the decisions of their predecessors in the chain. Thinking about modern governance as a chain of delegation provides a useful way to clarify who is accountable to whom in modern democratic societies.

The second set of ideas from which this theoretical framework is built comes from a quarter-century of formal modelling in economics and political science. This literature clarifies some fundamental properties of the relationship between institutions, information and political decision making.[3] This work reminds us that while the style of governance and shape of delegation chain vary from country to country, *there is a logic of delegation that is common to all modern governments.* Of particular interest is the fact that we can use formal logic to help explain why some acts of delegation undermine accountability while others do not.

Combining these two sets of ideas leads to the following argument:

> If the EU and EEA affect the abilities of principals and agents within a country's chain of delegation, then the EU and EEA can affect political accountability within that country's borders. Therefore, if we can be clearer about how outside forces affect domestic principals and agents, then we can be clearer about how the EU and EEA affect Member State self-governance.

From this argument I conclude that the EU and the EEA need not weaken domestic accountability. To be sure, national governments have transferred some powers to these outside forces. However, these international organisations can also give domestic political actors the bargaining leverage or credibility they need to increase accountability within national borders.

This conclusion is reached by using a theoretical framework to show that the EU and EEA affect domestic accountability by affecting *reversion points* and *information* that are relevant to domestic acts of delegation. By reversion point I mean the policy that prevails if a principal and agent, who together can change a policy outcome, cannot agree on which change to pursue. When outside forces change a domestic reversion point, they also change the relative bargaining leverage of domestic principals and agents (that is, they also change who is accountable to whom domestically). To clarify how the EU and the EEA affect Member State self-governance, we derive conclusions about the conditions under which externally driven reversion-point shifts increase accountability as well as the conditions under which such shifts decrease accountability. Attention is then turned to information. I explain how outside forces can affect the credibility of domestic information providers and, subsequently, the information that domestic principals possess about their agents. When outside forces increase the credibility of the people who provide information to domestic principals, domestic accountability can increase.

In the end, we can all agree that the Nordic countries – and indeed all EU and EEA Member States – have transferred some governing authority to the EU and the EEA. However, this transfer does not imply that Member States have weakened their powers of self-governance. Outside forces such as the EU and the EEA can give domestic actors bargaining leverage and credibility that they would otherwise lack. These forces make it possible for domestic actors to commit to new types of agreements and provide new types of collective goods. When these forces also make government actions more transparent, they shift domestic balances of power towards political principals and towards greater accountability.

The logical basis of the argument – a formal model of delegation – is presented in the next section. The model is then used to identify factors that determine whether or not agents are accountable to their principals. In conclusion, the model's logic is used to clarify how outside forces affect domestic acts of delegation.

A THEORY OF DELEGATION

In this section, a theory is described whose purpose is to clarify how the EU and the EEA affect Member State self-governance. First, a precise definition of an important aspect of national self-governance is given and then the theory's logical foundation – a simple formal model of delegation – is presented. The findings from the model are then used to clarify how outside forces affect domestic accountability.

Agency Loss: A Measure of Accountability

The purpose of this article is to address the question: 'How do the EU and the EEA affect national level governance?' It focuses, in particular, on how the EU and the EEA affect the extent to which any one actor in a country's chain of delegation is *accountable* to any other actor earlier in the chain. Therefore, the dependent variable is accountability.

To clarify how the EU and the EEA affect national-level governance, we must be precise about what we mean by *accountability*. We must be precise because the word accountability, like many words, is used in different ways by different people. Some people use the term accountability to describe *a process of control*. For example, we may say that civil servants are accountable to ministers if the ministers can influence the civil servants' actions. Other people use the term accountability to describe *a type of outcome*. For example, we may say that civil servants are accountable to ministers if the civil servant acts in the minister's interests. It is important to recognise, however, that the 'process' and 'outcome' definitions of accountability mean different things. To see the difference, note that a civil servant can provide outcomes that the minister likes without the minister exercising any control (for example, the civil servant and minister share precisely the same policy goals, and the civil servant ignores the minister when making a decision). Similarly, a minister can exercise great control over a civil servant without achieving a desirable outcome (for example, a minister makes a credible threat to remove a civil servant if a certain level of public service is not achieved, but circumstances render the civil servant unable to achieve the goal).

I use the term accountability to refer to a type of outcome rather than a process of control. This is because outcomes, rather than process, are the core concern of most people who participate in debates about the domestic effects of the EU and the EEA. So, while the models presented generate conclusions about both process and outcomes, this article describes the conclusions that pertain to outcomes.

There are several metrics available for characterising outcomes. This article adopts a conventional metric called *agency loss*. Agency loss is the difference between the actual consequences of delegating to the agent and what the consequence would have been had the agent been a perfect agent. By perfect agent I mean an agent who does what the principal would have done if the principal possessed unlimited information and resources. Using the metric of agency loss alerts us to the difference between the actual outcome of delegation and the best that the outcome could have been for the principal. It provides a simple way to describe how a wide range of factors affects accountability.[4]

A Simple Model

A simple model of delegation is now described. While this model has its origins in economics,[5] the version presented here is based on work by Romer and Rosenthal.[6] In the model, delegation is a game between two players, a principal and an agent. The principal represents a person or persons who have delegated a particular task. The agent represents the person or persons to whom the principal's authority has been delegated. Put another way, by delegating, the principal (for example, a minister) gives her agent (that is, civil servants within her ministry) the ability to take certain actions on her behalf.

The sequence of events in the Romer–Rosenthal model is as follows and is depicted in Figure 1. The agent moves first by using his delegated authority to make a decision. The agent can be thought of as making a decision to change what was done in the past. Formally, we portray the agent's action as proposing a new policy, $X \in [0, 1]$. This policy is an alternative to *the reversion point*, $RP \in [0, 1]$ (that is, the pre-existing policy *status quo*). The principal then either accepts the agent's proposal or rejects it in favour of maintaining the reversion point (that is, she chooses X or RP). The principal's decision to reject the agent's action can be thought of as an outright veto of an agent's decision or as a decision to sanction the agent by an amount sufficient to induce the agent to revert to old ways.[7] To draw inferences about agency loss from such a model we employ the Nash equilibrium concept. Ordeshook writes that: 'A Nash equilibrium is a set of strategies – one for each player – such that each strategy in the set is a best response to all the others.'[8] Thus, when we describe principal and agent

FIGURE 1
A DELEGATION MODEL

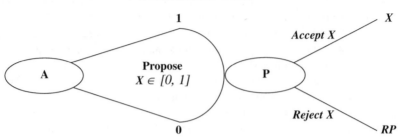

behaviours below, the behaviours in question are the principal's best response to his perception of the agent's action and the agent's best response to his perception of the principal's likely action.

We assume that the principal and agent have preferences about what the outcome of their interaction should be. We represent these preferences by assuming that each player seeks to maximise a single-peaked utility function. We call the peak of each player's utility function his or her ideal policy. We denote the principal's ideal policy as P ∈ [0, 1] and we denote the agent's ideal policy as A ∈ [0, 1]. Put another way, we assume that the principal and agent each prefer that the outcome of delegation be as close as possible to their own ideal policy outcome. It is further assumed, for the moment, that the principal and agent have complete information about all aspects of their interaction. Later we will show how gaps in the principal's information affect agency loss.

The main benefit of the Romer–Rosenthal model is that we can use it to deduce some fundamental dynamics of a delegation relationship, and the associated dynamics of agency loss. These dynamics are described below. The model reveals four mutually exclusive and collectively exhaustive situations. Figure 2 depicts these situations. What differentiates each situation from the others is the relationship between the principal's ideal policy, the agent's ideal policy and the reversion point.

In Situation 1, the principal and agent have identical ideal policies. In equilibrium, the agent proposes the principal's (and the agent's) ideal policy and the principal accepts the agent's proposal. In this situation, there is no agency loss – the agent is a perfect agent.

In Situation 2, the principal and agent have different ideal policies, but both players' ideal policies are on the same side of the reversion point. Put another way, the principal and agent agree on the desired direction of policy change but not on the magnitude of such change. Moreover, the principal's ideal policy is farther from the reversion point than it is from the agent's

FIGURE 2
GRAPHICAL DEPICTIONS OF THE POSSIBLE SITUATIONS

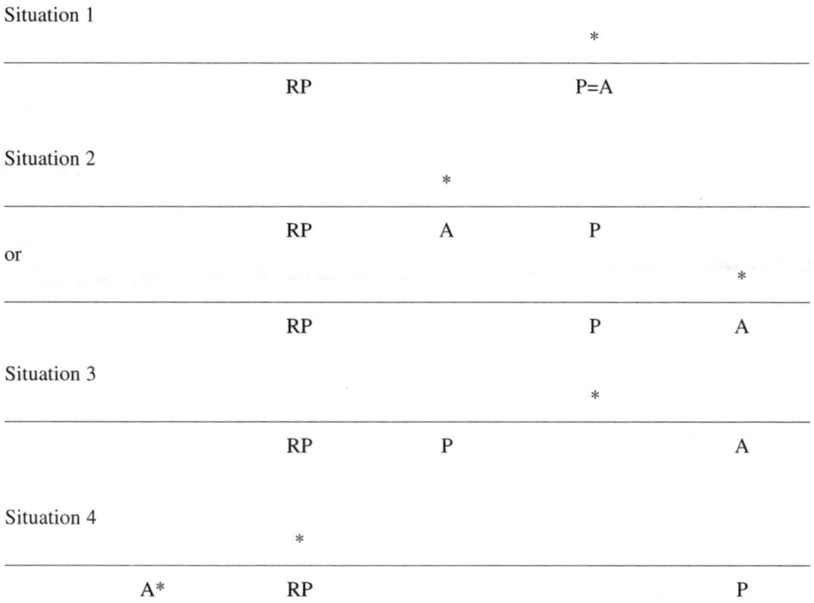

Situation 1

		*		
RP		P=A		

Situation 2

	*		
RP	A	P	

or

			*
RP		P	A

Situation 3

		*	
RP	P		A

Situation 4

	*		
A*	RP		P

Note: The star indicates the predicted outcome of delegation in the (complete information) Romer and Rosenthal model.

ideal policy. This implies that the principal prefers the agent's ideal policy to maintaining the reversion point. In equilibrium, the agent chooses his ideal policy and the principal accepts it. This occurs because the agent knows that the principal prefers some degree of change (that is, the agent's ideal point) to no change at all (that is, the reversion point). The agency loss in Situation 2 is the difference between the agent's ideal policy and the principal's ideal policy.

Situation 3 differs from Situation 2 in only one respect. In Situation 3, the principal's ideal policy is closer to the reversion point than it is to the agent's ideal policy. This means that the principal would rather maintain the reversion point than accept the agent's ideal policy. Since the agent knows this, he *will not* propose his ideal policy. He will, however, propose a change. In equilibrium, the agent chooses the policy closest to his own ideal policy that the principal will accept.[9] The agency loss in Situation 3 is at least as great or greater than the agency loss in any of the previous cases and is just less than the difference between RP and P.

In Situation 4, the principal's and the agent's ideal policies are on opposite sides of the reversion point. In this situation there is no alternative to the reversion point that is mutually agreeable to the principal and the agent. In equilibrium, the outcome is the reversion point and the agency loss is RP – P.

What can we learn about how the EU and EEA affect national-level governance from this simple model? The first thing to notice is that as we move from any lower numbered situation to any higher numbered situation, agency loss increases (when it changes). The second thing to notice is that moving domestic principals and agents from a lower numbered situation to a higher numbered situation implies either (1) an increase in the distance between A and P or (2) an increase in the distance between P and RP relative to the distance between A and P. Put another way, agency loss grows (when it changes) as either the agent's ideal policy or the reversion point moves away from the principal's ideal policy. That agency loss grows with the distance between P and A is straightforward – as the agent finds himself having less common policy interests with the principal, the agent gains fewer rewards from serving the principal's interests rather than his own. That agency loss can grow with the distance between P and RP follows from the fact that *bad reversion points make a wider range of proposals seem attractive* (that is, beggars can't be choosers).

Consider, for example, cases where the EU promulgates new regulations that affect industries, labourers and consumers. When these same actors, or their elected representatives, enter the political arena, their bargaining power *vis-à-vis* other actors may change. Suppose that a Labour party's constituents are negatively impacted by an EU regulation (that is, a policy reversion point has moved farther from Labour's policy ideal). If Labour is a principal in a chain of delegation, then the set of possible agent proposals that Labour prefers to the new reversion point is larger than the set of proposals that Labour preferred to the previous reversion point. When this set grows, opportunistic agents can benefit. In particular, the agent can take actions that are better for Labour than the new reversion point, but worse for Labour than the old reversion point, and still expect that Labour will accept them. When this happens, the action of outside forces causes increased agency loss. Similar logic reveals that if an EU policy moves a domestic reversion point closer to Labour's ideal point, then – other things being equal – the actions of the outside force decrease agency loss.

Extending the Simple Model to Incorporate Information Problems

If, in the empirical circumstances we care about, principals and agents have complete information, the Romer–Rosenthal model provides a complete and exhaustive description of the extent of agency loss emanating from any act of delegation. A common problem inherent in delegation, however, is that information can be hard to come by. In particular, political principals are regularly characterised as lacking information about their agent's actions.[10] The model is now extended by allowing the principal to lack information about her agent's action.

If the principal lacks such information, then even if she has the veto powers described in the Romer–Rosenthal model, she may not be able to wield these powers effectively. In particular, her lack of information may lead her to reject agent actions that are better for her than the reversion point or to accept agent actions that are worse for her than the reversion point.

In previous work an extension of the Romer–Rosenthal model has been offered that shows how the principal's lack of information affects the extent of agency loss.[11] Readers interested in the precise correspondence between the principal's information and the outcome of delegation can consult that paper. For our purposes here it is sufficient to summarise that paper's insight.

The Lupia model stipulates that if the principal lacks information about the agent's proposal in a Romer–Rosenthal type of delegation, then the agent always proposes his ideal point – regardless of its impact on the principal. This agent behaviour is different from that which is described in the Romer–Rosenthal model, particularly in Situation 3.

In Situation 3 of the Romer–Rosenthal model, the agent proposes an alternative to the reversion point that represents a compromise between himself and the principal. He offers the compromise because he knows that if he proposes his own ideal policy, the principal will reject it. In the equivalent situation in the Lupia model, the agent – who is now dealing with an uncertain principal – lacks an incentive to compromise. This follows because the agent can commit to no strategy other than proposing his own ideal – even if he were to promise a compromise, he could renege on his promise at the last possible moment and the principal would not have sufficient information to stop him. The principal, in turn, reacts by basing her decision about whether to accept or reject the agent's action on her prior beliefs about the agent's ideal point. That is, the principal acts as if the agent can commit only to proposing his own ideal policy. If the expected utility from choosing the agent's ideal policy is greater than the utility from choosing the reversion point, then the principal accepts the agent's action, otherwise she does not.

Table 1 shows how incorporating the principal's uncertainty affects agency loss. The left side of the table repeats the Romer–Rosenthal conclusions about the relationship between the reversion point and agency loss. The middle columns of the table display Lupia's agency loss results in the best case given an uncertain principal. In the best case, the principal can

TABLE 1
COMPLETE INFORMATION VERSUS INCOMPLETE INFORMATION

Complete Information Romer-Rosenthal 1978		Incomplete Information Best Case – Lupia 1992		Incomplete Information Worst Case – Lupia 1992	
Outcome	Agency Loss	Outcome	Δ Loss vs. Comp. Info.	Outcome	Δ Loss vs. Comp. Info.
Situation 1 P	None.	P	None.	RP	|P-RP|
Situation 2 A	- |A-P|	A	None.	RP	|A-RP|
Situation 3 ε closer to P than RP	- |RP - P| - ε	RP	ε	A	|A-(|RP-P|+ε)|
Situation 4 RP	- |RP - P|	RP	None	A*	|A*-RP|

Note: A* denotes the agent's ideal point in the situation where it and the principal's ideal point are on opposite sides of RP. In this situation, A* is worse for the principal than RP. ε denotes a number that is greater than zero, but very small.

guess the agent's behaviour correctly despite her uncertainty. The columns on the right display Lupia's agency loss results in the worst case given an uncertain principal. In the worst case, the principal's uncertainty leads her to make mistakes – to reject agent actions that would benefit her and accept agent actions that hurt her. Each set of columns show the policy outcome of delegation as well as its corresponding agency loss (that is, its utility consequences for the principal).

What can we learn about how outside forces affect domestic accountability from Table 1?[12] The first thing to notice is that uncertainty does not necessarily increase agency loss. As a result, the fact that the principal lacks some information about the agent's actions is, in itself, insufficient to generate additional agency loss. In the worst case, however, uncertainty significantly increases agency loss. In fact, Situation 4 with incomplete information generates the greatest agency loss possible in the model (that is, the agent takes actions that are bad for the principal and the principal accepts them). The lesson, therefore, is that an under-informed principal is not sufficient to cause agency loss. *What matters is whether or not the principal knows enough to wield whatever power she may have over the agent effectively.* Moreover, this lesson implies that an outside force can affect domestic accountability by affecting the principal's level of uncertainty – a point to which we will soon return.

The simple model and its extension reveal two ways in which outside forces affect agency loss.

•   First, outside forces can affect the relationship between the principal's ideal policy and the reversion point.[13] For example, if the EU or EEA shift a policy reversion point closer to a principal's ideal policy, then these outside forces can reduce agency loss.

- Second, if these outside forces provide the principal with information sufficient to wield her veto powers effectively, then outside forces can reduce agency loss. For example, in Situation 4, improving the principal's information reduces agency loss: from -|A*-P| to -|RP-P|. In situation 3, it reduces agency loss from -|A-P| to -|RP-P|. Moreover, in Situations 1 and 2, improving the principal's information prevents the principal from making a mistake – that is, it prevents her from vetoing a proposal that makes her better off than RP. Next, examples are provided of how outside forces affect the reversion points and information relevant to domestic political actors. These examples clarify the relationship between information, incentives, and behaviour in delegation contexts and reveal how the EU and the EEA affect domestic accountability.

HOW OUTSIDE FORCES MOVE DOMESTIC REVERSION POINTS

The EU takes many actions that affect the bargaining leverage that domestic political actors have *vis-à-vis* each other. Some of these actions do so by affecting the reversion point relevant to domestic acts of delegation. This section describes a piece of scholarship that clarifies how a branch of the EU, the European Court of Justice (ECJ), can affect domestic reversion points. This work explains how and why the ECJ gained the ability to affect many domestic reversion points.

K.J. Alter describes the evolution of the European Court of Justice (ECJ).[14] She shows how the ECJ evolved from an institution with relatively little authority into one that now influences how individuals challenge *national* law in national courts. Her research describes one way in which the EU, through the ECJ, shifts reversion points relevant to domestic delegation relationships.

Alter begins her argument with the premise that Member States 'want the ECJ to keep EU bodies in check'.[15] She then shows how the ECJ was able to increase its independence from Member State politicians. As she explains, the Member States created an ECJ that was not strong enough to gain such power by decree. She then shows that the ECJ gained powers by forming a coalition with a powerful set of domestic actors – national courts.

A compelling basis of Alter's argument is that 'judges and politicians have fundamentally different time horizons, which translates into different preferences for judges and politicians with regard to the outcome of individual cases'.[16] This difference between the time horizons of ECJ judges and Member State politicians created a window of opportunity for the ECJ.

This window allowed the ECJ to let present-day politicians escape the costs of possible transgressions of EU policy in exchange for establishing precedents for expanded ECJ influence. In particular, she asserts that 'Member States understood that the legal precedent established might create political costs in the future … [b]ut were willing to trade off potential long-term costs so long as they could escape the political and financial costs of judicial decisions in the present'.[17] Over time, the ECJ used this type of decision making to develop legal doctrine and construct 'the institutional building blocks of its own power and authority without provoking a political response'.[18]

The evolution of ECJ doctrine included a coalition-building element. The ECJ's coalition partner was the national courts. As Alter argues:

> In the early years of the EU legal system, national politicians turned to extralegal means to circumvent unwanted decisions; they asserted the illegitimacy of the decisions in a battle for political legitimacy at home, instructed national administrations to ignore ECJ jurisprudence, or interpreted away any difference between EC law and national policy. The threat that national governments might turn to these extralegal means, disobeying an ECJ decision, helped contain ECJ activism. With national courts enforcing ECJ jurisprudence against their own governments, however, many of these extralegal avenues no longer worked. Because of national judicial support for ECJ jurisprudence, national governments were forced to frame their response in terms that could persuade a legal audience, and thus they became constrained by the legal rules of the game.[19]

The coalition of the ECJ and national courts allowed the EU to increase its influence over domestic reversion points by 'limiting the possible responses of national governments to [ECJ] decisions within the domestic political realm'.[20] While, in the early part of this period, a principal or agent who disliked EU actions could circumvent an EU-impacted reversion point, in the later part of this period the coalition of courts prevented such circumventions. When the ECJ and national courts protected reversion points that were relatively far from that of the affected principal, the presence of the EU increased agency loss. By contrast, when the ECJ and national courts protected reversion points that were relatively close to the affected principal, the presence of the EU decreased agency loss. Mazey makes a similar argument, showing how EU actions affected national-level gender equality policies.[21]

HOW OUTSIDE FORCES AFFECT INFORMATION

The EU and the EEA can affect a domestic principal's information in at least two ways. First, it can provide a new source of information for the principal. Kite, for example, suggests that after EU membership, the Swedish parliament, via its European Affairs Committee, actually began to receive more (rather than less) information about some areas of foreign policy.[22] This is because the Swedish cabinet is required to report to the European Affairs Committee about positions that it takes in the EU Council of Ministers. This has had impacts for some foreign policy questions (such as foreign trade) insofar as matters previously handled largely within the Ministry of Foreign Affairs itself are now presented before a parliamentary committee. Second, outside forces can affect the incentives of those domestic actors charged with providing information to political principals. How this can come about is a theoretical question upon which we now focus.

In the 30 years since Harsanyi introduced modern notions of uncertainty to game theory,[23] scholars have produced many enlightening advances in how information affects political decision making. The advances most relevant to the question at hand clarify how institutions affect what is said, what is believed, and who can learn what from whom.[24] A description follows of what this work implies about how outside forces affect domestic accountability by affecting the principal's information.

A principal may lack the information she needs to distinguish agent actions that help her from agent actions that hurt her (that is, she may lack knowledge sufficient to reduce agency loss). Such a principal can obtain relevant information in three ways: direct monitoring, attending to *what the agent says* about his activities, or attending to *third party testimony* about the agent's actions. Each of these options can provide a principal with valuable knowledge about her agent. However, each option also has drawbacks. Most political principals lack the time and energy to engage in direct monitoring of their agents. Therefore, they are forced to learn what they need to know from others.

Relying on others for information, however, can entail substantial peril. Not all people from whom political principals can seek advice are equally trustworthy or knowledgeable. Therefore, a principal who wants to exert some degree of control over her agent's actions must be very selective about which advice she follows. She has an incentive to seek information from sources that provide credible reports of agent activities and to avoid information from those who provide vague or misleading reports. Outside forces can help by *offering alternate means for assessing credibility.*

Through their actions, outside forces can affect what people *choose* to say and what people *choose* to believe. Thus, outside forces affect credibility. How these forces work should be familiar to any member of an advanced industrial economy. For example, every day millions of people buy goods from, and sell goods to, people about whom they know little or nothing. Each of these transactions requires some degree of trust (for example, that the currency offered as payment is legitimate and that the merchandise has its advertised characteristics). Since buyers and sellers do not know each other well, they must have an alternate and effective means for evaluating credibility. Outside forces (that is, forces which do not directly participate in individual transactions) can take actions that provide buyers and sellers with substitutes for unobservable personal characteristics. For example, laws and customs realign strangers' incentives, giving people a basis for trust in billions of situations where it would not otherwise exist. The outside forces that promulgate and enforce these laws provide the basis for credibility that makes advanced economies possible.

What types of actions can the EU take to affect a domestic principal's ability to learn about her agent's activities? In particular, how do EU actions affect the incentives of those on whom domestic principals rely for advice about their agent's actions? These questions are answered by describing how verification, penalties for lying, and observable and costly efforts affect what domestic principals can learn about their agents. Individually, these forces can change what people say to a principal and can affect what a principal believes. Collectively, these three types of actions cover the range of effects that outside forces can have on communication. The following discussion is kept brief and intuitive.[25]

Verification works by posing the threat that the principal can discern true signals from false ones. This threat changes the speaker's incentives in the following way: as the probability of verification increases, the probability that he can benefit from sending a false signal decreases. Therefore, *verification decreases the expected value of making false or vague statements.* When the threat of verification distinguishes speakers from one another on the basis of their willingness to reveal what they know, the threat of verification provides the principal with a more effective way to judge the credibility of others.

Outside forces increase the likelihood of verification when they provide new actors with incentives to verify existing information. An agreement such as the EEA, for example, gives actors within Member States incentives and opportunities to act as verifiers on certain activities in other Member States. A domestic agent, who, in the absence of the threat of verification, would pursue a personal agenda rather than the agenda of his principals, must now consider the potentially verifying activities of actors in other EEA nations. When EEA or EU membership increases the population of potential verifiers, domestic agents are faced with a higher likelihood that their principals will detect and reject his actions. In such a case, the emergence of the EU and the EEA can help to reduce agency loss.

Penalties for lying help a principal gain information about her agent's actions by giving everyone involved a reason to believe that the principal can distinguish truth tellers from liars. In general, a principal who believes that the speaker faces a penalty for lying can make one of the following two inferences upon hearing a statement from the speaker: (1) the statement is true; or (2) the statement is false and the value to the speaker of lying is greater than the expected penalty if caught. When penalties for lying have this effect, they provide a window through which the principal can perceive the speaker's incentives, and judge his credibility, with greater accuracy. As a result, when outside forces increase domestic penalties for lying they can reduce agency loss.

When outside forces induce people to take *observable and costly efforts*, they can also affect domestic actors' information about each other. The logic underlying this effect closely follows the old adage: 'actions speak louder than words.' When a speaker takes a costly action (that is, exerts effort), he reveals information about how much a particular outcome is worth to him.[26] When we can distinguish the claims of others by the amount of effort they put into making the statements, we have yet another tool for assessing credibility.

Actors in the EU can affect the likelihood that certain claims by domestic actors are verified, can affect the magnitude of a penalty for lying, can make certain types of costly efforts easier to observe, and can make certain types of observable efforts more costly. When the emergence of the EU has these effects, it affects a principal's ability to assess the credibility of others. A principal who can better assess credibility is better able to learn about her agent's actions and, therefore, is better able to increase domestic accountability.

An example of the EU affecting domestic delegation relationships through affecting who can learn from whom can be seen by examining European Affairs Committees (EACs). As Raunio has shown,[27] EACs have increased in importance in all EU Member States. In addition to providing information about EU activities directly, EACs have caused certain governments to document more of their goals and policy positions.[28] These increases in documentation provide a basis for verification, penalties for lying or costly effort that did not exist before. During a later policy debate or an election, this additional documentation may affect the credibility of domestic agents' claims. To the extent that these claims are made by agents (that is, ministers) who know that they can be held accountable by others (that is, MPs or voters), the fact that the EU has induced greater documentation may translate into reduced agency loss.

CONCLUSION

In every Member State of the EU or the EEA, governance requires a chain of delegation. If agents in this chain of delegation are accountable to their principals, then the chain links the interests of political actors at various levels of government. In many discussions about the EU and the EEA, a common hypothesis is that the emergence of these outside forces necessarily reduces Member State governments' effectiveness. This article rejects this hypothesis.

Outside forces can affect the incentives of domestic principals and agents. They do this by shifting domestic reversion points. Such shifts can change the balance of power between domestic principals and agents. When outside forces shift a reversion point closer to a principal's ideal policy and away from her agent's ideal policy, they also increase the principal's bargaining leverage *vis-à-vis* her agent, and can lead to increased domestic accountability. However, in cases when outside forces shift a reversion point farther from a principal's ideal policy, they can decrease the principal's bargaining leverage and lead to decreased domestic accountability.

Outside forces can also affect domestic political actors' information. The EU and EEA can either provide information directly or change individuals' incentives in ways that affect who is credible to whom. For example, when membership in the EU or the EEA increases the likelihood of verification, the magnitude of penalties for lying, or the observability or costs of certain actions, they can help domestic principals distinguish between credible and non-credible advice. When principals gain this ability, the presence of the EU and the EEA increases domestic accountability.

This analysis of how the EU and the EEA affect domestic accountability is brief, its focus on reversion points and information is narrow. However, it is sufficient to reject an important null hypothesis – that the emergence of the EU or the EEA necessarily weakens the prospects of accountable national-level governance. While the extent to which EU and EEA actors have shifted domestic reversion points or information is an empirical question, that they have done so and will continue to do so is a certainty. Our attempts to explain or increase domestic accountability should incorporate this reality.

NOTES

1. See, for example, T. Bergman, 'National Parliaments and EU Affairs Committees: Notes on Empirical Variation and Competing Explanations', *Journal of European Public Policy*, Vol.4, No.4, (1998), pp.373–87; L. Martin, *Democratic Commitments: Legislatures and International Cooperation* (forthcoming); T. Raunio, 'Always One Step Behind? National Legislatures and the European Union', *Government and Opposition*, Vol.34, No.2 (1999), pp.180–202.

2. See, K. Strøm, 'Delegation and Accountability in Parliamentary Democracies' (University of California: Manuscript, n.d.); K. Strøm, W.C. Müller and T. Bergman, *Delegation and Accountability in Parliamentary Democracies* (University of California: Book manuscript, n.d.).
3. For example, K.A. Shepsle, 'Institutional Arrangements and Equilibrium in Multidimensional Voting Models', *American Journal of Political Science*, Vol.23, No.1 (1979), pp.27–60; D.C. North, *Structure and Change in Economic History* (New York: Norton, 1981); O. Williamson, *Markets and Hierarchies: Analysis and Antitrust Implications* (New York: The Free Press, 1975).
4. In the text I use the agency loss metric for its simplicity. However, a problem with the agency loss metric is that it focuses on an unrealistic reference point – the actions of a perfect agent. If people forget about this reference point when using the metric to interpret a study of delegation, then delegation will often seem to be a bad idea. However, the presence of agency loss need not imply that delegation is undesirable. Many political principals, such as voters or MPs, do not have the ability to provide all of the services that they ask their agents to provide. That is, most voters, legislators and ministers lack the time or energy to be perfect agents for themselves. So even if no delegation takes place, outcomes are likely to deviate from the ones that perfect agents would provide (that is, policy outcomes absent delegation are equivalent to policy outcomes with delegation and agency loss). As a result, I believe it better to interpret delegation outcomes by comparing them to a more realistic reference point – what would have happened if the principal had chosen not to delegate. In other work, I have used such a metric. In A. Lupia and M.D. McCubbins, *The Democratic Dilemma: Can Citizens Learn What they Need to Know?* (New York: Cambridge University Press, 1998), and A. Lupia and M.D. McCubbins, 'When is Delegation Abdication: How Citizens Use Institutions to Make Their Agents Accountable', *European Journal of Political Research* (Special Issue edited by T. Bergman, W. Müller and K. Strøm, forthcoming 2000) we define delegation as *successful* if the outcome of delegation improves the principal's welfare relative to the policy reversion point (that is, what would have happened had the principal and agent been inactive). We define delegation as *failed* if the outcome of delegation decreases the principal's welfare relative to the policy reversion point. The main difference between the agency loss metric and the success/failure metric is that the reference point for the former is a hypothetical outcome that rarely exists – a perfect agent – while the reference point to the latter is an entity that always exists – the reversion point.
5. See, W.A. Niskanen, *Bureaucracy and Representative Government* (Chicago, IL: Aldine-Atherton, 1971).
6. T. Romer and H. Rosenthal, 'Political Resource Allocation, Controlled Agendas, and the Status Quo', *Public Choice*, Vol.33, No.1 (1978), pp.27–44.
7. I follow convention by modelling delegation as a situation in which the agent makes proposals and the principal acts as a veto player. This convention allows the consequences of delegation to be described in the simplest possible terms. Fortunately, the results reported in the text are affected in straightforward ways by increasing the principal's range of action. Generally, the greater the principal's amendment powers, the greater her ability to reduce agency loss.
8. P.C. Ordeshook, *A Political Theory Primer* (New York: Routledge, 1992), p.97.
9. If RP is greater than A and P, then the agent will propose $P - |RP\text{-}P| + \varepsilon$, where $\varepsilon > 0$ and small. If RP is less than A and P, then the agent will propose $P + |RP\text{-}P| - \varepsilon$.
10. See, for example, M. Weber, 'Economy and Society', in H.H. Gerth and C. Wright Mills (eds.), *From Max Weber: Essays in Sociology* (New York: Oxford University Press, 1946); R.A. Dahl, *Pluralist Democracy in the United States: Conflict and Consent* (Chicago, IL: Rand McNally, 1967).
11. A. Lupia, 'Busy Voters, Agenda Control, and the Power of Information', *American Political Science Review*, Vol.86, No.2 (1992), pp.390–404.
12. To draw the proper inference about agency loss from Table 1, note that notation of the form $-|X - P|$ refers to the utility level of the principal given his ideal policy, $P \in [0,1]$, and the outcome of delegation, $X \in [0,1]$. So, for example, when the outcome of delegation is the principal's ideal policy, as it is in the complete information version of situation 1, then the

principal's utility level is $-|P-P|$ or 0. When the outcome of delegation is the agent's ideal policy, as it is in several instances in the table, then the principal's utility level is $-|A-P|$. Now, recall that agency loss is the difference between the actual consequences of delegating to the agent and what the consequence would have been had the agent been a perfect agent. Hence, agency loss in Table 1 is the difference between the principal's actual utility level from delegating to the agent and P, what the principal's utility level would have been had the agent been perfect.

13. Note that I shall focus on how outside forces affect the relationship between P and RP, but not the relationship between P and A. The reason for this focus is that the reversion point is a policy and the EU can affect policy in observable ways. By contrast, the agent's ideal point may come from the agent's ideology, beliefs, or any number of psychological processes. While membership in the EU and the EEA may affect the psychological processes of domestic principals and agents, they do so in ways that tend to fall outside the focus of contemporary economic and positive political theory. Exceptions to this rule include North, *Structure and Change in Economic History*, E. Gerber and J.E. Jackson, 'Endogenous Preferences and the Study of Institutions', *American Political Science Review*, Vol.87, No.3 (1993), pp.639–56, and M. Hinich and M.C. Munger, *Ideology and the Theory of Political Choice* (Ann Arbor, MI: University of Michigan Press, 1994).

14. K.J. Alter, 'Who Are the Masters of the Treaty?: European Governments in the European Court of Justice', *International Organization*, Vol.52, No.1 (1997), pp.121–47.

15. Alter, 'Who Are the Masters of the Treaty?', p.126.

16. Alter, 'Who Are the Masters of the Treaty?', p.122.

17. Alter, 'Who Are the Masters of the Treaty?', p.143.

18. Alter, 'Who Are the Masters of the Treaty?', p.122.

19. Alter, 'Who Are the Masters of the Treaty?', p.122.

20. Alter, 'Who Are the Masters of the Treaty?', p.122.

21. S. Mazey, 'The European Union and Women's Rights: From the Europeanization of National Agendas to the Nationalization of a European Agenda?', *Journal of European Public Policy*, Vol.5, No.1 (1998), pp.131–52.

22. C. Kite, 'Making Foreign Policy After Membership: '"Post-Yes" Politics in Sweden', *The European Policy Process Occasional Paper*, No.24 (1996). Human Capital and Mobility Network, Essex, UK. See also the contributions in this volume.

23. J. Harsanyi, 'Games with Incomplete Information Played by "Bayesian" Players, I: The Basic Model', *Management Science*, Vol.14, No.3 (1967), pp.159–82.

24. For example, A.M. Spence, *Market Signaling: Informational Transfer in Hiring and Related Screening Processes* (Cambridge, MA: Harvard University Press, 1974); J.S. Banks, *Signaling Games in Political Science* (Chur, Switzerland: Harwood Academic Publishers, 1991); Lupia and McCubbins, *The Democratic Dilemma: Can Citizens Learn What they Need to Know?*.

25. For those interested in greater detail, see Lupia and McCubbins, *The Democratic Dilemma: Can Citizens Learn What they Need to Know?* .

26. For example, if a knowledgeable speaker pays $100 for the opportunity to persuade us, then we can infer that the difference in expected value to the speaker between what the speaker expects us to do after hearing his statement and what he expects us to do if we do not hear his statement is at least $100. Therefore, even if he ultimately delivers his statement in a language that we do not understand, the speaker's payment informs us that our choice is important to him.

27. Raunio, 'Always One Step Behind?: National Legislatures and the European Union'.

28. E. Damgaard and A.S. Nørgaard, 'The European Union and Danish Parliamentary Democracy', this volume.

The European Union and Danish Parliamentary Democracy

ERIK DAMGAARD and
ASBJØRN SONNE NØRGAARD

Denmark entered the EC in 1973 and thereby delegated power to a supranational organisation. Membership was made possible by the constitutional amendment of 1953, which foresaw the need for integrated international co-operation in the post-1945 world. The constitution states (§ 20) that: 'Powers vested in the authorities of the Realm under this Constitutional Act may, to such extent as shall be provided by statute, be delegated to international authorities set up by mutual agreement with other states for the promotion of international rules of law and co-operation.'

From a Danish constitutional point of view, we are talking about a revocable 'delegation' because a law can be passed that simply recalls the delegation of power approved by the parliament (Folketinget) and referenda in 1972, 1986, 1993 and 1998. It is quite another matter whether a recall is possible in practice, given the enormous political, economic and social costs it would entail. Perhaps, then, one could argue that Danish authorities have *de facto* 'abdicated' with respect to the power formally delegated to the EC/EU.

On the other hand, Denmark is a member of the Union to which it has – from this point of view – irrevocably transferred powers. In various formal and informal ways, Denmark is represented in the bodies of the European Union, including the Council of Ministers, the Commission, the European Parliament, the Court, and so on. The delegated powers are therefore transferred to an organisation in which the country has voting rights. As long as unanimity was the dominating decision mode in the Council of Ministers delegating power was no problem, provided that the national Danish system of accountability worked as it should. However, the increasing use of (qualified) majority voting in the Council after the Single European Act (SEA, 1986) and the Maastricht Treaty (MAT, 1993), with the associated Edinburgh Agreement (granting Denmark some opt-outs from

Erik Damgaard is Professor and Asbjørn Sonne Nørgaard is Assistant Professor in the Department of Political Science at the University of Aarhus, Denmark.

the MAT), certainly could create problems in terms of national sovereignty. But, again, integration also creates opportunities for influence that a small nation would not otherwise enjoy.

In this article we look closer at the overall question of how more than a quarter-century's EU membership has affected national decision-making processes. The specific questions to be addressed concern membership's effects on delegation and accountability relationships between voters, MPs, the cabinet and the civil service. We use the general approach selected for the country contributions to the present volume. For each principal–agent link (voters–MPs, MPs–cabinet, cabinet–ministers, minister–civil servants) in an ideal type chain of delegation and accountability, we are interested in the *ex ante* and *ex post* instruments of control available to Danish principals, and in how these instruments and their use have changed with EU membership. Thus, while the main focus is on accountability as a process of representation, we also refer to accountability as a policy outcome of representation.

VOTERS AS PRINCIPALS, MPs (AND MEPs) AS AGENTS

This section first discusses the institutional constraints on the ideal-type description of MPs and MEPs (Members of the European Parliament) as agents of voters. Parties, and to a lesser degree referenda, interfere with the pure principal–agent relationship. Given the context of this institutional reality, we discuss the extent to which the authority delegated to the MPs/MEPs has been revoked by voters. Whereas in relation to EU issues the principal – that is voters – is highly assertive, the withdrawal of delegated power over EU matters has had few repercussions for the relationship between voters and their agents in the national parliament.

Formal and Informal Constraints on MPs' and MEPs' Role as Voter Agents

Although political parties are not mentioned in the Danish constitution, any discussion of voters as principals and MPs as agents has to take into account the critical role played by parties. MPs are elected on the basis of a party platform. The role of MPs as agents of voters is thus a highly mediated relationship. Constitutionally, MPs are bound only by their consciences, but in practice party discipline is strong and party voting in the Folketinget is the predominant behavioural rule for Danish MPs. This norm is facilitated by the fact that a party's parliamentary group and leadership control the distribution of positions in the party hierarchy.[1] However, party discipline is also partly a result of electoral rules, which recognise political parties.

The Danish two-tier PR electoral system has comparatively low threshold requirements,[2] the minimum of two per cent of the total national vote being the most important,[3] and it allows preferential voting on open party lists. Still, the overwhelming majority of MPs do not get enough personal votes to win a seat. Hence, they are elected partly by way of party votes.

Although the parties can distribute party votes according to a preferential formula, in most parties the party vote is distributed equally among the candidates. Those with the highest personal vote therefore get elected. This gives voters a strong influence over exactly who gets elected, even if the transferred party vote is crucial for getting a seat. However, before the voter can exercise this control, local and regional party organisations have already selected the candidates.[4] Given the general decline in party membership,[5] this important function has become the prerogative of the still smaller group of local party cadres.

Thus, MPs' accountability goes beyond accountability to voters on election day. MPs are also agents of their local party organisations and parliamentary groups, both of whom can penalise and reward an MP in various ways. *Ex ante* and *ex post* control is intertwined in a process involving several principals who control nomination, election and appointment.

Adding the EU level further complicates the principal–agent relationship. First, voters as principals have MP/MEP agents in two parliaments with partially overlapping authority. Traditionally, the MEPs have been looked upon as 'second-rate parliamentarians'.[6] However, the emergence of supranational authority and the increasing powers of the EP in some Pillar 1 issues have changed this. MEPs are in the process of becoming genuine agents of some significance, although national agents – because of their influence on the government's behaviour in the Council (cf. section II below) – are still more important. Second, the frequent use of referenda allows Danish voter-principals to express their attitudes on various issues without going through their agents.

There is no mention of the EU in the Danish constitution. Election to the European Parliament is regulated by a 1977 act.[7] Like the laws on national and local elections, it presumes the existence of political parties, and the electoral rules are the same as the ones used in local government elections. In electing the 16 Danish MEPs the whole country is treated as a single multi-member district. As in all other elections, a PR system is used. As in local elections, alliances among lists are allowed in the one-tier EP elections. Candidates are distributed among lists according to the d'Hont formula (divisor 1,2,3…n). Because there are only 16 MEPs, the effective threshold is higher than in national elections. According to the method suggested by Lijphart, the effective threshold is 4.7 per cent for European Parliament elections.[8]

As in national elections, the parties can distribute party votes in an EP election according to a preferential formula that allots the party vote to a particular candidate. However, as in national elections, most parties distribute the party vote among the candidates in proportion to their individual vote. Preferential voting may therefore be decisive. Typically, only one or two top candidates are known to the general public. These well-known candidates get the lions' share of the preferential votes. Other elected candidates on the list may have received relatively few preferential votes. Preferential voting for little known candidates may thus be quite effective in cases where the party list gains more seats.[9]

The link between MEPs and voters is thus also mediated by parties, though the exact character of the role of parties as selectors of candidates is uncertain. The issue of candidate nomination is largely unregulated by law. In general, local and, in particular, regional party organisations play a role in finding and suggesting candidates, but the national level is also involved in ranking candidates and deciding which formula to apply for distributing party votes. The general picture is a little unclear due to the fact that there are two anti-integrationist movements that run for the EP, but not for national political office.

A recent study of the candidates running for the EP can shed some light on the issue of candidate selection.[10] Responses from 105 of 183 Danish candidates for the 1994 EP election indicate that regional party leaders have more power in candidate selection than national and local party leaders. However, on average the candidates perceive 'national party factions' and 'local party members' to be as important as regional party leaders in selecting candidates. The role of national party factions and party members may be related to the fact that some parties have to balance their lists to reflect the relative power of sceptics-*cum*-opponents and supporters of the EU among voters and party members.

Still, the exact way to nominate candidates may not be that important since '(t)he European parliament is still a dead end for a national politician in his prime',[11] and therefore the competition for nomination is probably not that fierce. Of course, with the increasing powers and status of the EP, this may be in the process of changing.

The EP parliamentary groups may also exercise some influence on MEPs, for instance by controlling committee appointments.[12] Generally speaking, the EP party groups have been seen as weak bodies which bear little resemblance to traditional political parties.[13] Evidence indicates that party groups in the EP are fairly cohesive as compared to the US Congress, but they are still less cohesive than in national parliaments in western Europe.[14]

For a Euro-sceptic country like Denmark, the spoils that the EP party groups control are probably too weak to challenge the status of national parties and voters as the most important principals. Assuming that EP 'parties' belong to the pro-integrationist European elite, evidence indicates that their impact on Danish MEPs is weaker than in most other countries. Comparing differences of opinion between MEPs and the electorate on three issues of integration, congruence is 'closest in Denmark and Italy'.[15] Thus, the power of EP parliamentary groups as principals seems comparatively weak in the Danish case.

Bringing into the picture the somewhat exceptional practice of frequent referenda on EU-treaty matters, the principal–agent relationship among Danish voters and MPs/MEPs becomes even more confused.

Four of the five referenda on EU treaty matters have been (seen as) constitutionally mandated. Sovereignty delegated to international authorities 'to such extent as shall be provided by statute' (§20) requires a referendum unless a five-sixth majority in the Folketinget have approved the treaty. Three referenda (1972, 1992, 1998) have referred to this rule, albeit without knowing whether the necessary majority actually existed.[16] A fourth referendum – in 1993 on the second Maastricht Treaty, which included the Danish opt-out clauses – referred to other articles in the constitution (§ 42(5), cf. § 19). In this case an ordinary law was passed mandating a binding referendum to be held. Finally, the 1986 referendum on the Single European Act was merely 'consultative' (under § 42(6)). It was suggested by then prime minister Poul Schlüter when he realised that the treaty could not muster a majority in the Folketinget. In practice, the 1986 referendum was also binding.[17]

As a legal institution the practice of referenda may be somewhat unclear. However, as a political institution constraining the autonomy of the Folketinget it has become strong. The principal–agent delegation of authority is revoked in EU treaty matters, and the Danish voter-principals are generally not in agreement with the policy positions of MP-agents when they exercise this power.

How EU Politics Affect the Voter–MP Relationship

With MPs and MEPs confronting principals other than voters, and with voters having an opportunity to express their views without using their agents, the congruence between voters and MPs becomes an interesting empirical question. How does EU politics affect the voter–MP relationship, and to what extent do differences in policy preference give rise to a distinct EU dimension in Danish party politics?

To begin with, it may be noted that the turnout for EP elections is much lower than for national elections and EU-related referenda. The mean

TABLE 1

RESULTS OF EP AND THE CLOSEST FOLKETING ELECTIONS, 1979–99: BALANCE OF EURO-POSITIVE AND EURO-NEGATIVE PARTIES IN EP AND FT

	FT-79	EP-79	FT-84	EP-84	FT-88	EP-89	FT-94	EP-94	FT-98	EP-99
Liberals *	12.5	14.5	12.1	12.4	11.8	16.6	23.3	17.7	24.0	23.3
Conservatives *	12.5	14.0	23.4	20.8	19.3	13.3	15.0	19.0	8.9	8.5
Centre Democrats *	3.2	6.2	4.6	6.6	4.7	8.0	2.8	0.9	4.3	3.5
Christian People's P. *	2.6	1.8	2.7	2.8	2.0	2.7	1.8	1.1	2.5	2.0
Radicals *	5.4	3.3	5.5	3.1	5.6	2.8	4.6	8.5	3.9	9.1
Social Democrats *	38.3	21.9	31.6	19.5	29.8	23.3	34.6	15.8	35.9	16.5
Progress Party *	11.0	5.8	3.6	3.5	9.0	5.3	6.4 #	2.9 #	2.4 #	0.7
Danish People's P. #	–	–	–	–	–	–	–	–	7.4	5.8
Justice Party #	2.6	3.4	1.5	–	–	–	–	–	–	–
Socialist People's P. #	5.9	4.7	11.5	9.2	13.0	9.1	7.3	8.6	7.6	7.1
Left Wing #	6.0	3.5	3.5	1.3	4.7	–	3.1	–	2.7	–
People's Movement Against EC #	–	20.9	–	20.8	–	18.9	–	10.3	–	7.3
June Movement #	–	–	–	–	–	–	–	15.2	–	16.1
Euro-positive Parties	85.5	67.5	83.5	68.7	82.2	72.0	82.1	63.0	79.5	62.9
Euro-negative Parties	14.5	32.5	16.5	31.3	17.7	28.0	16.8	37.0	20.5	37.0
Euro-negative (EP-FT)		+18		+14.8		+10.3		+20.2		+16.5

Note: *: Euro-positive Parties; #: Euro-negative Parties. Although the SPP advocated a 'yes' to the second Maastricht referendum, the official party line has remained sceptical towards the EU. In 1994, one per cent of the popular vote went to Jacob Haugaard. In 1998 0.4 per cent of the vote went to Democratic Renewal, a stern Euro-negative party.

Source: Statistisk Årbog, various years; Folketingets Årbog, 1997/98; www.eu-oplysningen.dk

turnout for EP elections in the period 1979–99 was 49.9 per cent (50.4 per cent for the 1999 EP election), whereas it was 85.3 per cent for national elections during the same period. Turnout was 82.0 per cent for the five referenda held between 1972 to 1998.[18] This indicates that MEPs are seen as less important agents as compared to MPs, and perhaps that the development of a European loyalty and identity is still fairly weak. Furthermore, as indicated by Table 1, there is a distinct difference in voting behaviour with regard to the Folketing elections and the EP.

As the table reveals, voters give different directions to their MP agents and their MEP agents. That is, their general party preferences and loyalties do not determine their voting behaviour in EP elections. Evidence from the 1979 and 1984 EP elections showed that voter turnout was higher among voters in anti-EC parties and that those voters who disagreed with their national party abstained more often.[19] The problem is worst for the Social Democrats, who have been split on the EU issue since 1972. In the early 1970s MPs and voters were divided on the issue of membership, while in the 1990s voters (and particularly Social Democratic voters) are divided on the issue of further integration.[20] In the 1998 referendum only about 55 per cent of Social Democratic voters followed the unified party recommendation to vote 'yes' for the Amsterdam Treaty. In the 1999 EP election the Social Democratic share of the vote was less than half of the share won in the Folketing election of 1998 (see Table 1).

TABLE 2

PERCENTAGE MPS IN PARLIAMENT RECOMMENDING 'NO' TO REFERENDUM AND PERCENTAGE 'NO' AMONG VOTERS, 1972–98

	MPs recommending 'no' (%)	Voters saying 'no' (%)
1972: Joining the EC	9.8 (Socialist People's Party)	36.7 (+26.9)
1986: Single European Act	56 (SD, Radicals, Socialist People's Party, Left Socialists)	43.8 (–12.2)
1992: Maastricht Treaty	15.4 (Socialist People's Party, Progressive Party)	50.7 (+35.3)
1993: Maastricht Treaty with opt-out clauses (Edinburgh)	6.9 (Progressive Party)	43.3 (+36.4)
1998: Amsterdam Treaty	20 (Socialist People's Party, Unity List, Progressive Party, Danish People's Party)	44.9 (+24.9)

Sources: Siune et al., 1994: 33; Pedersen, 1996; Statistisk Årbog, various years;

Still, voters in all the major parties, with the exception of the Socialist People's Party, perceive their MPs to be more pro-integrationist than they are themselves.[21] In general, MPs believe the same thing.[22] The difference between the number of MPs recommending a 'no' vote in EU referenda and voter behaviour mirrors this discord among MPs and their principals.

Comparing Tables 1 and 2 makes it clear that voter behaviour in EU-related referenda is more in accordance with voter behaviour in EP elections than in the Folketing elections. Thus, there is an EU conflict dimension – though probably not a deep cleavage – which is evident in voting concerning EU politics as such, but which is apparently not strong enough to impact on the voter–MP relationship in national politics. This claim needs to be elaborated.

First of all, the significance of the difference between voting behaviour in EP and the Folketing elections should not be exaggerated. The low turnout in EP elections is one indication of how important Danes consider the European Parliament. Besides, voting behaviour in EP elections also seems to be a way for voters to inform national politicians of their Euro-scepticism. As corroborative evidence for this interpretation, it may be noted that Danish voters do not think highly of the EP. Danes have been among those Europeans who see the EP to be of little importance. Since 1992, they have been the only ones who, on balance, hope that the EP will become even less important in the future.[23] This separates voters somewhat from their national MP agents, who hope for a stronger role for the EP in the future.[24] The electorate's view on and hopes for the EP reflects a deep opposition to further political integration in the EU.[25]

Second, that the difference in opinion between MPs and voters does not cause more stress in Danish politics is due to the fact that EU politics has never been a priority issue among Danish voters. The EU consistently ranks low in surveys about the most important issues in Danish politics.[26] A study on the 1994 general election[27] found that EU politics had no impact on the election outcome. It concludes more generally that 'the European referenda and elections tend to stand, as it were, in parentheses in Danish voting behaviour'.[28]

Although EU issues have not directly determined voting behaviour – nor are they likely to do so in the near future – they may have an indirect impact. In combination with immigration policy, the 'policy distance' from the governing party on EU issues has the strongest impact on voters' political distrust in government.[29] It may be conjectured that the entry of the new right-wing party, the Danish People's Party, in 1998, and the general increase in support for the extreme right is related to political distrust, and thus indirectly to EU-scepticism in an unholy alliance with a fierce anti-immigration policy stance.

In sum, EU politics has made its mark on Danish politics. MEPs are new agents of voters, and voters send them partially conflicting signals compared to national MPs. When voters act as their own agents in referenda, their behaviour also differs quite markedly from that of their usual MP-agents in national politics. Whereas this apparent inconsistency is primarily due to the low saliency of EU in national politics, it may also be interpreted as a message to national MPs about their principal's preferences on one particular policy issue – something which is usually impossible in representative democracies. In addition, a recall of delegated powers, that is, the possibility that the parliamentary majority is defeated in a referendum, is something Danish MPs fear. Finally, with the strong presence of anti-integrationist movements among Danish MEPs, Danish voters may have more sources of information on EU matters than voters in many other member countries. For these reasons, Danish voter-principals' control over their national MPs in EU-*cum*-international affairs may actually have increased.

PARLIAMENT AS PRINCIPAL AND CABINET AS AGENT

As long as it is remembered that political parties are the driving forces in parliamentary politics, it makes sense to look into questions concerning the committees, procedures and resources of the Folketing.

Parliamentary Organisation

The Danish parliamentary committee system was reformed in 1972 with the creation of some 20 permanent committees covering the policy areas of the various government departments.[30] One of the new committees was the Market Relations Committee ('Markedsudvalget'), since 1994 the European Affairs Committee ('Europaudvalget'). Today there are 22 permanent committees with substantial policy tasks. They all have 17 members (and a number of substitutes, typically about ten) with a party composition reflecting the relative sizes of the parliamentary groups.

Committee members may discuss any matter within their jurisdiction whether a formal proposal is being considered or not. They may ask for written information from the responsible minister, and they may request the presence of the minister in a committee meeting to answer questions (called a 'consultation'). Of course, they may also use the control instruments generally available to MPs, such as written and oral questions and interpellations.[31] In short, the committees have ample opportunity to interfere with the legislative and administrative activities of ministers who are responsible for the work performed by their civil servants.

The committees are not unitary actors but rather arenas that structure the activities of party representatives.[32] As such they are very important bodies, especially for opposition parties. Except for one majority government (January 1993–September 1994), all Danish governments since 1971 have had to rely on the support of one or more opposition parties. The minority status of governments undoubtedly increases the importance and influence of committees, not least the European Affairs Committee (EAC) because of the way it is integrated into the Danish European policy-making process.

The Accession Act of 1972 requires that the government report to the Folketinget on developments in the European Communities. It further states that: 'The government informs a committee set up by the Folketing about proposals for Council decisions which become directly applicable in Denmark, or the fulfilling of which requires the approval of the Folketing.' However, more precise rules for parliamentary involvement were agreed upon by all parties in government and opposition after a political crisis in February 1973.[33] Thus, the very first report of the Market Relation Committee (29 March 1973) stated that: 'Prior to negotiations in the EC Council of Ministers on decisions of a wider scope, the government submits an oral mandate for negotiation to the EEC Committee. If there is no majority against the mandate, the government negotiates on this basis.'

This basic rule has been observed by all subsequent governments and, today, might possibly be considered a part of Danish constitutional law. Parliament wanted to control (*ex ante*) the behaviour of the government in the Council. The goal was to prevent the government from committing Denmark to a policy that was opposed by a majority in parliament, just as the country is not to have a government that is unacceptable to a parliamentary majority.

The EAC is clearly the most important committee in EU affairs. It is involved in all EU matters and is the only committee that can give a bargaining mandate to a minister. Thus the EAC delegates limited power to the government, which is accountable to the committee and to parliament. To ensure that there is no parliamentary majority against a government position, mandates are determined by calculating the number of parliamentary seats which party representatives on the committee represent.

Membership on the EAC is generally considered very attractive by MPs. A 1992 questionnaire among MPs showed that the committee was regarded as the most important, followed, at some distance, by the Finance Committee.[34] The importance of the EAC can be illustrated further by its staffing. Whereas the other permanent committees usually employ an

FIGURE 1
THE EU COMMITTEE: EU COMMITTEE MEETINGS; EU COMMITTEE
CONSULTATIONS; AVERAGE MEETINGS/CONSULTATIONS PER COMMITTEE.
PERCENTAGES OF ALL PERMANENT COMMITTEES, 1972/73–1997/98

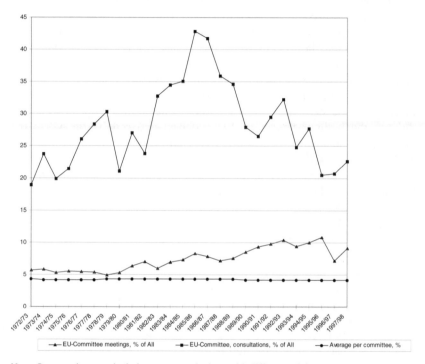

Note: One meeting may include more consultations with different ministers.

Source: Folketinget, Årbog og Register, various years.

academic staff of one or two persons, the EAC employs an academic staff of six and a clerical staff of five. One of the academic staff is an official representative of the Folketinget at the EU. S/he is stationed in Brussels and reports to the EAC on EU work, particularly the activities of the European Parliament and Commission.

Although the EAC clearly is the central committee in EU matters, other committees may also play a role. However, with a few exceptions, notably the Environment Committee, their input has so far been limited. Since 1994, documents to the EAC have simultaneously been sent to the relevant permanent committee. However, it is up to the committees whether and how they deal with the issues within their respective fields. Special procedures pertain to Pillar 2 (common foreign and security policy) and Pillar 3 (co-operation on legal, police and asylum policy) of the Maastricht Treaty. In these cases, the government informs the Foreign Policy Committee and the Legal Affairs Committee, respectively, in addition to the EAC.

To see how the EAC works as of early 1999 we can briefly outline the procedures followed in decision-making.[35] The EAC meets every Friday except in August, thus it meets even when the Folketinget is not in session. The meetings may last for two to five hours. The frequency of meetings and, notably, the number of EAC consultations with ministers is therefore high compared to that of other permanent committees (see Figure 1).

The most important topics on the EAC agenda are the Council meetings to be held the following week. The minister opens by going through the main issues in an EU proposal and reports on where the negotiations stand. If a decision is expected in the Council, the minister will give a detailed account ending with a request for a bargaining mandate. The mandate is confidential and not put down on paper, but the Secretariat produces summary minutes that are sent to the party spokesmen. Members of other committees can read them in the Secretariat. The minutes obviously help the committee in exercising *ex post* control over the behaviour of the minister. After the opening presentation there is a question-and-answer session. The discussion of an item is not concluded with a formal vote, but the chairman usually notes that there is no majority against the proposed bargaining mandate, which may have been changed during discussion.

It is quite common that ministers are joined by civil servants (there are no top-level political appointees such as junior ministers or secretaries of state in Denmark) when appearing before a committee. This is particularly true in the case of EAC meetings, where civil servants always participate. This is due to the special tasks of the EAC. It deals with a great number of matters from a variety of ministries; the issues up for discussion are often very complex; and the committee gives bargaining mandates to ministers. There is no direct communication between committee members and civil servants, although the minister and the committee chairman may allow some exceptions to this general principle. The rule is that civil servants assist ministers who are responsible to parliament.[36]

Over the years the EAC has received increasing amounts of information from the government, so-called 'notes'. These are written by the relevant ministry and forwarded to the EAC via the Ministry of Foreign Affairs, which co-ordinates Danish EU policies. 'Basic notes' deal with new directive proposals, Green Papers, White Papers and other topics that the government considers important. 'Topical notes' deal with the items that are on the agenda for Council meetings and must be forwarded to the EAC at the latest one week before the committee is to discuss them.

FIGURE 2
THE EU COMMITTEE: WRITTEN QUESTIONS TO THE MINISTER; WRITTEN
CONSULTATION QUESTIONS; NO. OF DOCUMENTS TO THE COMMITTEE.
PERCENTAGES OF ALL PERMANENT COMMITTEES, 1972/73–1997/98

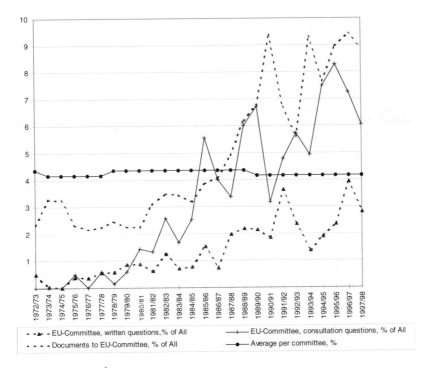

Source: Folketinget, Årbog og Register, various years

Figure 2 presents data on the activity of the EAC compared to the average level of activity for all committees. The percentage of written questions for consultations, as well as the percentage of documents received, has been well above the average since the mid-1980s, that is, since the launching of the internal market initiative.

About one week after a council meeting the minister reports back to the EAC with his summary of the meeting. Such summaries have been published since 1993. The EAC also receives the press release issued by the secretariat of the Council, which usually contains information on how the individual member states voted. These documents help the committee to control whether the minister has stayed within his mandate. If necessary, committee members may use the control instruments reported in Figure 2 or even ask for an interpellation debate in the Folketing.

EU directives that are adopted are implemented according to the national rules of the member states. If they require legislative action, a bill will be read three times in plenary sessions and handled by the relevant permanent committee between the readings. However, in Denmark most directives are implemented by way of administrative regulations, as various laws typically delegate considerable powers to the ministers. This procedure might create an 'agency loss' problem for the Folketing, but since 1996 a note is sent as soon as possible to the EAC and the relevant permanent committee describing how directives submitted to the EAC for a negotiating mandate have been implemented. In this way *ex post* control is exercised.

Ministers as well as all committees may initiate plenary debates on proposed EU directives and other topics, but such debates have been relatively few and not very successful. The most important plenary EU discussions are conducted as interpellation debates which may end with a formal parliamentary resolution on Danish EU policy. Interpellation debates that involve EU aspects of policy became more frequent in the 1990s. In the period 1990-1998 there were about ten per year, which is almost one-fourth of all interpellation debates.

Cabinet as Agent

Danish executive–legislative relations have not changed significantly because of EC/EU membership. On the contrary, it might be argued that existing coalition patterns have been reinforced. The Folketing delegates power to the cabinet, but in the prevailing tradition of minority rule it retains the power to decide, on each major issue, whether or not the cabinet should have its way. In this sense, the principal really controls the agent.

Most observers tend to agree that the Danish system of EU decision making works fairly well in promoting Danish interests and in terms of parliamentary control. Nonetheless, possible problems have been identified from the perspective of parliamentary control. A report[37] based on analyses of five cases, deliberately selected to show that problems could indeed exist, pointed to some shortcomings in control. The EAC gets involved late in the decision-making process; relevant and exhaustive information is not always provided; it may be difficult to check whether the minister has behaved within the bounds of the bargaining mandate; permanent committees are not properly included in decision making. Incidentally, it is worth noting that some of these complaints might also apply to the normal national policy-making process.

Steps have been taken since 1994 to solve some of the possible problems, and there is still room for improvement. Thus, after extensive discussions, a report[38] from the EAC in February 1999 introduced a number of innovations implemented from 1 March. First, the permanent committees were to have a more important role at an early stage of the decision-making process. Various procedural suggestions were made, without imposing rigid rules or interfering with the exclusive right of the EAC to decide on bargaining mandates at the later stage of the process. Thus, each of the committees still has to decide about how they want to become involved. Second, public meetings (in addition to the existing private ones in which bargaining mandates are formulated) of the EAC are to be introduced. All interested MPs as well as Danish MEPs can participate in these meetings, which are also open to the media and general public. Third, Danish MEPs are to be granted the right to have matters placed on the agenda of relevant permanent committees and the EAC. (It is not quite clear how this will be assured.) Fourth, public hearings on Green and White Papers from the Commission are to be increasingly used. A first such hearing took place in April 1999, as a joint initiative of the EAC and two other committees.

It is probably fair to conclude that these new initiatives represent a persistent and determined effort to adapt parliamentary institutions and procedures to the challenges created by EU membership. However, the extent to which the initiatives ensure that parliament becomes more active in the early phases of the EU decision-making process remains to be seen.

CABINET AS PRINCIPAL AND INDIVIDUAL MINISTERS AS AGENTS

The role of the prime minister as cabinet leader has been strengthened. The prime minister is Denmark's member of the European Council. Prior to Council meetings, the PM appears before the EAC to inform it about the subjects on the agenda and about the government's positions. If, in rare cases, specific decisions are expected, the PM will propose a mandate for negotiation. After the European Council meeting, the PM will again appear before the EAC to report on the outcome of the summit. The PM also plays an important role at intergovernmental conferences. The IGC on the Amsterdam Treaty is the most recent example. The Danish PM was very actively involved in the treaty negotiations.

Danish cabinet power is exercised through individual ministers responsible for their departments. Ministers are quite autonomous within their jurisdictions, but also constrained by the cabinet headed by the prime minister and by their possible coalition partners, as collective cabinet responsibility is also the norm. The constitution states that the jurisdictions of ministers shall be settled by the prime minister. Therefore, parliament cannot interfere with the distribution of offices and jurisdictions among the ministers of government. Ministers need the approval of the cabinet for important proposals and decisions and approval of the Minister of Finance for new expenditures, but otherwise they basically act on their own.

In principle, the ministerial jurisdictions are mutually exclusive, but conflicts of interests are not unknown because many issues are of interest to more than one minister. In fact, the whole procedure for making EU decisions, with special committees and other co-ordination instruments, reflects this state of affairs. The special committees include civil servants from different ministries and, sometimes, representatives of important interest organisations (more about this in the next section). In 1993 the cabinet determined that the individual ministers could not unilaterally decide which interest organisations to include in the special committees. In four controversial special committees the cabinet decided to include some organisations as permanent members, but in most areas the cabinet apparently left the decision to the individual ministers.[39] Thus, even if the cabinet as a whole retains its prerogative to intervene in general, the principle of broad ministerial autonomy prevails.

In EU affairs, just as in domestic policy making, individual ministers (with their civil servants) are crucial actors within their policy fields. The Ministry of Foreign Affairs is mainly responsible for overall policy co-ordination. The PM has a small secretariat, staffed by civil servants, that attempts to monitor the activities of the various ministries, but it rarely interferes directly into their affairs.

The Danish system of parliamentary control in EU policy making, with the EAC as the central body, is actually a system focusing on the proposals, decisions and actions of individual ministers (and thereby indirectly the whole cabinet). According to the constitution, not only the PM but also individual ministers are directly accountable to the Folketing. It states that: 'A minister shall not remain in office after the Folketing has approved a vote of no confidence in him'. Therefore, all the control instruments available to parliament and MPs (see above) can also be used to monitor the EU activities of individual ministers.

CABINET/MINISTERS AS PRINCIPALS AND CIVIL SERVANTS AS AGENTS

The Danish administrative organisation largely retained its structure after entering the EC/EU. The principle of individual minister responsibility for affairs belonging to his ministry is still in place. Furthermore, Danish ministries resemble classical Weberian hierarchies in the sense that the political superior, the minister, can give general as well as specific orders to his staff, unless specifically prevented from doing so by law. In comparison to, for instance, the Swedish system, this administrative structure guarantees – at least in principle – that all civil servants through the chain of command and delegation act on behalf of their political principal also in EU matters. All agencies are under a minister.

Inter-Ministerial Co-ordination versus Ministerial Autonomy

The traditional administrative principles are only partially changed as a consequence of the central co-ordinating role of the Foreign Ministry. A new system of decision making that did not quite fit with the traditional distinction between international and domestic politics was introduced to handle EC matters.[40] The system was designed after intense discussions before Denmark entered the EC in 1973 and is still in force. It is a fairly complex system that aims at combining decentralised administration with overall national co-ordination at all levels.

At the bottom of the system are about 30 so-called 'special committees'. A special committee is chaired by the ministry formally responsible for the policy area. The Ministry of Foreign Affairs is represented in all committees, and the other members are civil servants from ministries with an interest in the special committee's policy area (such as agriculture, labour market and social affairs, transportation, and so on) and representatives from important interest organisations who may be more or less formal members of the committees.[41] The main tasks of special committees are to prepare political decisions, co-ordinate the policies of the various ministries and consult with interested organisations. Since 1989 the special committees produce a 'background note', which is the first statement on how civil servants in the ministries should act in the early phases of the decision-making process in the EU. In addition, background notes generally form the basis for the 'basic notes' sent to the EAC.[42]

The special committees are usually well informed about forthcoming proposals from the Commission and may therefore start working on an issue before a formal proposal exists. Some of the members may also be members of the EU Commission's corresponding advisory committees as well as members of working groups under the Council of Ministers.

A special committee reports to 'its' ministry, which again makes recommendations to the EU Committee, consisting of top civil servants from the roughly ten ministries most involved in EU matters. The EU Committee is chaired by the Ministry of Foreign Affairs. Other ministries are invited if they are affected by specific proposals. The EU Committee normally meets every Tuesday, and has done so since 1973. The EU Committee may be regarded as an important link between the special committees and the cabinet's Foreign Policy Committee, which meets every Thursday. The Foreign Policy Committee decides on the general policies and specific proposals to be presented to the Folketing's EAC, as described above.

In the EU Council of Ministers, Denmark is represented by the minister in charge of the policy area under consideration at the meeting. However, quite frequently the minister is represented by his/her permanent secretary (that is, the top civil servant of the ministry). In either case, it is the minister who informs the EAC about discussions and the results of the meeting.

The balance between co-ordination and individual ministerial autonomy is evident also at the EU level. The Danish permanent representation in Brussels has about 40 civil servants.[43] Only about one-third of them are employed in the Ministry of Foreign Affairs, with the rest coming from other Danish ministries.

In sum, the principle of ministerial autonomy is also strong in relation to EU matters. It is the individual ministries which

(1) chair the special committees and provide them with secretarial assistance;
(2) send agents (often from agencies under the ministry) to the Commission's expert committees during the early preparatory stages of the EU decision-making process;
(3) appoint (in general) representatives to the working groups of the Council;
(4) appoint their own attaché to the permanent representation in Brussels and keep in contact with him;
(5) draft Danish negotiation instructions (which are then approved by the top civil servant inter-ministerial EU Committee, the Foreign Ministry and the cabinet);
(6) participate (through their minister) in the relevant Council meeting.[44]

Formal and Informal Constraints on Ministers as Principals of Civil Servants

In practice, civil servants may enjoy considerable autonomy under some general guidelines issued by the minister. In EU decision making this delegation of authority may be rather important because a position which has become integrated into a Commission proposal is hard to reverse at a later stage of the process without loss of credibility. Moreover, without the veto weapon a Danish minister may even be prevented from doing so.

Given constraints on *ex post* control by the minister, and thus by implication constraints on the EAC, the issue of *ex ante* control becomes more important. From the perspective of delegation and subsequent accountability, ideally, the civil servant should get a mandate from his minister early in the policy process unless there is unambiguous precedence establishing how to approach an issue currently on the agenda. However, fear of administrative overload as well as political and administrative expediency – notably the possibility of being able to adapt the Danish position to changing circumstances in the preparatory phases of the decision-making process without having to pay attention to a narrow political mandate – suggest that the principal should not be consulted until later in the process unless the pending issue is controversial. In a recent book, two close observers of Danish EU policy making concluded: 'In practice a balance has developed according to which the main rule is that an issue is not presented to the minister in an early phase, but that the civil servants take a position on the basis of existing political directions.'[45] This indicates that civil servants have some, albeit politically bounded, autonomy in interpreting what is in the best interests of their principal.

The autonomy of the ministries, and in particular the civil servants, should not be exaggerated, at least not in high priority issues. Knowing their minister's point of view and political preferences, civil servants will most likely incorporate their principal's anticipated reaction when acting on his behalf.[46] Not least because serving their minister loyally most likely improves their own career opportunities. The ministers, on their part, know that eventually the issue will appear in the special committee, where the positions of other ministries and important external interests have to be taken into account as well. Besides, as an agent of a minority coalition government, broader political concerns also have to be observed, at least if the Commission proposal entails elements that may be politicised in the national political arena. Thus, in terms of outcomes the chain of accountability may very well be intact. Moreover, the individual ministers and civil servants are subject to some *ex ante* control via the special committees, the EC Committee, and ultimately the EAC insofar as the cabinet has chosen to inform it early in the decision-making process.

Whereas other ministries have been committee members since 1973, organised interests have gradually become more and more integrated into the special committees. In the early days of membership, organisations were only consulted on an *ad hoc* basis and largely at the discretion of the ministries, except in the areas of social and labour market affairs where the traditional social partners participated.[47] In the wake of the Internal Market Initiative, a 1986 government decision introduced an 'early warning system' stating that organised interests broadly defined could demand to be heard as early as possible.[48] And, as mentioned in the preceding section, a new government decision in 1993 formalised the permanent representation of some interest organisations.

Today there are 27 special committees on EU issues, of which 13 have permanent representation by interest organisations.[49] The inclusion of external interests still varies considerably across sectors. The largest special committee is the one on the environment, which consists of 56 permanent members – 19 from the public sector and 37 representing interest organisations. In some cases, 'the preliminary draft for a negotiating mandate' prepared by the ministry in charge of the special committee is discussed with the most important organised interests even before it is presented to the special committee.[50]

How can the early involvement of the special committees and organised interests be interpreted in terms of delegation and accountability? The answer is contingent upon which *status quo ex ante* situation one compares it to and which principal's perspective one takes. The inclusion of organised interests in early phases of the decision-making process should not be seen as fundamentally challenging the role of ministers with regard to civil servants. The participation of organised interests may also be a way for weak cabinets, and thus weak ministers, to increase their autonomy *vis-à-vis* the EAC in the Folketing. There is some indication that depoliticisation was actually one of the motives for integrating the organised interests in the preparatory phase of policy making.[51]

Thus, not surprisingly, the special committees rank high among the bodies that MPs think should have less influence on EU matters.[52] Nor may it come as a surprise that, traditionally, 'Danish private interests often rely on the support of official representatives'.[53] Still, in recent years Danish organised interests have also increased their direct links to the EU, for example by establishing their own offices and joining so-called Euro-groups that represent their interests.[54]

However, if one compares this with a situation in which no interest organisations participate in policy preparation, there are good reasons to expect that parliament will not experience a great agency loss after all. First of all, the privileged inclusion of some organised interests early on in the decision-making process was quite common before EC membership, and it is still common in a host of domestic policy areas. Seen from this perspective, it is unclear whether the bureaucracy has become more or less accountable to its minister and ultimately to parliament and voters.

Second, if the relevant comparison is with the first years under qualified majority rule – that is, after 1986 but before organised interests became as closely integrated in the special committees as they are today – parliament may not have lost, but rather gained control. Because of a lack of information when policy proposals are drafted in the EU, MPs have never been able to exercise close *ex ante* control, not even in Denmark. With the need for early policy advocacy, the participation of organised interests – and through their growing participation in Euro organisations[55] – MPs get information earlier and through more sources. Furthermore, it is probably of higher quality. This will actually improve the chain of accountability. If some interests feel left out, chances increase that they will pass on important information to plausible allies in parliament, who may or may not take action on the information. In short, the MPs' possibilities for obtaining information may have improved, thus suggesting that accountability to parliament may also have improved.

Third, it is also possible that the government position presented before the EAC is based on a genuine grand compromise, with consensual backing of all important affected interests. This may or may not lead to information being passed on to parliament. However, in that case it would be hard to envision a stern opposition in parliament, thus indicating that outcome accountability might remain intact after all. The fact that MPs actually may gain information and that plausible MP interests already may have been expressed by the interest organisations should not lead us to forget that qualified majority rules in the EU *de facto* suspend national governments' veto. That is what makes early policy advocacy by civil servants necessary in the first place.

To varying degrees, organised interests and civil servants also participate in the implementation of directives. As noted earlier, most directives are implemented by administrative regulations issued under a framework law delegating rule-making authority to the minister. When this is the case, organised interests usually participate through formal or informal corporatist contacts.[56] Some directives in social and labour market policy can even be implemented by way of collective agreements (Article 137, section 4). This also happens in Denmark. However, even if parliament may not be able to recall the power delegated to the EU to issue directives, surely the Folketing can decide on another implementation structure if it so wishes.

CONCLUSION

The transfer of Danish national authority to the supranational EC/EU in 1972, 1986, 1992/93 and 1998 has reduced the sovereignty of national decision makers, but it has also created possibilities for the enactment of desired policies that cannot be decided upon by national actors alone. It has also given Demark certain voting rights in the decision-making bodies of the EU.

Danish membership had quite dramatic effects on voter–MP relationships. Some parties were divided over membership, and a Danish Euro-party system developed alongside the traditional party system. Several referenda, one of which was unsuccessful, were held to assure the legitimacy of the delegation of power in an electorate that holds sceptical views on the desirability of political integration. To assure support for the Maastricht Treaty, it was necessary to introduce some exceptions for Denmark by way of the Edinburgh Agreement.

Although membership did not change the normal patterns of parliamentary coalition formation, it did introduce an elaborate and quite sophisticated system for parliamentary control of government and ministers in EU matters, with the EAC as the cornerstone. In a similar way, while the existing administrative structure was largely upheld, a new set of procedures and committees were added to handle better the EU issues that did not fit well with the traditional distinction between foreign and domestic policy. This latter change created new tasks for civil servants and interest groups to perform as agents of the minister and the cabinet.

We may identify possible problems of accountability in all the principal–agent relationships dealt with here. In the terms introduced by Lupia,[57] we have mainly focused on accountability as a process of control, indicating the various *ex ante* and *ex post* mechanisms in operation. As Lupia suggests, one might also talk about accountability in terms of outcomes. However, the two aspects of accountability could very well be related and we tend to think that effective control mechanisms (which sometimes also includes the well-known rule of anticipated reactions) are more likely to result in favourable outcomes than are defective mechanisms.

On balance we find that Danish voters have been quite effective in relation to their elected representatives with regard to overall EU issues. The principal has certainly not abdicated, and it is not easy to imagine how voters could be more influential than they presently are. We also think that parliamentary control of government is quite effective, although the permanent committees could play a larger role. Minority cabinets are highly dependent upon legislative majorities, and the EU has directly or indirectly provided the Danish parliamentary principal with crucial and relevant information.[58]

We are less sure about the accountability relationships between ministers and civil servants with respect to the workings of the special committees. This possible problem can perhaps best be analysed in terms of outcomes. If ministers want national consensus in the various areas of policy before commitments are made in the EU, perhaps that is what they get through the co-operation of civil servants and interest groups in the special committees. If so, the result is as it should be. If the cabinet and parliament agree, everybody should be happy.

The voters cannot, and should not, be asked about hundreds and thousands of proposals. Presumably, however, they care about outcomes in important areas. It seems that, although they are sceptical of political integration, they favour practical solutions to concrete problems concerning the environment, the economy and employment, without caring too much about whether the solutions are made in Denmark or the EU. If the EU, in such areas, changes the 'reversion points' (Lupia) in the right direction through majority voting in the Council, Danish voters will not object.

NOTES

1. See E. Damgaard, 'How Parties Control Committee Members', in H. Döring (ed.), *Parliaments and Majority Rule in Western Europe* (Frankfurt: Campus Verlag, New York: St. Martin's Press, 1995), pp.308–25.
2. See A. Lijphart, *Electoral Systems and Party Systems. A Study of Twenty-Seven Democracies 1945–1990* (Oxford: Oxford University Press, 1995).
3. There are two other ways to gain representation: (a) either a list gets sufficient votes to get a district seat in one of the 17 multi-member constituencies (district seats are distributed according to a modified Sainte-Lagüe formula); or (b) the list gets the average vote per district seat in two of three main areas in the country; cf. J. Elklit, 'Danske valgsystemer: Fordelingsmetoder, spærreregler, analyseredskaber' (Paper, Aarhus: Department of Political Science, 1997), p.43.
4. See L. Bille, 'Candidate Selection for National Parliament in Denmark 1960–1990. An Analysis of the Party Rules', in T. Bryder (ed.), *Party Systems, Party Behaviour and Democracy. Scripta in honorem professoris Gunnar Sjöblom sexagesimum annum complentis* (Copenhagen: Copenhagen Political Studies Press, 1993).
5. See J. Elklit, 'Faldet i medlemstal i danske politiske partier', *Politica*, Vol.23, No.1 (1991), pp.60–83.
6. See J. Fitzmaurice, 'Denmark', in R. Morgan and C. Tame (eds.), *Parliaments and Parties. The European Parliament in the Political Life of Europe* (London: Macmillan Press Ltd., 1996), pp.236–58.
7. Law No. 609, 14 Dec. 1977
8. Lijphart, *Electoral Systems and Party Systems*, p.22.
9. See M.N. Pedersen, 'Euro-parties and European Parties: New Arenas, New Challenges and New Strategies', in S.S. Andersen and K.A. Eliassen (eds.), *The European Union: How Democratic Is It?* (London, Thousand Oaks, New Delhi: Sage Publications, 1996), pp.15–40; and J. Blondel *et al.*, 'Representation and Voter Participation', *European Journal of Political Research*, Vol.32, No.2 (Oct. 1997), pp.243–72.
10. See P. Norris and M. Franklin, 'Social Representation', *European Journal of Political Research*, Vol.32, No.2 (Oct. 1997), pp.185–210; and H. v.d. Kolk *et al.*, 'Appendix: The European Elections Study 1994', *European Journal of Political Research*, Vol.32, No.2 (Oct. 1997), pp.283–9.
11. Pedersen, 'Euro-parties and European Parties: New Arenas, New Challenges and New Strategies', p.37.
12. See T. Raunio, *Party Group Behaviour in the European Parliament. An Analysis of Transnational Political Groups in the 1989-94 Parliament* (Tampere: University of Tampere, 1996).
13. Pedersen, 'Euro-parties and European Parties: New Arenas, New Challenges and New Strategies'.
14. Raunio, *Party Group Behaviour in the European Parliament*, pp.136–8.

15. M. Marsh and B. Wessels, 'Territorial Representation', *European Journal of Political Research*, Vol.32, No.2 (Oct. 1997), pp.227–41; cf. also R.S. Katz, 'Representation Roles', *European Journal of Political Research*, Vol.32, No.2 (Oct. 1997), pp.211–26.
16. See K. Siune *et al.*, *– fra et nej til et ja* (Aarhus: Politica, 1994), p.32.
17. Recently the Supreme Court asserted its constitutionally granted power to rule on the constitutionality of giving up sovereignty (§ 20). Although the specific ruling confirmed the legality of the Maastricht Treaty it is a new practice in Danish jurisprudence that the Supreme Court exploits its power to conduct a 'constitutionality review' of Danish laws.
18. Blondel, 'Representation and Voter Participation', p.244; Siune, *– fra et nej til et ja*, p.33; and http://www.inm.dk/eu98, 1.6.1998.
19. See T. Worre, 'The Danish Euro-Party System', *Scandinavian Political Studies*, Vol.10, No.1 (1987), pp.79–95.
20. Siune *et al.*, *– fra et nej til et ja*, p.101; and O. Borre and J.G. Andersen, *Voting and Political Attitudes in Denmark* (Aarhus: Aarhus University Press, 1997), ch.10.
21. Borre and Andersen, *Voting and Political Attitudes in Denmark*, p.292.
22. See T.K. Jensen, 'Partierne, Europaudvalget og europæiseringen', *Politica*, Vol.27, No.4 (1995), pp.464–80.
23. See O. Niedermayer and R. Sinnott (eds.), *Public Opinion and Internationalized Governance* (Oxford: Oxford University Press, 1995), pp.292–5.
24. Jensen, 'Partierne, Europaudvalget og europæiseringen', p.475.
25. Siune *et al.*, *– fra et nej til et ja*, pp.124–32.
26. See K. Siune, *EF på dagsordenen* (Aarhus: Politica, 1991), pp.53, 99, 103 and 152; and Borre and Andersen, *Voting and Political Attitudes in Denmark*, pp.88–9.
27. The election most likely to have been influenced by the EU dimension, because MPs sent the Maastricht Treaty to a second referendum, thus plausibly leading to a feeling that the first result was not taken seriously.
28. Borre and Andersen, *Voting and Political Attitudes in Denmark*, p.294.
29. Borre and Andersen, *Voting and Political Attitudes in Denmark*, pp.307–8.
30. See E. Damgaard, *Folketinget under forandring* (Copenhagen: Samfundsvidenskabeligt Forlag, 1977).
31. See E. Damgaard, 'Parliamentary Questions and Control in Denmark', in M. Wiberg (ed.), *Parliamentary Control in The Nordic Countries. Forms of Questioning and Behavioural Trends* (Jyväskylä, Finland: The Finnish Political Science Association, 1994), pp.44–76.
32. See H. Jensen, 'Committees as Actors or Arenas? Putting Questions to the Danish Standing Committees', in M. Wiberg (ed.), *Parliamentary Control in The Nordic Countries. Forms of Questioning and Behavioural Trends* (Jyväskylä, Finland: The Finnish Political Science Association, 1994), pp.77–102; and H. Jensen, *Arenaer eller aktører? En analyse af Folketingets stående udvalg* (København: Samfundslitteratur, 1995).
33. The Danish minister of agriculture had agreed to a deal on export bacon in the Council of Ministers which was not acceptable to the opposition parties. The (minority) government decided to yield to the demands of the opposition by accepting rules of procedures designed to prevent such cases in the future. See F. Laursen, 'Parliamentary bodies Specializing in European Union Affairs: Denmark and the Europe Committee of the *Folketing*', in F. Laursen and S.A. Pappas (eds.), *The Changing Role of Parliaments in the European Union* (Maastricht: European Institute of Public Administration, 1995), pp.43–60; and S. Auken *et al.*, 'Denmark Joins Europe. Patterns of Adaptation in the Danish Political and Administrative Processes as a Result of Membership of the European Communities', *Journal of Common Market Studies*, Vol.14, No.1 (Sept. 1975), pp.1–36.
34. Jensen, *Arenaer eller aktører? En analyse af Folketingets stående udvalg*.
35. Further information may be found in N.-J. Nehring, 'The Illusory Quest for Legitimacy: Danish Procedures for Policy Making on the EU and the Impact of a Critical Public', in G. Sørensen and H.-H. Holm (eds.), *And Now What. International Politics After the Cold War. Essays in Honour of Nikolaj Petersen* (Aarhus: Politica, 1998), pp.60–81; N.C. Sidenius *et*

al., 'The European Affairs Committee and Danish European Union Politics', in M. Wiberg (ed.), *Trying to Make Democracy Work. Nordic Parliaments and the European Union* (The Bank of Sweden Tercentenary Foundation & Gidlunds Förlag, 1997), pp.9–28; H. Hegeland and I. Mattson, 'To Have a Voice in the Matter: A Comparative Study of the Swedish and Danish European Committees', *Journal of Legislative Studies*, Vol.2, No.3 (Autumn 1996), pp.198–215; F. Laursen, 'Parliamentary Bodies Specializing in European Union Affairs: Denmark and the Europe Committee of the *Folketing*', pp.43–60; D. Arter, 'The Folketing and Denmark's "European Policy": The Case of an "Authorising Assembly"', *Journal of Legislative Studies*, Vol.1, No.3 (Autumn 1995), pp.110–23; and Note published by Secretariat of the EAC, October 1996.

36. *Forholdet mellem minister og embedsmænd.* Betænkning nr. 1354 (Copenhagen: Statens Information, 1998).

37. J.G. Christensen *et al.*, *Åbenhed, offentlighed og deltagelse i den danske EU-beslutningsproces. Rapport udarbejdet til brug for Rådet for europæisk politiks høring den 18. april 1994 i Landstingssalen på Christiansborg* (Rådet for Europæisk Politik, 1994), p.45.

38. 'Beretning om større åbenhed i den danske EU-beslutningsproces m.v.' afgivet af Europaudvalget den 19. Februar 1999.

39. L.N. Rasmussen, *Korporative institutioner under forandring, Et casestudie af udviklingen i samspillet mellem interesseorganisationer og forvaltning omkring formuleringen af den danske EF-politik i perioden efter 1986*, Speciale (Aarhus: Department of Political Science, 1999), pp.78–9; cf. P. Nedergaard and J.Ø. Møller, *Hvem bestemmer hvad i EU?* (Aarhus: Forlaget Systime, 1996), p.105.

40. See, for example, J.Ø. Møller, 'Den danske EF-beslutningsproces i praksis', *Nordisk Administrativt Tidsskrift*, No.3 (1982), pp.258–79; C.B. Jacobsen, 'Den danske forvaltnings EU-opbygning. Struktur og relationer til organisationer og EUs institutioner', *Nordisk Administrativt Tidsskrift*, Vol.75, No.3 (1994), pp.211–23; Nedergaard and Møller, *Hvem bestemmer hvad i EU?*; Nehring, 'The Illusory Quest for Legitimacy: Danish Procedures for Policy Making on the EU and the Impact of a Critical Public', pp.60–81; and Rasmussen, *Korporative institutioner under forandring.*

41. Jacobsen, 'Den danske forvaltnings EU-opbygning. Struktur og relationer til organisationer og EUs institutioner', p.216; and Rasmussen, *Korporative institutioner under forandring*, pp.74–9.

42. Rasmussen, *Korporative institutioner under forandring*, pp.80–82.

43. As of 1996, cf. Nedergaard and Møller, *Hvem bestemmer hvad i EU?*.

44. Christensen *et al.*, *Åbenhed, offentlighed og deltagelse i den danske EU-beslutningsproces*, pp.7–8; Jacobsen, 'Den danske forvaltnings EU-opbygning. Struktur og relationer til organisationer og EUs institutioner', 214; and Nedergaard and Møller, *Hvem bestemmer hvad i EU?*, pp.105–6.

45. Nedergaard and Møller, *Hvem bestemmer hvad i EU?*, p.107.

46. Cf. *Forholdet mellem minister og embedsmænd*, pp.209–12.

47. Møller, 'Den danske EF-beslutningsproces i praksis', p.263.

48. Rasmussen, *Korporative institutioner under forandring*, pp.77–82.

49. Rasmussen, *Korporative institutioner under forandring*, pp.71–4; and Jacobsen, 'Den danske forvaltnings EU-opbygning. Struktur og relationer til organisationer og EUs institutioner'.

50. Christensen *et al.*, *Åbenhed, offentlighed og deltagelse i den danske EU-beslutningsproces*, pp.7–8 and 32–3; Nedergaard and Møller, *Hvem bestemmer hvad i EU?*, p.105.

51. Rasmussen, *Korporative institutioner under forandring.*

52. Jensen, 'Partierne, Europaudvalget og europæiseringen', p.477.

53. See H. Bregnsbo and N.C. Sidenius, 'The National Lobby Orchestra', in M.P.C.M. Van Schendelen (ed.), *National Public and Private EC Lobbying* (Aldershot, Brookfield USA, Hong Kong, Singapore, Sydney: Dartmouth, 1993), pp.183–200.

54. See N.C. Sidenius, 'A Collective Action Problem? Danish Interest Associations and Euro Groups', in J. Greenwood aand M. Aspinwall (eds.), *Collective Action in the European Union. Interests and the New Politics of Associability* (London and New York: Routledge, 1998), pp.81–107.
55. Cf. Sidenius, 'A Collective Action Problem? Danish Interest Associations and Euro Groups'.
56. See A.S. Nørgaard, *The Politics of Institutional Control: Corporatism in Danish Occupational Safety and Health Regulation and Unemployment Insurance, 1870–1995* (Aarhus: Politica, 1997), pp.285–8.
57. See A. Lupia, 'The EU, The EEA, and Domestic Accountability: How Outside Forces Affect Delegation within Member States' (this volume).
58. Cf. Lupia, 'The EU, The EEA, and Domestic Accountability: How Outside Forces Affect Delegation within Member States'.

Building Elite Consensus: Parliamentary Accountability in Finland

TAPIO RAUNIO and MATTI WIBERG

The Finnish political system combines parliamentary democracy with a strong presidency and is therefore often characterised as semi-presidential. The birth of parliamentary democracy is closely linked to the struggle for independence, which was won in December 1917. The Constitution of 1906 established universal suffrage and replaced the old four-estate assembly with a one-chamber parliament, the Eduskunta. The first parliamentary elections were held in 1907. In the summer of 1917 the Constitutional Committee approved a regulation on parliamentary governance which was subsequently enshrined in the 1919 Constitution Act. Section 2 reads: '(1) Sovereign power in Finland shall lie with the people; the people shall be represented by the Parliament. (2) Democracy shall entail the right of the individuals to participate in and influence the development of society and their living conditions. (3) The exercise of public authority shall be based on law. In all public activity, the law shall be scrupulously observed.'[1] According to Section 3, '(1) the legislative power shall lie with the Parliament; the Parliament shall decide also on State finances. (2) The executive power shall lie with the President of the Republic and the Government; the Ministers must enjoy the confidence of the Parliament. (3) The judicial power shall lie with independent court of law; the highest courts of law shall be the Supreme Court and the Supreme Administrative Court.'[2]

Since the Second World War Finnish parliamentarism has been constrained by two major factors. During the Cold War, foreign policy – and to a lesser extent domestic policy – was heavily influenced by the need to anticipate reactions from Moscow. Secondly, the president has wide-

The authors would like to express their sincere thanks to the other project participants for their insightful comments. Special thanks also to Mr Niilo Jääskinen, the Counsel of the Grand Committee, Head of the Secretariat for EU affairs of the Parliament of Finland, and Mrs Auni-Marja Vilavaara, Government Counsellor in the Prime Minister's Office, for sharing their expertise.

Tapio Raunio is a Post-doctoral researcher in the Department of Political Science at the University of Helsinki, Finland and Matti Wiberg is Professor of Political Science at the University of Tampere, Finland

ranging powers over both foreign and domestic policy. While recent constitutional amendments have strengthened parliamentarism, the president continues to enjoy considerable authority, even in domestic policy matters. Nonetheless, it is correct to say that Finland is moving more towards parliamentarism and away from semi-presidentialism.

VOTERS AS PRINCIPALS AND MPs AS AGENTS

European Community (EC) membership was hardly even discussed in Finland before the Soviet empire began to collapse. However, when the tide turned, it turned very quickly. Finland joined the European Free Trade Association (EFTA) and the Council of Europe as late as 1989. Public debate on the EC began in earnest after Sweden decided in 1990 to apply for membership. Finland applied for membership in March 1992. The public realised the significance of the decision. According to a survey carried out in May–June 1993, 81 per cent identified the membership question as the most important and consequential decision in decades.[3] During the referendum debate, supporters of membership emphasised the need to secure Finland's influence and cultural ties with the West, and the benefits for trade. Opponents focused on the loss of sovereignty and negative economic impacts, especially in the agricultural sector, where the Common Agricultural Policy (CAP) was expected to lead to heavy down-sizing.[4] The main reason why membership in the European Economic Area (EEA) – which came into effect in January 1994 – did not create any real debate in Finland was because it does not cover foreign policy or agriculture.

The 1994 Membership Referendum

A consultative referendum on EU membership was held on 16 October 1994. Turnout was 74 per cent, with 56.9 per cent voting in favour of membership and 43.1 per cent voting against. Core support for membership came from the more educated urban south. The two political parties most favourable to membership were the National Coalition (KOK) and the Swedish People's Party (RKP), with, respectively, 89 and 85 per cent of party supporters favouring membership. The leadership of the Social Democratic Party (SDP) supported membership and 75 per cent of SDP party voters took a similar stand in the referendum. The Centre Party (KESK) was divided over the issue. After party chairman and then Prime Minister Esko Aho announced that he would resign if the party rejected membership, a party congress held in June 1994 adopted a pro-membership position. However, only 36 per cent of the party's supporters voted for membership in the referendum. The Left Alliance (VAS) and the Green League (VIHR) did not adopt formal positions prior to the referendum.

Twenty-four per cent of the VAS supporters and 55 per cent of the Greens voted 'yes'. The only anti-membership Eduskunta parties were the small Christian League (SKL) and the Rural Party (SMP).[5] The Eduskunta approved membership on 18 November 1994, with 152 voting in favour of membership and 45 against. One member was absent and one abstained (the Speaker does not vote).

Oversized Coalitions and Decentralised Electoral Politics

Finnish governments tended to be short-lived until the 1970s, but since then cabinets have stayed in office for the full four-year mandate period. Recent governments have been broad coalitions that bring together parties from across the political spectrum. The only exception to this is the 1991–95 bourgeois centre-led coalition, which did not include any leftist parties. The left–right dimension dominates Finland's rather highly fragmented party system. There are five major parties: SDP, Centre, KOK, VAS and RKP. As a rule, recent governments have been formed around two of the first three (that is, SDP, Centre, KOK). The Green League is a newcomer, becoming – in 1995 – the first European green party to gain seats in a cabinet. During the 1990s the rural–urban and national–international cleavages have acquired new importance, largely due to integration.

The Finnish parliament, the Eduskunta, has 200 members elected from 14 multi-member electoral districts. They are elected in direct, proportional elections held every fourth year. The autonomous province of Åland is entitled to one seat. Voters choose between individual candidates from non-ordered party lists. The candidate selection mechanism is decentralised and largely controlled by district organisations. When Finland joined the EU in January 1995, Finland's first 16 European Parliament members (MEPs) were nominated from among national MPs, with parties given representation on the basis of their Eduskunta seats. The first direct election of members of the European Parliament was held in October 1996. Six parties won seats: SDP, KESK, and KOK got four seats each, VAS got two, and RKP and VIHR each got one. The country was divided into four electoral districts, but parties nominated only nationwide candidates. Turnout was 60.3 per cent. In the 1999 European elections, the whole country was one constituency. Only 31.4 per cent cast their votes. Seven parties gained seats: KESK and KOK four, SDP three, VIHR two, and VAS and the Christian League one each. The system for transforming votes into seats is the same d'Hondt method as is used in national parliamentary elections.

Party and Public Opinion on Integration

Finnish parties stress in their political rhetoric that the EU remains an association of independent states and play down its legislative powers. All

Eduskunta parties support membership, but no party favours a federal Europe. The main parties all support limited increases in EU power. The Green League has altered its position quite radically since the referendum, arguing that the Economic and Monetary Union (EMU) needs to be counterbalanced by EU-level minimum-standards legislation in the fields of social, environmental and taxation policy. Party leaders have played a crucial role in convincing their more Euro-sceptical supporters to toe the official party line. This was particularly true for the rainbow coalition government that came to power in 1995 (composed of the SDP, KOK, VAS, RKP, VIHR and led by the SDP's Paavo Lipponen), which was determined to bring Finland into the inner core of the EU. After the 1999 election, the same parties have continued to govern with only minor portfolio changes.

Because parties must be seen as being capable of participating in responsible government, party elites have had to adapt to the new circumstances created by the EU and EMU. The Centre Party, in opposition after 1995, kept its options open by refusing to bind itself to the pro-European policy of the government, while avoiding a clearly negative stand. A good example is the party's EMU policy. While Centre was against Finland's membership in the third stage from 1999, after the Eduskunta vote it indicated that it respected the will of the parliamentary majority and would not demand Finland's resignation from the EMU. Such behaviour, with the party leadership taking a more pro-integration position than the voters, is mainly due to the fact that party elites do not want to exclude their parties from future government negotiations.[6]

Public opinion continues to be divided over the EU. The CAP and the Agenda 2000 initiative in particular cause considerable anxiety, especially so among the rural segments of the public. Finnish public opinion is more sceptical about the EU than is true for most of the other EU states. This has been revealed in all Eurobarometer polls conducted since Finnish membership. Support for membership and the perceived benefits of membership have always been roughly ten per cent lower than support across the Union on average. Party elites and the government have taken a gamble on European issues, adopting positions that have been opposed by a majority of voters. Finnish policy on EMU membership is illustrative of the split between the public and elites. The Eduskunta approved Finland's EMU membership on 17 April 1998. The vote was 135 in favour and 61 opposed. There was one abstention and two members were absent. Despite this, public opinion polls conducted during 1995–98 repeatedly revealed that only about 40 per cent of the population favoured joining the EMU.[7] Table 1 shows the distribution of votes in national parliamentary and European elections in the 1990s.

TABLE 1
DISTRIBUTION OF VOTES IN NATIONAL PARLIAMENTARY AND EUROPEAN
ELECTIONS, 1991–99 (%)

PARTY	1991	1995	1996 EP	1999	1999 EP
Centre Party of Finland (KESK)	24.8	19.8	24.4	22.4	21.3
Social Democratic Party (SDP)	22.1	28.3	21.5	22.9	17.8
National Coalition (KOK)	19.3	17.9	20.2	21.0	25.3
Left Alliance (VAS)	10.1	11.2	10.5	10.9	9.1
Swedish People's Party (RKP)	5.5	5.1	5.8	5.1	6.8
Green League of Finland (VIHR)	6.8	6.5	7.6	7.3	13.4
Christian League (SKL)	3.1	3.0	2.8	4.2	2.4
Finnish Rural Party (SMP)	4.8	1.3			
Liberal People's Party (LKP)	0.8	0.6	0.4	0.2	
Young Finns (NUORS)		2.8	3.0	1.0	
True Finns (PS)			0.7	1.0	0.8
Åland Island[1]	0.3	0.4	0.4	0.4	0.3
Others	2.4	3.1	2.7	3.6	3.1
TOTAL	100.0	100.0	100.0	100.0	100.0

Note:
[1] The autonomous Åland region has one MP in the Eduskunta. This representative is not formally a representative of the Swedish People's Party, but in practice sits with the RKP group.
Three parliamentary groups were formed during the 1995-99 legislative term: the Leftist Faction (3 MPs), a splinter group of the Left Alliance, and two independent members – Mr Pertti Virtanen and Mr Risto Kuisma. Only the latter retained his seat in the 1999 elections. The Young Finns failed to gain seats in the 1999 elections.

Source: Statistics Finland

PARLIAMENT AS PRINCIPAL AND CABINET AS AGENT

Decision making in the Eduskunta is based on a continuous interplay between committees and party groups. Parliamentary party groups are rather cohesive, and have become increasingly independent of their extra-parliamentary parties. The distribution of committee seats among the political parties is proportional and based on the distribution of seats among the parties in the chamber. Because of the decentralised, candidate-centred electoral system, larger party groups always include stubborn and troublesome MPs that leaders of the parliamentary party groups cannot easily control. This has been particularly evident in recent EU debates.

Internal Organisation of the Eduskunta

Committees are the principal arenas for examination and scrutiny of legislative initiatives. The Eduskunta has 14 specialised standing committees, plus the Grand Committee,[8] which is the main committee responsible for handling EU matters. All legislative proposals must be referred to a committee for deliberation before a final vote to approve or reject can be taken. The final committee report on a legislative proposal contains both a recommendation to the Eduskunta and an extensive statement explaining the position of the majority. Committee members opposed to the majority resolution may add their dissenting opinions to the report. The decision rule in committees is simple majority. The committee report is almost always accepted by the chamber. Virtually all MPs are members of at least one committee. Ministers are not entitled to seats in committees. However, the members of the Council of State (that is, cabinet ministers) have the right to participate in committee meetings unless a committee decides otherwise. Committee quorums are two-thirds of the members of the committee. A committee may declare its proceedings open to the public if this is seen as necessary to collect relevant information.[9] The parliament may also establish temporary committees. The Eduskunta has not created any temporary committees to address EU issues. However, in September 1995 the Grand Committee set up a special sub-committee to deal with the 1996–97 Intergovernmental Conference (IGC).

The right of the parliament to receive information from the government is regulated in the Constitution:

> (1) The Parliament shall have the right to receive from the Government the information it needs in the consideration of matters. The competent Minister shall see to that Select Committees and other parliamentary organs have access, without delay, to the necessary documents and other information in the possession of the authorities.
> (2) A Select Committee shall have the right to receive accounts from the Government or the appropriate Ministry on a matter within its competence. The Select Committee may issue a statement to the Government or the Ministry on the basis of the account.
> (3) In addition, the right of the Parliament to information on international affairs shall be governed by the provisions elsewhere in this Constitution.[10]

Since the early 1980s Finnish governments have stayed in office for the whole mandate period. While opposition parties have constantly criticised the government of the day, governments have been able to rule without much effective dissent from the Eduskunta. Nevertheless, the MPs have a variety of ways to control the executive, the most important of which are no-confidence votes and parliamentary questions. There are three types of votes of no confidence: those following interpellations, government-initiated votes, and votes held without prior warning during plenary debates. The most important are votes following interpellations. Although the last government resignation due to an interpellation vote occurred in 1958, interpellations remain the most important method of realising in practice the idea of parliamentary responsibility. Members have the right to table written and oral questions as well as questions to the Council of State. The representatives ask questions on virtually all kinds of issues. Other scrutiny mechanisms include parliamentary motions and speeches and debates following government reports.[11]

Scrutinising European Matters

Within the Eduskunta, adapting to EU membership began in connection with EEA membership.[12] Finland had to implement all relevant EC/EEA legislation – basically all legislation related to the single market – and this led to a huge increase in the number of laws enacted each year. In 1995 the Eduskunta approved an all-time high of 777 laws. From 1996 onwards the trend reversed, confirming that the peak in the mid-1990s was due to the need to implement EU legislation. Figure 1 shows the amount of new legislation enacted in Finland between 1945 and 1998.

Membership created a new situation for the Eduskunta and political parties. Foreign policy decision making had previously been the exclusive domain of the president. Integration changed the situation to the advantage of the government and the Eduskunta. In December 1993 the Eduskunta passed an amendment to the Constitution Act (HM § 33a, 15.12.1993/1116) which entitles 'Parliament to take part in the national preparation of matters to be decided in international bodies as legislated in the Parliament Act'. According to the same amendment:

FIGURE 1
ANNUALLY ENACTED LAWS, 1945–98

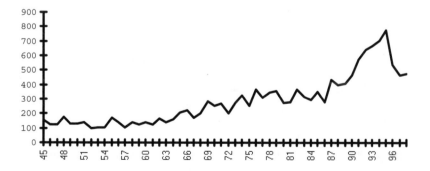

the government is empowered, notwithstanding the provisions of section 33, to make decisions concerning national preparation of issues arising within international organs and, to the extent that such a decision is not subject to parliamentary approval nor requires regulation by decree, also to decide on other related measures.

These changes, combined with chapter 4a of the Parliament Act (VJ 4a, 1551/94) which extended the government's powers to include national preparation of matters relating to the EU's common foreign and security policy, have significantly altered Finnish foreign policy decision making. Before EU membership, the president could block any foreign policy proposal that he opposed, thus maintaining the *status quo*. EU membership changed this. It has considerably narrowed the areas in which the president has sole authority. According to the new constitution:

(1) The foreign policy of Finland shall be directed by the President of the Republic in co-operation with the Government. However, the Parliament shall accept the international obligations of Finland and their renouncement, as well as decide on the implementation of the international obligations in so far as provided in this Constitution. The President shall decide on war and peace by the consent of the Parliament. (2) The Government shall see to the national preparation of the decisions to be made in the European Union, as well as decide on the concomitant Finnish measures, unless the decisions require the adaptation of the Parliament. The Parliament shall participate in the national preparation of decisions to be made in the European Union, as provided in this Constitution. (3) The communication of important foreign policy positions to foreign States and international organisations shall be seen to by the Minister with competence over foreign affairs.[13]

European integration has also reduced the powers of the Ministry of Foreign Affairs insofar as some of its previous competence has been shifted directly to specialised ministries.

The Grand Committee (*Suuri valiokunta*) and the Committee for Foreign Affairs are the main committees responsible for European questions. The former handles first (EC) and third pillar (JHA) issues, the latter second pillar (CFSP) matters. The Grand Committee has 25 members and 13 substitutes. It convenes on Wednesdays at 1pm and on Fridays at 2pm. The Grand Committee tends to attract prominent Eduskunta members. Following both the 1995 and 1999 elections the Committee membership included five Chairmen of standing committees, and representatives from the leadership of the three main party groups (SDP, KESK, KOK). Spokespersons from the opposition groups have found it particularly worthwhile to receive information on European questions and to express their own political views before the committee. The Grand Committee is an agent of the whole Eduskunta.

The involvement of the Grand Committee in EU matters is three-fold. It scrutinises the behaviour of Finnish representatives in the European Council; gives instructions to cabinet ministers attending meetings in the Council of Ministers; and participates in national policy formulation on issues decided at the European level. The Constitution defines the Parliament's role in European matters as follows:

(1) The Parliament shall consider the proposals for acts, agreements and other measures which are to be decided in the European Union and which otherwise, according to the Constitution, would fall within the competence of the Parliament. (2) The Government shall communicate the proposals referred to in paragraph (1) to the Parliament without delay after receiving notice of them, so as to have the Parliament take a position on them. The proposals shall be considered by the Grand Committee and usually by one or more other Select Committees, which issue statements to the Grand Committee. However, a proposal pertaining to foreign and security policy shall be considered by the Select Committee for Foreign Affairs. Where necessary, the Grand Committee or the Select Committee for Foreign Affairs may issue a statement on the proposal to the Government. In addition, the Speaker's Council may decide on the matter being taken up for debate in plenary session; no decision shall nevertheless be made by the Parliament. (3) The Government shall provide the appropriate Select Committees with information on the consideration of matters in the European Union.[14]

The following provides a brief analysis of how the procedures work in practice.[15]

European Council Meetings

According to the Constitution, 'the Prime Minister shall provide the Parliament or a Select Committee with information on matters to be discussed in a European Council beforehand and without delay after the Council. The same provision shall apply when amendments are being prepared to the treaties on the establishment of the European Union'.[16] In practice, the Prime Minister must inform the Grand Committee in advance of questions to be addressed by the European Council. After European Council meetings, he or she must also provide the plenary session or the Committee with information on what took place.

Instructing the Government before Meetings of the Council of Ministers

The Grand Committee convenes – usually on Fridays – to get information from ministers about Council meetings scheduled for the following week. Committee members receive the agendas of the meetings – as approved by COREPER – in advance. They also receive memoranda prepared by the competent ministries detailing Finland's position on the issues to be discussed. The ministers must give the Committee the chance to express its opinion on all matters discussed by the Council before final decisions are taken in the Council of Ministers. The Grand Committee has insisted on this, and this parliamentary scrutiny reserve has been used by ministers and ministries in negotiations with other national ministries and in EU institutions. This was particularly true during the 1996–97 IGC. After Council meetings the Committee receives a report on the meeting. Ministers must be prepared to appear before the Committee and to explain in detail any deviations from the given policy guidelines.

Advance scrutiny of issues to be discussed at Council meetings means, in most cases, discussing the relevant issues and their implications while the matters are being considered by the Council and the EP. Actual voting instructions are only given at the final stage of the process and constitute a small percentage, albeit an important one, of all instructions. These voting instructions by the Grand Committee are not constitutionally binding. Politically, however, they are important because the government must enjoy the support of the legislature. In instructing the government, the Committee can issue different types of mandates. The Grand Committee usually leaves the government some degree of flexibility, thus giving ministers a certain amount of freedom of manoeuvre. The Grand Committee also recognises the fact that Council decisions are often complex package deals. Therefore, various outcomes and their probability and acceptability are debated. This is reflected in the behaviour of the Finnish government in the Council, which is mainly characterised by flexibility and the desire to build compromises. Moreover, the Grand Committee focuses its scrutiny on selected issues, often those of special interest to eminent MPs. The overwhelming majority of European matters do not cause any controversy.

National Policy Formulation on EU Matters

The Council of State must inform the parliament without delay of any proposal for a Council decision. The Council of State must also send the Grand Committee information on the preparation of any issue relating to the EU that might belong to the competence of the parliament. In practice this usually means the EU Commission's legislative proposals. The Council of State sends a formal letter to the Speaker. The letter includes a summary and normally the full text of the proposal, together with its relevance and consequences for Finland. In some cases the Eduskunta has complained that the information provided by the government is too extensive, making it difficult for MPs to identify the key points of proposal. The Speaker forwards the matter to the Grand Committee and requests the competent specialised committee or committees to give their opinion to the Grand Committee. The specialised committees prepare their opinions in light of information about the government's tentative position and after having heard expert testimony. It is uncommon for the Grand Committee to deviate from the opinion of the specialised committee. It has been estimated that in approximately 90 per cent of the cases the Grand Committee accepts the opinion of the specialised committees.[17] When more than one specialised committee delivers an opinion, the Grand Committee summarises and mediates. After debating the issue, the Grand Committee formulates a position (which is a parliamentary recommendation, not a formal decision), in the form of a summary from the chairman. The government representatives are notified of the decision. The Grand Committee, its secretariat, and the specialised committees monitor the progress of the initiative. The government has often failed to inform the parliament of legislative amendments enacted by the Council and the EP, forcing the committees to take steps to acquire the relevant information. Finally the Grand Committee has an opportunity to express its views to the minister prior to the decisive Council meeting.

The strength of the Finnish system is the proactive and early involvement of specialised standing committees, which greatly increases the ability of the parliament to influence the position of the government. More centralised arrangements which give specialised committees a much smaller role – such as those found in the majority of Member States – fail to benefit from the cumulative expertise of the standing committees. A decentralised system, on the other hand, forces all representatives to engage in EU deliberations.[18]

The functional capacity of the Grand Committee has been enhanced by its secretariat. In 1999 the Grand Committee employed three committee counsels and one technical secretary. The Foreign Affairs Committee had one committee counsel. When additional staff are required, the Grand Committee primarily relies on the staff of the specialised committees. Committee counsels with personal experience with EU matters have been especially important, suggesting that it would facilitate parliamentary scrutiny if each committee had one functionary who specialised on European issues. The existence of high-quality telecommunications, information and documentation services is also important. The Eduskunta has its own EU information service.

The plenary can become involved both before and after decisions are taken at the European level. The plenary session of parliament may, after a proposal by the Speaker's conference, request the Grand Committee to submit EU Commission proposals to the whole parliament, along with all information provided to the Committee by the Council of State. The plenary may debate the proposals, but does not make formal decisions in such cases. A formal Act of Parliament, that is, a decision made after plenary debate, is necessary when the implementation of EU directives requires legislation. Treaty changes also require the consent of national parliaments. While routine EU legislation is rarely debated on the floor, far-reaching political decisions such as the EMU and Agenda 2000 have inspired long plenary debates. MPs who do not sit on the Grand Committee have voiced concerns about the difficulty of following European matters, and have argued that more EU issues should be debated on the floor.

During the first four years of membership the Eduskunta's ability to control, *ex ante*, the government and contribute to national policy making on European issues has been impeded by the fact that the government's superior administrative resources and regular participation in the Council gives it the opportunity to become well informed before issues are brought to the Eduskunta. This also applies to domestic legislation, but is more serious with regard to European issues because MPs primarily focus on national politics. In the early years of membership this was occasionally compounded by the fact that information arrived late and without being translated into the official languages. However, the situation has recently improved, as has the overall competence of the state bureaucracy on European matters. The Eduskunta currently scrutinises virtually all EU legislative initiatives. The wisdom of such extensive involvement can be questioned. Better *ex ante* control, established for example through advance meetings with ministries, might enable the parliament to focus its efforts on selected matters.[19]

An unresolved problem is party groups' lack of resources. Party groups can partially compensate for their meagre resources through regular contacts with their MEPs. All seven parties with EP seats have several meetings each year between MEPs and leading party organs. In addition, in most parties MEPs belong to the executive party organs. While there is less institutionalised co-operation between the Euro-parliamentarians and the Eduskunta, the MEPs are in regular contact with their parties' Grand Committee members.

While the Eduskunta cannot be categorised as a strong policy-influencing legislature, it has subjected the government to significant scrutiny with regard to EU matters. The parliament has taken a more critical approach towards integration than the Lipponen government. Debates on the EMU and the 1996–97 IGC are good examples. In the latter case, the position of the Eduskunta was similar to the government's. The Grand

Committee and the Foreign Affairs Committee produced detailed statements (16 and 24 pages respectively) on Finland's political goals and priorities.[20] The former Grand Committee Chairman, Erkki Tuomioja (SDP), is one of many who have criticised the government more than once for its Euro-mindedness. A remark made by Prime Minister Lipponen illustrates the situation rather well: 'Why are there so many so critical views even when the Government has such a majority in the committees?' Until February 1999 there were some cases in which the government – apparently due to misunderstandings – did not follow instructions from the Grand Committee. On these occasions the government pursued its own policy preference.

Committee scrutiny of European matters differs in one important respect from domestic legislation: the government-opposition dimension does not play the only significant role in either the Grand Committee or specialised committees. The government is usually attacked by individual MPs from both opposition and government parties rather than by a united opposition or even united party groups. The Grand Committee has refused to act as the government's rubber-stamp and insists that all relevant information is to be made available to both the government and opposition representatives. The main goal is understood to be to achieve parliamentary – and thus national – unanimity, which can be translated into additional influence in the Council.[21]

TABLE 2
THE SHARE OF PARLIAMENTARY QUESTIONS AND INTERPELLATIONS ON EU
ISSUES, 1991–98

Year	Written Question	Oral Question	Council of State's Question Hour	Interpellation
1991	5/443	6/190	2/64	-/4
1992	35/765	14/261	9/126	-/5
1993	20/731	7/140	7/95	1/4
1994	104/907	49/293	11/74	1/8
1995	36/445	17/138	5/75	-/1
1996	42/1011	17/165	8/107	-/3
1997	53/357	23/195	17/98	1/3
1998	77/1534	18/242	4/50	1/5
Total (%)	372/6193 (6.0 %)	151/1624 (9.3 %)	63/689 (9.1 %)	4/33 (12.1 %)

Source: Eduskunta records.

Table 2 shows the share of parliamentary questions and interpellations that dealt with EU matters between 1991 and 1998.[22] Integration issues feature in about ten per cent of all questions. A large percentage of these concern either agriculture or regional policy. Neither the Centre-led Aho government (1991–95) nor the Lipponen government (1995–99) have faced any major internal crisis or parliamentary rebellions over integration matters.

CABINET AS PRINCIPAL AND INDIVIDUAL MINISTERS AS AGENTS

The Prime Minister is the head of the cabinet. It used to be that the president could appoint the PM and other ministers and even dismiss the parliament. According to a constitutional amendment from 1991, the dissolution of the Eduskunta and sacking of individual ministers require a 'reasoned initiative', that is, a proposal by the PM to the president. If the Prime Minister resigns, the whole cabinet is dissolved. Cabinet meetings are chaired by the PM. Five members constitute a quorum. Decisions are taken by simple majority rule, with each minister having one vote of equal weight. When the vote is tied, the position of the PM is decisive. Since Finnish post-war governments have tended to be broad coalitions, the PM needs to have good bargaining skills in order to work out agreements between the coalition partners. In coalition governments, the PM cannot appoint or dismiss individual ministers without the consent of the government parties.

Besides plenary meetings, the cabinet co-ordinates its work through four statutory ministerial committees (*ministerivaliokunta*): Cabinet Foreign and Security Policy Committee, Cabinet Finance Committee, Cabinet Economic Policy Committee, and Cabinet European Union Committee. The EU committee is a newcomer, established following Finland's accession to the Union in 1995. All committees are chaired by the PM. While these ministerial committees do not possess the formal authority to take decisions on behalf of the whole government, they perform a very important function by preparing decisions which are given the final seal of approval by a plenary session of the whole cabinet or by a ministry.[23]

Finland currently has 12 ministries, each headed by a minister. The cabinet used to include not more than 17 ministers, but the 1995 cabinet had 18. The 1999-appointed second Lipponen government again has 17 ministers. Those ministers who do not head a ministry are called ministers without portfolio. They have the same status as other ministers. There have been no major changes in portfolios or ministerial jurisdiction as a result of EU membership because these matters were settled during membership negotiations. The Minister of Foreign Trade (Ole Norrback, RKP) became the Minister of European Affairs in 1995, but actual competence on

European matters has been given to and guarded by a number of individual ministers. Thus the 1999-nominated Lipponen government does not have a specific Minister of European Affairs.

Individual ministers have strong influence over their fields of competence. Their autonomy has increased since the 1970s. At the same time, individual ministers also have collective responsibility for cabinet decisions, as regulated in the Constitution: 'The Ministers shall be responsible for their official actions to the Parliament. Every Minister participating in the consideration of a matter in a Government session shall be responsible for any decision made, unless he/she has expressed an objection to be entered in the minutes.'[24]

Ministerial Independence under a Powerful Prime Minister

European Union membership has reinforced two changes already under way: ministerial independence and a more powerful role for the prime minister. The political weight of the PM has increased during the 1990s. Strong oversized governments now tend to stay in office through the whole mandate period. Also of significance in this regard is Finnish participation in the European Council. The PM is now an influential actor in foreign policy, an issue area which previously was the domain of the president.

Decision making on European issues is heavily sectionalised, with each ministry enjoying much freedom of action within its own sphere of competence. Individual ministers enjoy strong authority over their domains, and are relatively independent from the rest of the government. This fragmentation of authority and lack of co-ordination between the ministries has become visible, for example in the allocation of EU structural funds. The departmentalisation mirrors the situation that exists in Brussels. The work of the Council is also very sectionalised, with little horizontal interaction, thus each sector has gradually built its own policy community. The Ministry of Finance would like to see more co-ordination, but other ministries have protected their jurisdictions. Lack of co-ordination between ministers is compensated for by the fact that civil servants, who are very influential in policy preparation, have their own inter-ministerial networks where they can find out the views of their colleagues in other ministries during preparation of European matters.

Finland is normally represented in the Council at the ministerial level. If the minister is unable to attend a Council meeting, the following may take her or his place: another minister appointed by the government, Finland's permanent representative to the EU (since 1995 Antti Satuli), or a person designated by the permanent representative. Finland's permanent mission to Brussels has 78 employees, and they are in constant contact with their counterparts in Helsinki. The permanent mission has performed a crucial role during Finland's years as a new EU member. It not only participates in COREPER, but also acts as an important source of information for Finnish civil servants, ministers and MEPs. Apart from the Finnish EU Commissioner, the cabinet does not organise the selection of Finns assigned to work in EU institutions, for instance in the Commission. This is the responsibility of the EU organs themselves. The government's main interest is to make sure that Finland has enough qualified candidates to fill all EU posts earmarked for Finns.

A specific delegation and accountability problem is Finland's representation in the European Council. The Eduskunta's Committee for Constitutional Affairs decided prior to membership that the prime minister should represent Finland in the European Council summits. However, the president, Martti Ahtisaari (SDP), has refused to accept this. In May 1995 the prime minister published an announcement formulated jointly with the president's office, stating that the PM would always attend the summits and the president would attend when he wanted to do so. The Parliament has not made any decisions or statements on the issue. The dispute is important from the point of view of parliamentarism because the President is not accountable to the Eduskunta.

CABINET/MINISTERS AS PRINCIPALS AND CIVIL SERVANTS AS AGENTS

The 12 ministries are all divided into various sections and offices. The minister directly controls central state agencies under his/her jurisdiction. Ministers are aided by a chief secretary (*kansliapäällikkö*), who is a career civil servant, though not entirely without partisan views. The chief secretary's task is to oversee the functioning of the ministry. The delegation of authority to individual ministers is replicated in the ministries, where ministers have in some cases delegated considerable authority to the top civil servants. While political responsibility is the minister's, civil servants can be held accountable for actions they undertake in their official duties.

Perhaps more than the ministers, the bureaucracy needed to adjust quickly to new circumstances after membership.[25] Apart from preparing for EMU and the 1996–97 IGC, Finland was scheduled to take on the responsibilities of Council Presidency during the latter half of 1999. Preparations for the Presidency began as early as 1996. The main changes in administrative organisation were carried out in connection with EEA membership. While EU membership has demanded the establishment of some new organisational structures, the overall organisation of the state bureaucracy has not changed. European matters have increased the workloads of most bureaucrats, especially in those ministries most heavily involved in EU affairs, such as Agriculture, Finance, and Foreign Affairs. The overall size of ministerial staffs has increased, in particular in the Ministry for Agriculture and Forestry. Altogether 540 new ministerial staff employees were hired during 1995–97 as a result of EU membership.

The Foreign Ministry has overall responsibility for handling European matters. The Ministry is in charge of co-ordinating ministerial EU policies and is home to the EU Secretariat. The main inter-ministerial co-ordinating body is the Committee for EU Matters located in the Foreign Office. It has 17 members: chief secretaries from the ministries, the Prime Minister's Office, the Office of the President, the Bank of Finland, the Office of the Attorney General and Åland. The Committee for EU Matters has played a rather marginal role, as shown by the low attendance record of the chief secretaries. The Committee had 38 sections in 1999, each operating under an appropriate ministry. The sections are consultative and their function is to co-ordinate EU matters. Sections also include representatives from relevant interest groups. Officials present matters to sections for discussion and inform them of issues under preparation. In practice the sections' main role is to approve decisions prepared by the ministries. When there is agreement on a policy, the section procedure is sufficient for determining Finland's final position. In other cases the matter is presented to the Committee for EU Matters and/or the Cabinet's European Union Committee, with the latter usually serving as the forum for resolving conflicts.

An important administrative reform that will most likely enhance the capacity of the whole state bureaucracy and the Parliament to process European issues is the decision of the 1999-appointed Lipponen government to move the EU Secretariat and thus the overall responsibility for handling EU matters from the Foreign Office to the Prime Minister's Office. This will tie Finnish EU politics more closely to its proper context – national economic and social policy. The Prime Minister's Office has already carved out a prominent role for itself, in particular in relation to the European Council summits.

According to a recent report based on extensive interview data, individual middle-level civil servants have a central role in the preparation and processing of European legislation.[26] Ministers seldom have a significant impact on the substance of the issues, and the same applies even to high-level civil servants. This seems to imply that there is room for improvement in intra-ministerial political co-ordination. Indeed, civil servants seem to want more political steering from the politically accountable actors. They are unwilling to bear the burden of sensitive EU decisions.

The parliament monitors civil servants through regular hearings in the specialised committees. For example, the Environment Committee has regular meetings with civil servants from the Environment Ministry. Such consultation enables MPs to learn about issues under preparation and thus improves *ex ante* parliamentary control. Meetings also serve as occasions for conflict management, where possible differences between the ministries and the parliament are discussed. This mainly explains why there is so little conflict between the government and the Grand Committee. While civil servants appreciate the legitimacy bestowed by parliamentary hearings, they also think that the hearings cause unnecessary work and delays.

National representatives to the Commission and Council working groups and comitology committees are recruited on the basis of policy competence. They are bound by standard official regulations and their mandate is the same as their mandate in the national political process. Following meetings in Brussels they report back to their immediate superiors. Participation in EU policy making has required considerable staff training, with particular emphasis on linguistic skills. This has resulted in the emergence of a new bureaucratic Euro-elite, consisting mainly of younger, internationally oriented civil servants.

Public authorities take the implementation of EU legislation seriously. It would not be misleading to characterise the Finnish authorities as 'norm neurotics' in this respect. The EURODOC system, an electronic database on EU governance, is actively used to monitor the current implementation situation. Many public authorities also carry out extensive semi-scientific studies in order to better implement European legislation.

CONCLUSION

Recent changes in the Finnish political system – partly caused by EU membership – have strengthened the Eduskunta's control of the political agenda. Constitutional amendments have given the parliament a larger role in EU decision making, and parliamentary scrutiny of policy preparation by ministries has improved since Finland joined the Union. Ministers and bureaucrats enjoyed more freedom of action before membership. Membership has therefore led to positive spill-over effects.

How has the EU influenced the national chain of parliamentary democracy? While it is difficult to estimate the success of the principal at different stages of the delegation process, the following conclusions are supported by empirical evidence:

(a) Integration has not altered the role of the individual voter. Voters have not gained more impact on agenda formation. The parliamentary elections have not been fought over European issues and Finnish parties remain weakly Europeanised. Turnout in the EP elections has been low, particularly in the June 1999 elections. Integration policy has remained an elite issue, without active involvement from ordinary citizens. In this respect Finland is no different from its fellow European countries.

(b) The parliament's freedom of manoeuvre has been notably reduced in matters where the EU already has significant powers: agriculture, environment, finance, internal market and trade. In other sectors, such as social and cultural policies, the impact of the Union is only symbolic. European questions therefore affect MPs to a varying degree, depending on their policy specialisation.

(c) The powers of the Cabinet and especially the role of the PM have been strengthened due to integration. The role of the PM has been highlighted and emphasised, particularly in foreign policy, as never before in Finnish political history. This has taken place at the expense of the president. The lack of effective parliamentary opposition due to oversized cabinets has increased the government's ability to control the political agenda, although the government needs to anticipate MPs' reactions to a greater extent than before.

(d) Ministers in charge of core integration sectors suffer from a serious work overload. Ministers travel back and forth to Brussels on an almost weekly basis, which reduces the time they have to deal with domestic political issues, particularly in their constituencies and in party organisations. The only remedy is to increase ministerial resources, for example by introducing a system of junior ministers.

(e) Agencies and civil servants are the true winners in the politico-administrative game. This is because the growth of expertise and professionalism requires dedication to detailed issues. European legislation is often rather technical, thus civil servants are the only actors competent to deal with substantive questions. The elected politicians have insufficient resources to balance this bureaucratic hegemony. No cure is in sight. Politicians do not have any resources for policy planning independent of the bureaucratic administration. They are therefore dependent upon bureaucrats, who often have their own policy goals, ones that are not necessarily formulated by democratically accountable politicians. This applies not only to the Finance Ministry. Bureaucrats often exercise significant political power by presenting their decisions as minor policy adjustments, which ministers then sign. Integration issues have strengthened this development due to the detailed and technical nature of most European legislation. However, such bureaucratisation is less evident in Finland than it is in other Member States. This is largely explained by the forceful activity of the Eduskunta and the ministers.

In sum, we argue that powers have been delegated from the voters to parties and parliamentary party groups and from them to the governing parties. Governing parties delegate to individual ministers and ministries and the state bureaucracy in general. The power shifts have not been large, but they are nonetheless significant. The Eduskunta has simultaneously been strengthened and has lost power to the government and civil servants. The *ex ante* control instruments have been rather effective, but they cannot compensate for the overall transfer of powers that have taken place.

The Eduskunta does not really need to bark or bite because the preparation of EU issues is based on a continuous dialogue between the ministries and the parliament. Both sides recognise the need to achieve a convergence of views. The broad oversized cabinets have also reduced the impact of the opposition. No bitter power struggles have emerged between different actors in the delegation chain. The public view of the delegation process seems to be a rather realistic and well-informed one in comparison to that which is found in other Member States.

What are the consequences for regime legitimacy? Integration issues have been difficult for all Member States, as results of various referenda reveal. No serious political force demands that Finland leave the Union. If integration decisions have had any impact on regime legitimacy, we claim that they are more positive than negative.

What kind of procedural or other innovations would strengthen the role and organisation of the national parliament *vis-à-vis* all relevant agents? Any measure that somehow reduces the state administration's role in agenda formation and evaluation of the implementation of EU legislation should be welcomed by anyone interested in strengthening the role of the parliament. The use of the parliamentary plenary as a forum for national debate needs to be emphasised in this context. But this is something only the parliament itself can pursue. A better and more pro-active system of monitoring the cabinet and individual ministers is important in this context, but no promising suggestions have been made. Neither has there been any serious interest in developing such mechanisms.

It is difficult to suggest how all EU-related procedures could be made more effective, open and transparent. It is naive to believe that such simplistic measures as requiring civil servants to improve their reporting to the Eduskunta would immediately bring more light and insight into the policy process. There are only marginal national improvements to be made in this area. All reforms that make EU policy making more effective and transparent help also to make the national decision-making process more effective. The Nordic principle of direct access of all citizens to all state documents should be made the norm for EU governance.

NOTES

1. The Constitution of Finland Section 2, 11.6.1999/731. Previously the constitution consisted of four different laws: the Form of Government Act (1919), the Parliament Act (1928), the Act Concerning Ministerial Responsibility (1922) and the High Court of Impeachment Act (1922). The new unified constitution will be implemented on 1 March 2000. Amendments will strengthen the parliamentary dimension of the political system, though the modifications are more technical than substantial. While the letter of the law will not undergo any major changes, much will depend on more informal, evolving practice. See www.eduskunta.fi for the current version of the Finnish constitution.
2. The Constitution of Finland Section 3, 11.6.1999/731.
3. Elinkeinoelämän valtuuskunta (EVA), *Suomalaisten EY-kannanotot* (Helsinki, 1993).
4. See M. Jakobson, *Finland in the New Europe* (Westport: Praeger, 1998); A.T. Jenssen, P. Pesonen and M. Gilljam (eds.), *To Join or Not to Join: Three Nordic Referendums on Membership in the European Union* (Oslo: Scandinavian University Press, 1998); P. Pesonen (ed.), *Suomen EU-kansanäänestys 1994: Raportti äänestäjien kannanotoista* (Helsinki: Ulkoasiainministeriö, Eurooppatiedotus ja Painatuskeskus, 1994); and D. Arter, 'The EU Referendum in Finland on 16 October 1994: A Vote for the West, not for Maastricht', *Journal of Common Market Studies*, Vol.33, No.3 (1995), pp.361–87.
5. R. Sänkiaho, 'Puoluesidonnaisuutta vai sitoutumattomuutta', in P. Pesonen (ed.), *Suomen EU-kansanäänestys 1994: Raportti äänestäjien kannanotoista* (Helsinki: Ulkoasiain-ministeriö, Eurooppatiedotus ja Painatuskeskus, 1994), pp.164–73.
6. See T. Raunio, 'Facing the European Challenge: Finnish Parties Adjust to the Integration Process', *West European Politics*, Vol.22, No.1 (1999), pp.138–59.
7. See the public opinion surveys conducted by EVA at www.eva.fi.
8. The Grand Committee is called Grand simply due to the fact that it has more members than other standing parliamentary committees.
9. See M. Wiberg and M. Mattila, 'Committee Careers in the Finnish Parliament, 1945–1994', in L.D. Longley and A. Ágh (eds.), *The Changing Roles of Parliamentary Committees* (Appleton: International Political Science Association, Research Committee of Legislative Specialists, 1997), pp.167–79.
10. The Constitution of Finland Section 47, 11.6.1999/731.
11. For information on control instruments see V. Helander and G.-E. Isaksson, 'Interpellations in Finland', in M. Wiberg (ed.), *Parliamentary Control in the Nordic Countries: Forms of Questioning and Behavioural Trends* (Jyväskylä: The Finnish Political Science Association, 1994), pp.201–46, and, in the same volume, M. Wiberg, 'To Keep the Government on Its Toes: Behavioural Trends of Parliamentary Questioning in Finland 1945–1990', pp.103–201.
12. This section draws on previous work by the authors. See M. Wiberg and T. Raunio, 'Strong Parliament of a Small EU Member State: The Finnish Parliament's Adaptation to the EU', *Journal of Legislative Studies*, Vol.2, No.4 (1996), pp.302–21; T. Raunio and M. Wiberg, 'Efficiency Through Decentralisation: The Finnish Eduskunta and the European Union', in M. Wiberg (ed.), *Trying to Make Democracy Work – The Nordic Parliaments and the European Union* (Stockholm: Gidlunds, 1997), pp.48–69; and T. Raunio and M. Wiberg, 'Parliaments' Adaptation to the European Union', in K. Heidar and P. Esaiasson (eds.), *Beyond Congress and Westminster: The Nordic Alternative* (Columbus, OH: Ohio State University Press, 2000, forthcoming).
13. The Constitution of Finland Section 93, 11.6.1999/731.
14. The Constitution of Finland Section 96, 11.6.1999/731.
15. Suuri valiokunta, Lausunto 3/1995 vp (SuVL 3/1995 vp): Euroopan unionin asioiden käsittelystä suuressa valiokunnassa ja sille lausunnon antavissa erikoisvaliokunnissa, 22.11.1995.
16. The Constitution of Finland Section 97(2), 11.6.1999/731.
17. See R. Lampinen and I. Räsänen, 'Eduskunnan asema EU-asioiden valmistelussa', in R. Lampinen, O. Rehn and P. Uusikylä (eds.), *EU-asioiden valmistelu Suomessa* (Helsinki: Eduskunnan kanslian julkaisu 7/1998), pp.121–32.

18. See T. Raunio, 'Always One Step Behind? National Legislatures and the European Union', *Government and Opposition*, Vol.34, No.2 (1999), pp.180–202.
19. See R. Lampinen and I. Räsänen, 'Eduskunnan asema EU-asioiden valmistelussa'.
20. See Committee for Constitutional Law, Opinion No.6/1996 Session, to the Foreign Affairs Committee on the Report of the Council of Ministers No.1/1996 Session, 28 March 1996; Grand Committee, Opinion No.2/1995 Session (SuVL 2/1995 vp), Preparing for the Inter-Governmental Conference of the European Union, Opinion of the Grand Committee to the Council of Ministers, 22 Nov. 1995; Grand Committee, Opinion No.2/1996 Session, to the Foreign Affairs Committee, 10 April 1996; and Foreign Affairs Committee, Finland and the Intergovernmental Conference, concerning the report of the Council of Ministers 'Finland's Points of Departure and Objectives at the 1996 Intergovernmental Conference', 26 April 1996 (UaVM 7/1996-VNS 1/1996 VP). The government's goals for the IGC are found in Council of Ministers Report, 'Finland's Points of Departure and Objectives at the 1996 Intergovernmental Conference', 1996.
21. Information from Grand Committee Chairman, Erkki Tuomioja, 14.12.1998. This view seemed to be shared by the whole Committee.
22. Note that the findings are based on a key word search by using the word 'EU-#', and therefore questions not containing that word are excluded. We are grateful to Laura Niemi at the Eduskunta for her assistance in compiling the data.
23. For information on cabinet decision making and legislative–executive relations, see J. Nousiainen, 'Finland: Ministerial Autonomy, Constitutional Collectivism, and Party Oligarchy', in M. Laver and K.A. Shepsle (eds.), *Cabinet Ministers and Parliamentary Government* (Cambridge: Cambridge University Press, 1994), pp.88–105; J. Nousiainen, 'Finland: Operational Cabinet Autonomy in a Party-Centered System', in J. Blondel and M. Cotta (eds.), *Party and Government: An Inquiry into the Relationship between Governments and Supporting Parties in Liberal Democracies* (Basingstoke: Macmillan, 1996), pp.110–27; and J. Nousiainen, 'Finnland: Die Konsolidierung der parlamentarischen Regierungsweise', in W.C. Müller and K. Strøm (eds.), *Koalitionsregierungen in Westeuropa – Bildung, Arbeitsweise und Beendigung* (Wien: Signum, 1997), pp.327–69.
24. The Constitution of Finland Section 60(2), 11.6.1999/731.
25. Much of the information in this section is based on R. Lampinen, O. Rehn and P. Uusikylä (eds.), *EU-asioiden valmistelu Suomessa* (Helsinki: Eduskunnan kanslian julkaisu 7/1998).
26. See R. Lampinen *et al.*, *EU-asioiden valmistelu Suomessa*.

Another Link in the Chain: The Effects of EU Membership on Delegation and Accountability in Sweden

HANS HEGELAND and INGVAR MATTSON

The Swedish constitution is founded on a fairly straightforward chain of delegation and accountability: citizens to parliament – the Riksdag – through the government to the ministries and state agencies. When Sweden joined the European Union (EU), this chain was blurred by the complicated pattern of links to EU institutions and organs that came into being. As a consequence, membership has reopened a classic constitutional question. Put in terms of principal–agent theory, the problem is how do we make sure that appointed politicians and bureaucrats do, in fact, act as representatives of the citizens?

The fundamental problem can be stated as a question: how can institutions be designed to grant governmental agents the discretion and ability needed to act efficiently in the interest of the citizens and yet impede those agents from pursuing there own interests at the expense of the citizens? Theory implies that the principal seeks to structure the relationship with the agent so that the outcomes produced through the agent's efforts are the best the principal can achieve, given the assumption that the agent seeks to maximise his or her return subject to the constraints and incentives offered by the principal.[1] Democratic states use many kinds of constitutional constraints to promote agent control, including bicameralism, minority rights, qualified majorities and so on. Brennan and Buchanan have suggested an even wider range of tools, for example, balanced budget requirements, independent monetary authorities and money supply rules, and constraints on the kinds of taxes that can be levied.[2]

The Swedish constitution includes few such constraints. Instead of constraining the agents' freedom of action, the basic principle for assuring that the principal's interests are fulfilled is a strong belief in representation and in decision making by majority rule. Anyone who studies the 1974 Instrument of Government (IG) will be struck by one fundamental feature

Hans Hegeland and Ingvar Mattson are secretaries to standing committees in the Swedish Riksdag and affiliated to Lund University of that constitutional reform. Any constraints that impede the manifestation of the will of the people should be abolished. The Riksdag is the foremost representative of the people and it is elected in proportional elections. The chain of principals and agents is assumed to be comparatively clear-cut. The will of the people, as is expressed in majority votes by the representatives of the citizens, shall prevail.

In order to make sure that the government and, indirectly, the bureaucracy, implements its decisions, the Riksdag has at its disposal a variety of supervisory instruments, including supervision of the government by the Standing Committee on the Constitution[3] and MPs' interpellations and questions to ministers.[4] These instruments are a form of institutional check. The Riksdag also has other instruments, such as contract design, screening and selection mechanisms, and monitoring and reporting requirements.[5] The use of these instruments varies from one policy area to another. It also tends to vary depending upon when a programme or law was enacted, since control methods seem to go in and out of fashion over time.

The instruments mentioned above are examples of typical *ex post* control. The Riksdag and other principals also have the authority to exercise control *ex ante*. Examples are building into programmes' and laws' goals, structures and personnel systems that promote agency compliance from the outset. The Riksdag has recently undertaken efforts to improve management by objectives and results in an effort to improve its *ex ante* control over state budget spending. Through strategic choices about organisational design, the Riksdag can get state authorities to do their bidding.[6]

Although the main feature of the IG is a relatively straightforward chain of delegation and accountability based on majoritarian principles, there are also some constitutional restrictions on simple majority rule. Shortly after the formulation of the new IG, a commission of inquiry, the Commission on Rights and Freedoms, was set up in response to demands to enshrine fundamental rights into the constitution. The Commission's proposals were largely implemented, but this did not end the matter. Various commissions have subsequently proposed additional constitutional amendments to safeguard minority rights.

Given that this is a broad picture of the main features of the chain of delegation and accountability in Sweden,[7] we will now describe in more detail the impact of EU membership in terms of the principal–agent dilemma. When Sweden became a member of the EU in 1995, the role of the Member States in EU decision making was stressed in official statements. Referring to the reasoning behind the decision of the German Constitutional Court on the Maastricht Treaty, the Riksdag stated that the transfer of power was not unconditional. In essence, the reasoning implied that the national chain of democracy was still the most important channel for political influence.[8]

The aim of this study is to describe and analyse the whole chain of delegation and accountability, with particular focus on the role of the Swedish Riksdag. The focus is on how the principal gives structure to the relationship with its agents so that the outcomes produced through the agents' efforts are the best the principal can achieve, given the assumption that the agents seek to maximise their return subject to the constraints and incentives offered by the principal. We will focus on the internal organisation of the Riksdag, the relationship of the Riksdag to the government and the ministries, and the relationship between the government and the bureaucracy. However, we will start with a more fundamental issue: how do citizens estimate and perceive their ability, as the utmost principal, to control EU institutions?

VOTERS AS PRINCIPALS AND MPs AS AGENTS

In the referendum on Swedish EU membership in November 1994, a 52.8 per cent majority voted yes; 46.8 per cent voted against. About one per cent (0.9) voted blank. Turnout was 83.3 per cent, which was higher than the turnout in previous Swedish referenda, but 3.5 percentage points lower than voter turnout in the general election held in September 1994.[9] Since the major political parties and interest groups favoured membership, the surprise was not the fact that a majority of the voters said 'yes', but rather that so many people voted 'no'.

According to various opinion polls, the primary principals in Sweden, that is, the voters, are indeed reluctant members of the EU.[10] According to Eurobarometer data from March 1998, 46 per cent of voters think that Swedish membership is a bad thing, 31 per cent support it, while 23 per cent are undecided. The typical supporter of Swedish membership is a young, wealthy male living in an urban area, whereas the typical opponent has the opposite characteristics.[11] It is worth noting that these profiles also characterise typical voters on the left–right dimension in Swedish politics. Survey data reveal an almost perfect correlation between voters' subjective conception of their position on the left–right scale and their attitude towards the EU membership.[12]

The left–right dimension was the most profound cleavage in Swedish society at the time of the breakthrough of democracy in the 1920s, and it continues to be the most important cleavage.[13] Seven parties are currently represented in the Riksdag, which means that they were supported by more than four per cent of voters in the 1998 election. The Social Democratic Party has been in government for most of the period since the 1930s, while the non-socialist parties have largely had the role of opposition. Conflict between the political parties has reflected the socio-economic conflict among the voters and has formed the conditions for the exercise of parliamentary control.

However, the conditions for accountability with regard to EU matters are different. The Left Party and the Green Party, who together obtained 16.5 per cent in the Riksdag election 1998 but 25.3 per cent in the EP election in 1999, form the opposition on many EU issues. The Green Party, which opposes Swedish EU membership more than any other political party, is also the most active party in EU matters in the Riksdag, at least in relation to its size. This means that the conflict dimension in EU matters is two-fold. On the one hand, the two most EU-negative parties in the Riksdag – the Greens and the Left Party – stand in opposition to the other five Riksdag parties, all of which, to varying degrees, support EU membership. On the left–right dimension, the non-socialist parties are in opposition. This dimension is visible in the Riksdag when economic issues are discussed, and even, for instance, when the EU Advisory Committee deliberates with the government prior to meetings in the ECOFIN – the EU Council meetings in which Member States are represented by their finance ministers. Almost without exception, these issues are marked by a conflict between the Social Democratic government and the non-socialist parties, especially the Conservatives (the moderate party) and Liberals. Still, the most salient conflict dimension in EU matters is between the EU-negative and EU-positive political parties.

The political parties are, however, not very representative of their voters with regard to Swedish EU membership. As is the case in other Nordic states, party leaderships are much more positive towards membership and the European integration project than are the parties' voters. This implies that, despite the correlation between the left–right dimension and the EU dimension, it may be difficult for a voter to find a political party that fits his views on both the EU dimension and the traditional right–left dimension. In these circumstances it is interesting to study how the voters have behaved in European elections.

The Swedish elections to the European Parliament (EP) are organised similarly to the general elections to the Riksdag. The traditional list system of proportional representation has, in recent years, been adapted to give voters the opportunity to indicate a preference for individual candidates among those nominated by the parties. In order to distribute seats, Sweden uses the adjusted odd-number method (divisors 1.4; 3; 5; and so on) which guarantees good proportionality. Only parties that receive at least four per cent of the nation-wide vote are entitled to take part in the distribution of seats. In Riksdag elections, individual candidates benefit from preference voting if they are chosen by at least eight per cent of voters who vote for their party in their electoral district. The threshold for EP elections is five per

TABLE 1
NATIONAL AND EUROPEAN ELECTIONS 1994–1999

Party	RD 1994 (%)	EP 1995 (%)	Diff 94–95 (%)	RD 1998 (%)	EP 1999 (%)	Diff 98–99 (%)
Social Democratic Party	45.2	28.1	–17.0	36.4	26.0	–10.4
Moderate Party	22.4	23.2	+0.8	22.9	20.7	–2.2
Left Party	6.2	12.9	+6.7	12.0	15.8	+3.8
Christian Democratic Party	4.1	3.9	-0.2	11.8	7.6	–4.2
Centre Party	7.7	7.2	-0.5	5.1	6.0	+0.9
Liberal Party	7.2	4.8	-2.4	4.7	13.9	+9.2
Green Party	5.0	17.2	+12.2	4.5	9.5	+5.0
Other parties	2.2	2.8	+0.6	2.6	0.5	–2.1
Voter turnout	86.8	41.6	–45.2	81.4	38.8	–42.6

Source: The National Tax Board (Riksskatteverket; http://www.rsv.se/)

cent. In contrast to national elections, the nation is not divided into several constituencies in EP elections.

When Sweden first became an EU member in 1995, however, MEPs were elected by the Riksdag. The 22 Swedish representatives were elected among the MPs, with each party getting seats in Brussels and Strasbourg in proportion to their seats in the Riksdag. The direct elections in September that same year changed the situation dramatically due to successful campaigns by the two parties most opposed to Swedish membership – the Green Party and the Left Party.

As a consequence of the direct elections, EU-positive MEPs were replaced by Euro-sceptics and opponents of Swedish membership. A study by Martin Brothén shows that the voters, as principals, delegated power (to the extent that MEPs have political power) to candidates who were more representative of their views about Swedish membership and future EU development than were candidates elected by the Riksdag. Eleven of the 22 directly elected Swedish MEPs had an EU-negative view.[14]

However, the main conclusion to be drawn from the first European elections is much more pessimistic than the fact that it led to a better match between voters' and MEPs' opinions on EU membership. The most noteworthy observation is record low turnout. Only 41.6 per cent of voters participated in the elections, compared to about 85 per cent who vote in regular Riksdag elections. Moreover, interest in EU-related issues was clearly lower in 1995 than it was during the 1994 referendum. One example of lack of interest is that only 41 per cent of those who did bother to vote reported that that they actually cared about the final result of the election.[15]

The 1999 EP election took a similar turn. In line with a general tendency throughout the Member States, voter turnout in Sweden continues to be low and decreasing. Only 38.8 per cent of the electorate participated compared to 81.4 per cent in the 1998 Riksdag election. Survey data indicate that many voters who are sceptical towards Swedish membership stayed at home. As a consequence, the number of Swedish MEPs who are negative to Swedish membership decreased. This means that the new group of Swedish MEPs is less representative with regard to general attitudes towards the EU than was the outgoing group. The two parties which are openly against Swedish membership lost two seats, despite the fact that they both got more votes in the EP election than in the last Riksdag election. It is also worth noting that the two largest parties, the Social Democrats and the Moderate Party, did not obtain as large a share of the vote as in the Riksdag election of 1998.

The negative attitude towards the EU has also been reflected in scepticism over Swedish participation in the third phase of Economic and Monetary Union (EMU). The Riksdag decided that Sweden should not participate in the EMU from 1 January 1999. This resolution, taken by the Riksdag in autumn 1997, was supported by a majority of citizens and has tended to keep the EMU issue from becoming fully politicised. At the beginning of 1999, when the Euro was introduced – by and large successfully – public opinion polls revealed a swing in popular opinion towards more favourable EMU attitudes. However, when the European Commission resigned in March 1999 support for Swedish participation in the EMU declined again. This suggests that, at present, attitudes towards the common currency are volatile and to some extent a function of attitudes towards the EU as a whole.

The ability and willingness of voters to exercise accountability seem weak. Already the low election turnout implies that European elections are less functional as a viable link in the delegation–accountability chain. Furthermore, similar to the experience in other Member States, the EP election campaigning dealt more with national issues than European ones. Citizens tended to vote either on the basis of their opinion about membership *per se* or on the basis of national issues. The role of the European Parliament is unclear to many voters, and when casting their votes they tend to express their view of either the EU or the performance of the national government. This makes elections to the European Parliament of limited usefulness as a means of exercising control in EU matters. Other channels, in reality the indirect link through the Riksdag, must fulfil this function.

PARLIAMENT AS PRINCIPAL AND CABINET AS AGENT[16]

When Sweden became a member of the EU, the Riksdag's Committee on the Constitution argued that the Riksdag can hold the government accountable for its actions in the EU, in accordance with the general principles of parliamentarism. The Committee stated that if the constitutional relationship between the two branches of government remained unchanged, the role of the Riksdag in EU matters would only be indirect and control would largely be limited to *ex post* measures. The Committee considered this to be insufficient, and argued that there were strong reasons to complement *ex post* control with new means of ensuring that the Riksdag could exercise an active and real influence over Swedish EU policy.[17]

A new institution was established – the Advisory Committee on European Affairs (the EU Advisory Committee). It was modelled after its Danish counterpart.[18] The Riksdag's Committee on the Constitution argued that the Riksdag would, in practice, gain influence over EU policy through the Advisory Committee. The Committee noted that it was reasonable to assume that the government would not pursue a policy contrary to that supported by the European Affairs Committee in deliberations.[19] At the same time, however, it was agreed that statements by the EU Advisory Committee could not be binding on the Riksdag as a whole, and that they lacked formal juridical effect.

The Left Party and the Green Party, the only two (of seven) Riksdag parties that campaigned against Swedish membership during the 1994 referendum, have argued that the Advisory Committee procedure for dealing with EU matters is not sufficient to ensure parliamentary influence.[20]

The Advisory Committee on European Affairs (the EU Advisory Committee)

The Advisory Committee on European Affairs and the government discuss both Sweden's positions on EU matters and how Sweden should negotiate in meetings of the Council of Ministers. The committee's role is regulated in the Riksdag Act, which states that the government is obliged to inform the Riksdag on EU affairs and to deliberate with the Advisory Committee. No distinction is made among the three EU pillars. The EU Advisory Committee has 17 members and approximately 25 substitutes. All seven party groups in the Riksdag are represented on the Advisory Committee. Almost every Friday the committee meets ministers who will participate in Council meetings during the following week. In all this involves about 35–40 committee meetings per year. The meetings normally last two to three hours, which means that the committee meets about 100 hours each year. Advisors from the ministries, who can answer more detailed questions about issues at hand, accompany the minister to committee meetings. The government submits in advance written information about matters on the agenda of the forthcoming Council meeting. At the committee meeting, representatives of the government often explain the views and position of the government and might also give an account of new developments. If members of the committee do not share the government's position, then they give their views on the matter at hand. Alternatively they may forward inquiries. At the end of the deliberations, the chairman summarises the discussions and notes whether the government has the support of a majority of the committee. The committee is assisted by a full-time staff of about seven persons.

Within a week of the Council meeting, the government submits an account of the meeting to the EU Advisory Committee. That report can facilitate the Riksdag's ability to control the government. However, the reports are not followed up systematically; rather, they are examined on an *ad hoc* basis – for example, when there has been a heated discussion on an issue at an earlier stage. MPs considered it attractive to sit on the committee, even if it meets on Fridays (when there is normally no session in the chamber), as well as during breaks in the Riksdag sessions.

In general, we are inclined to conclude that the EU Advisory Committee functions as intended. In a strict sense the EU Advisory Committee serves as an *ex ante* process, since the committee gives its view before Council meetings. Furthermore, most issues appear several times on the Council agenda, and thus on the agenda of the Advisory Committee, before a final decision is made. Before issues are brought before the Council, they have been considered in Council working groups and in COREPER. Swedish representatives have expressed their views in different arenas and there is a political cost, which might be fairly high, for changing the national position at the 'last minute' at a Council meeting. Thus, the committee comes into the process too late to be really capable of efficiently exercising *ex ante* activity. Yet, the very fact that the ministers know that they will be summoned to the committee might encourage them to adjust government policy to take into account the opinions of the Riksdag parties in order to avoid criticism.

When the organisational forms for dealing with EU matters in the Riksdag were decided, it was stressed that it is important that the Riksdag gets involved early in the process, before the decisions are made in the EU. The standing committees should perform this *ex ante* control of the government.

The Standing Committees

The important role of the standing committees in regard to EU matters has been underlined in official documents numerous times. After two years of Swedish EU membership, the obligation of the committees to monitor the activities of the EU within their respective subject areas was included in the Riksdag Act. The standing committees receive all new official documents from the Commission via the government. Memoranda containing factual information should accompany the more important proposals from the government. The memoranda should, *inter alia*, contain an account of the main content of the proposal and, if the government has taken a position on the issue, this should also be included in the memo. The government occasionally presents written accounts of its views in certain policy areas, for example agriculture. The committees arrange hearings with the government on EU matters in order to obtain additional information. The committees most involved in EU affairs are Agriculture, Foreign Affairs, Industry and Trade, and Transport. Communication between the standing committees and the EU Advisory Committee normally occurs via the parliamentary groups.

Ideally, the standing committees should react to and give their views on Commission proposals fairly early in the policy process. The committees could react to White papers and Green papers from the Commission, letting the government know their reactions before the government is required to take a position. If the view of the standing committee remains unchanged when the Commission presents its final proposal, the government ought to act in accordance with the committee view. Under this procedure, the EU Advisory Committee could then serve as the final formal instrument of control prior to Council decision making. That check could involve verifying that the voting intentions of the Swedish government are in accordance with earlier communications between the Riksdag (committees) and the government. Between 1995 and 1998 the Riksdag formulated approximately 20 resolutions in which it stated how the government ought to act with regard to a particular issue at the EU level. For instance, the Riksdag asked the government to pursue particular environmental issues in the EU. In reality, however, *ex ante* control – that is, clear instructions from standing committees to the government – does not function as well as intended.

Regarding *ex post* control exercised by the standing committees, the annual account of EU activities presented to the Riksdag by the government should be mentioned. Once the government has presented its account, every member of the Riksdag may offer motions based on it. The account and the motions are then scrutinised and discussed by the Committee on Foreign Affairs. Other standing committees are given the opportunity to present their own views. In 1999, the EU Advisory Committee delivered a statement on the report to the Committee on Foreign Affairs. The Foreign Affairs Committee report is then subject to debate and a formal decision in the chamber.

Reports from the Committee on Foreign Affairs have thus far not focused on the issue of controlling Swedish government actions in EU fora. If future accounts by the government contain more information on its performance in the EU, then this would give the principal – the Riksdag – a greater opportunity to control its agent *ex post* on an annual basis.

Parliamentary Control

While the Riksdag can actively influence government behaviour via deliberations with the government prior to important decisions in the EU, it can also use its other forms of parliamentary control to influence government activity. This mix of roles has unexpected drawbacks. If the principal becomes too involved in the agent's carrying out of its responsibilities, the principal might find itself in a position where it cannot put the whole responsibility for the agent's actions on the agent itself. There is a certain point at which the roles of the principal and the agent become blurred. At this point the principal cannot blame the agent without blaming itself as well. The Instrument of Government states that the government rules the country and is responsible to the Riksdag. The Riksdag must therefore balance two contradictory values. The government must, on the one hand, have the discretion necessary to govern. This implies that the Riksdag should not interfere too much with its day to day activities. Rather, the Riksdag should focus on controlling. On the other hand, confining itself to control after the fact might leave the Riksdag with little influence in very important matters.[21] Let us look into how the various instruments of parliamentary control are applied to EU issues.

The Committee on the Constitution examines ministers' performance of their duties and the handling of government business. The committee reports the result of its examinations to the chamber once or twice each year. Of the nearly 140 matters the Committee has examined during 1995–98, approximately 18, or 13 per cent, concerned actions by government on EU matters. For instance, the committee has given an account of the way the government organises its EU activities. The information the government had given to the EU Advisory Committee prior to deliberations about third pillar issues has also been examined by the committee. This examination led to an obvious increase in the amount of material the government sends to the EU Advisory Committee concerning the third pillar.

Every year, the Committee on the Constitution examines the publication of Swedish laws and statutes. The committee has stated that it will also analyse regulations from the EU which are published in the EU *Official Journal*. However, according to the Swedish constitution, the committee examines the Swedish government, which is hardly responsible for the publication of the *Official Journal*. If the committee is critical towards something with regard to the *Official Journal*, it can only make demands on the Swedish government and not on any EU institution. The publication of regulations may seem to be a minor question, hardly likely to cause any widespread public discontent, but it makes visible a missing link in the delegation–accountability chain. The national parliament lacks formal competence to exercise control over EU institutions. If the Riksdag finds

TABLE 2
EU-RELATED INTERPELLATIONS AND QUESTIONS

Interpellations Year	Per cent about EU matters	Total number
1994/95	32	154
1995/96	15	261
1996/97	16	372
1997/98	14	313
Questions Year	Per cent about EU matters	Total number
1994/95	12	736
1995/96	13	718
1996/97	12	839
1997/98	10	1103

Note: The column *per cent EU* shows what percentage of interpellations and questions concerned the EU.

Source: Own compilation of interpellations and questions.

reason to criticise something in the EU, it has to go through the government in order to bring about changes. However, the Swedish government is only one of 15 governments, and even if it tries to remedy problems raised by the national parliament it may very well find it impossible to do so.

In recent years, there have been plans in the Riksdag to increase the amount of time that the standing committees devote to following up and evaluating the implementation and effects of decisions made by the Riksdag. To the extent that the subject areas of the standing committees are also EU matters, we can expect this activity to include EU-related issues. However, to date ambitions in this regard outstrip actual behaviour.

Any member of the Riksdag may submit an *interpellation* or a *question* to a minister on any matter concerning the minister's performance of his duties. Table 2 shows the number of times EU matters have been discussed in questions and interpellations. The data is based on an analysis of all questions.

Of the 372 interpellations during 1996/97, 16 per cent concerned EU-related matters. Since 1995, the share of interpellations and questions dealing with EU matters has varied between ten per cent and 16 per cent, except for interpellations in 1994/95, when no less than 32 per cent concerned EU matters. Several of the EU-related interpellations occurred before the Swedish referendum on EU membership in November 1994.

There are also other types of debates in the chamber, which are not related to formal Riksdag competencies. Of the 30 specially arranged debates in 1995–98, five concerned EU matters. In such debates the government might, for example, inform the Chamber. This function is not part of the formal means of control as regulated in the constitution, but, nonetheless, it gives the opposition MPs an opportunity to ask the government critical questions. During 1995–98, the government informed the Riksdag on a variety of issues on 43 occasions, with 24 of these debates concerning EU matters, for example, information about meetings of the European Council.

The Parliamentary Auditors scrutinise central government activities.[22] The 12 auditors are to ensure that central government resources are used as efficiently as possible. They submit their major reports to the Riksdag. One area of auditor interest is EU-related issues. The auditors have, for instance, analysed the role of the government in implementing EU rules in Sweden. They have also published a report about how ministries work with EU matters.

The Parliamentary Ombudsman supervises the application of laws and other statutes in the public interest. Above all, individual citizens turn to the ombudsman. Even if the ombudsman ought to take into account relevant EU rules, this institution has not been much affected by Swedish EU membership.

Finally, there is the core principle of parliamentary government itself. If more than half of the members of the Riksdag declare that a particular minister does not enjoy their confidence, then the minister must resign. If the Riksdag declares that the prime minister does not enjoy its confidence, the government as a whole must resign. There have been four votes taken on a declaration of no confidence (1980, 1985, 1996 and 1998), but there was no majority for such declarations on any of these occasions. However, the mere possibility of a motion of no confidence might lead a minister to resign. A declaration of no confidence has not, to date, been brought up in connection with an EU matter and no minister has resigned due to any EU-related political conflict.

All instruments of control discussed here are primarily intended to function *ex post*. This does not mean that they do not have any role *ex ante*. The mere risk of being criticised by, for example, the Committee on the Constitution makes the government more likely to act in ways that satisfy the principal. However, while these means of control may be very efficient and well suited for the task of making the agent act in the interests of the principal, when the EU is added to the picture a new problem arises. Even if the government acts in order to fulfil the wishes of the Riksdag, it may not be able to find a majority in the EU for the views held by the Swedish Riksdag.

The Riksdag: Discussion

Obviously, the Riksdag has lost formal powers due to EU membership. However, it has also gained insight into issues in which it did not previously take much interest – at least not before they were, in practice, already settled. These issues include, for example, conventions in third pillar matters. The political parties also have close contacts with their MEPs, which means that the parties are less dependent on the government for information about EU issues. Furthermore, information technology has given the Riksdag new means for obtaining information. The political parties and the Advisory Committee on European Affairs actively collect information from the Internet and from different news databases.

As we have seen, the Advisory Committee on European Union Affairs focuses on meetings in the Council of Ministers. However, since it gets involved fairly late in the process, the extent to which it actually performs control *ex ante* can be questioned. With regard to the Riksdag's standing committees' treatment of EU issues, while it has improved since the first year of Swedish EU membership, the means available for the committees to formulate and state positions more authoritatively are somewhat problematic. On the other hand, the government is likely to anticipate the views and reactions of the Riksdag, which means that *ex ante* control is probably exercised indirectly.

CABINET AS PRINCIPAL AND INDIVIDUAL MINISTERS AS AGENTS[23]

When Sweden joined the EU, the official view was that the division of labour among the Riksdag, the government and the authorities should remain unchanged. No major administrative reforms of the Swedish Government Office took place when Sweden joined the EU. EU issues were to be integrated into each ministry. However, a new EU secretariat with a staff of approximately 20 was established in the Ministry for Foreign Affairs. Its task was to assist the Prime Minister's Office as well as the other ministries. Its head was recruited from the Finance Ministry and the staff came mainly from ministries other than Foreign Affairs. The Swedish permanent representation in Brussels has about 50 civil servants (May 1998). Some have complained that there are too many people stationed in Brussels.

Swedish ministries are fairly small entities. In April 1998 the ministries had a total of about 4,000 employees (1,500 of whom work at the Ministry for Foreign Affairs). Of these, some 140 hold political appointments. The others are civil servants who keep their positions even when governments change. In April 1994 the ministries employed only about 3,400. The ten ministries (plus the Prime Minster's Office and the Office for Administrative Affairs) have formed a common authority since 1997. One reason for creating a single authority was growing internationalisation, of which Swedish membership in the EU is a significant part.

Representatives of the Swedish Government Office travel approximately 5,000 times per year to Brussels and Luxembourg. Regardless of who represents the government, the Government Office is supposed to formulate instructions. Normally they take the form of guidelines from the responsible ministry, but they can also be a decision by the cabinet. Those who attend an EU meeting are required to submit a report to the Government Office within 24 hours after the meeting ends.

The Government Office was partly reorganised in March 1996, when the former Minister of Finance Göran Persson succeeded Ingvar Carlsson as prime minister. The overarching political co-ordination of EU matters was moved from the Ministry for Foreign Affairs to the Prime Minister's Office. The goals of the reorganisation were probably not fully realised, and in early 1999 new measures were taken to strengthen the co-ordinating role of the Prime Minister's Office. A new unit for EU affairs was created in the Prime Minister's Office. There are also closer contacts between the political leadership in Stockholm and the Swedish permanent representation in Brussels. The Prime Minister's Office is responsible for the political co-ordination of EU matters, among them the Swedish EU Presidency, from January to June 2001. There is, however, still also an EU secretariat in the Foreign Office.

The Foreign Office has had a fairly strong position in EU matters. Central EU issues, such as the enlargement of the EU, often requires close contact with other EU Member States. These contacts often go through the embassies, which are under the Foreign Office. Before some meetings in the Council, such as in the General Affairs Council and ECOFIN, there are often government briefings in the capitals of the EU Member States. At these briefings, representatives of the government inform the embassies about the positions the government will take on issues to be discussed at the Council meeting. The General Affairs Council deals with several matters, not only traditional foreign issues. On the other hand, the ECOFIN plays a more and more important role as economic integration grows. The introduction of the single currency in 1999 has given finance ministers an even more central role. If Sweden introduces the Euro, the Finance Ministry's influence will probably increase further.

The number of issues handled by the Government Office has increased considerably due to the EU membership. The demands for quickly formulating government positions have also increased. The goal is to decide on a Swedish position early in the process in order to give Sweden a better opportunity to influence the final decision. The Government Office has a system for common deliberations (*gemensam beredning*). This means that all relevant ministries have an opportunity to present their views. When it concerns EU matters, the Prime Minister's Office, the Foreign Office and the Finance Ministry are always given the opportunity to express an opinion. If the ministries cannot agree, the issue is discussed in cabinet. If there is still no agreement then the prime minister decides the issue.[24] This system for common deliberations is suitable for forming positions on EU matters. However, such decisions have not, in fact, been made as early as intended. Instead, during the first years of membership the focus in the Government Office has been on day to day work in the Council. This was probably due both to the fact that Sweden did not fully realise the importance of the work in the Commission and to the pressing need to manage the most urgent issues to be decided in the Council. There are also signs that there has been a lack of political leadership with regard to EU matters within the Government Office, at least in some policy areas.

With regard to the Riksdag, interesting changes in the foreign policy making process have occurred. Traditionally, it has been the government who has decided foreign policy in Sweden. The government informs the opposition parties about the most important issues of foreign affairs in the Foreign Affairs Advisory Council, whose members include party leaders and other top politicians. The Ministry of Foreign Affairs has to react quickly, perhaps in one day, to numerous foreign affairs questions arising out of the EU co-operation.[25] However, the Riksdag has gained additional insight into foreign policy due to EU membership. Before each General Affairs Council, the Foreign Minister informs and consults with the EU Advisory Committee. Regular information is also given to the Standing Committee on Foreign Affairs. This means that the government has lost some of its monopoly on foreign affairs. The growing internationalisation of the Riksdag in general,[26] through travelling and contacts with other national parliaments, has also strengthened the Riksdag *vis-à-vis* the government in the realm of foreign policy. This means that the principal can control the agent better than was possible previously, when the dominant source of information about foreign affairs was the agent.

As has been noted above, co-ordination between the ministries is crucial. Leadership from the prime minister is important. The PM cannot fully control what his colleagues do in the Council, but a consistent performance in the Council is necessary to avoid appearing Janus-faced. This may be particularly challenging for a PM in a coalition government. To date, Sweden has had single party minority government during its years of EU membership. Experience from coalition governments in 1976–82 and 1991–94 shows that the Prime Minister's Office plays a significant role in co-ordination between the parties in this kind of government.[27] The difficulty a PM has in controlling his ministers is not a new phenomenon – ministers usually have an information advantage – but EU membership gives it a new dimension.

CABINET/MINISTERS AS PRINCIPALS AND CIVIL SERVANTS AS AGENTS

In many ways, the most fundamental change in the ability of principals to control their agents in the chain of delegation and accountability after membership of the EU has occurred with regard to the public agencies. This is true for a number of reasons. For example, it is related to the fact that the principle of access to public documents and the openness of political institutions in Sweden is quite different from continental traditions, which dominate the EU. Moreover, Sweden is a centralised, unitary state, which means that multi-level principles are quite different from federal states. But the main reason for the increased difficulty of controlling the bureaucracy is associated with the fundamental principle that organises relations between the government and public authorities in Sweden. For historical reasons, public authorities are comparatively independent of the government. This means that the government cannot decide how a public body is to act in a particular case concerning the exercise of public authority against a private subject or a municipality, or in cases concerning the application of law.[28] Moreover, responsibility for managing a public authority is given to a board or director general. An individual minister cannot, as a general rule, determine how an agency should be organised or operate. Instead, to the extent that those tasks are issues for the government, they are matters for the ministers as a group, in cabinet meetings, to decide. As noted previously, the cabinet uses a collegial decision-making method.[29]

The original idea behind this form of organisation was that authorities were supposed to act independently from individual ministers. Civil servants were to operate in a way similar to the courts, applying rules laid down by law in the execution of their duties. Their tasks were to be performed independently and held accountable after the fact. The growth of the welfare state made it difficult to maintain the traditional role and function of civil servants. Many welfare state tasks, such as nursing, teaching, and so on, differ fundamentally from the traditional ones characteristic of the liberal state. Nevertheless, the constitutional relationship between principal and the public administration remains unchanged.

With EU membership, the tasks performed by civil servants have changed in at least two fundamental ways, both of which make it more difficult to hold them accountable. First, civil servants act as Swedish representatives in various situations, for instance in the Commission's commitology. Given the fundamental principle that ministers are not supposed to intervene in civil servants' tasks, how should the agent make sure that he or she acts in accordance with the wishes of the government? How can the government instruct Swedish representatives, co-ordinate their actions and control the execution of their tasks? Secondly, civil servants implement not only Swedish legislation, but EU legislation as well. Occasionally, this can lead to conflicts of interest. For instance, should time and other resources primarily be devoted to implementing national policies or EU policies?

As mentioned, Swedish civil servants participate at various stages in the EU decision-making process. At the preparatory stage, experts in different policy areas participate in working groups and expert groups set up by the Commission. The Swedish representatives often come from the relevant government agencies. They provide the Commission with expert knowledge and present a 'Swedish' view on different proposals. In the decision-making stage, the proposals are handled by working groups and high level groups. In these cases Sweden is represented mainly by civil servants from government ministries and the permanent delegation to the EU. In the implementation stage, civil servants from both ministries and agencies sit on the various commitology committees. It is obvious that these civil servants might exert influence.

Each year, hundreds of people from Swedish authorities participate in EU groups of all kinds. At the same time, the ministries are rather small. The principal's failure to control may be costly in political terms. The civil servants may present Swedish positions at an early stage of the decision-making process. Once Sweden has adopted a position it is politically costly to change it. The further advanced the process is, the more costly it is to deviate from a stated position. This is crucial for the delegation problem. Even if the agent has taken a position that the principal, be it the government or the Riksdag, does not favour, the high political cost of changing it significantly reduces the likelihood of doing so. The obvious implication is that the principal should give clear guidelines to the agent early in the policy process.

Swedish principals have exercised weak control over Swedish agencies and have had limited understanding of the agencies' collaboration with autonomous EU agencies. Control over the agencies as well as government support for them in their EU-related work is still seriously flawed. A combined case study and questionnaire survey revealed that several ministries believe there needs to be increased insight into agency activities and better control over and evaluation of the agencies' actions *vis-à-vis* EU agencies. The ministries do not think that they have the capacity and skills needed to develop goals and policies successfully for Swedish participation in EU organs, or for monitoring and evaluating the work of subordinate agencies.[30] As a consequence, the dependence of the Government Office on the agencies has increased as a result of EU membership. The factual knowledge that the agencies possess is needed in the detailed work in EU institutions and agencies.

In sum, the authorities work closer to the Government Office in EU matters than on other issues. It is also possible that authorities have a better chance of successfully pursuing their own policy preferences in EU matters than in national ones. There are, however, changes that have been brought about by EU membership which have increased the principal's insight into the work of the agent. Many of the issues that are decided in the Council of Ministers were formerly delegated to Swedish public authorities or the government. The government and the Riksdag – especially the EU Advisory Committee – now take an interest in these issues and study them more intensively when they are subject to Council decision. Particularly in the areas of agriculture and consumer protection, the Riksdag has gained insight into regulatory frameworks that the public authorities used to run more or less at their own discretion.

There are some 3,200 laws and other legal norms promulgated by the government, which are in force in Sweden. Of these, only 8.3 per cent concern EU matters in the sense that there is a reference to a Celex number of an EU rule. Most of these rules concern the areas of agriculture and foodstuffs.[31]

Interest organisations have traditionally played an important role in Swedish politics, and the major ones have had close contact with the government. EU membership has meant that interest groups have formed new channels of direct access at the European level. However, there are also close contacts between Swedish interest groups and the government in EU matters. Reference groups have been formed in the ministries to ensure that organised interests are heard on important EU issues.[32]

CONCLUSION

Swedish EU membership changed preconditions for controlling agents in the delegation–accountability chain in a number of ways. The effects of the changes in terms of accountability have varied. On the one hand, the Riksdag's ability to control the government and public administrators has decreased. This is true for many reasons. The latter participate in decision making – indeed determine legislation – in matters that used to be the prerogative of the Riksdag. To counterbalance this, the Riksdag has taken measures such as demanding continuous information from the government and establishing an EU Advisory Committee. On the other hand, the Riksdag has gained insight into areas that were previously the privilege of the government, such as foreign affairs, or public authorities, such as details of agriculture policy and regulation. While this latter change hardly outweighs the loss of authority, it is nonetheless worth noting.

In congruence with Lupia's propositions about the EU and domestic accountability, our results come close to those he derives from his theoretical model. Membership need not always weaken domestic accountability. Nevertheless, the changed conditions for accountability caused by EU membership are a challenge for the principals in the chain of delegation and accountability. This work points out some of these challenges and identifies some of the difficulties principals experience in responding to them.

As we have explained, both the government and the Riksdag focus on activities in the Council. The Riksdag has chosen an organisational solution with compulsory deliberations in the EU Advisory Committee before each Council meeting. Other than this, the government and its agents are required to present reports or other information on important Commission proposals. Thus, the organisational choice biases the work in the Riksdag towards the work in the Council. As a consequence, the Riksdag risks being brought into the policy process at a very late stage, when exerting influence is largely impossible. Efforts to bring standing committees into EU issues have thus far not produced the intended results.

It is important, especially for a small country like Sweden, to act consistently and in a co-ordinated fashion. It is an advantage to speak 'with one voice', so that representatives do not convey different, or even opposing, points of view. If Sweden takes a stand on an issue in a Council working group, the political cost of changing the position later, in COREPER or at a Council meeting, is quite high. Despite this, the focus of work in the Advisory Committee on European Affairs is Council meetings. Even if the same issue appears many times on Council meeting agendas, there is, in practice, limited opportunity for the Advisory Committee to force the government to change a position that the government has already stated in a Council forum.

Furthermore, the parliament faces significant difficulties in exercising *ex post* control over the government with regard to its actions in the Council and other EU institutions. The government representative who participates at a Council meeting can always claim that if Sweden had changed its view to accommodate the Advisory Committee, it would have paid too high a political cost. The Riksdag Committee on Constitution has stated that co-operation between the Riksdag and the government should be performed in a way that furthers the interest of the country. This can, in practice, give the government an advantage. It suggests that the Riksdag's ability to hold the government responsible for its actions at a particular meeting is limited.

This way of organising the role of the Riksdag in EU matters reveals a dilemma. The government must, on the one hand, have the discretion necessary to govern. Among other things, it must have discretion in order to act efficiently in Council negotiations. This implies that the Riksdag should not interfere too much with the actions of the government or tie the government's hands too tightly. Rather, the Riksdag should focus on controlling *ex post*. On the other hand, if the Riksdag limits itself to controlling after the event, then it may find that it lacks influence in very important matters. However, if the principal becomes much too involved in the agent's implementation of its tasks, then the principal might find itself in a position in which it is unable to hold the agent alone completely responsible for its actions. There is a certain point at which the roles of the principal and the agent are blurred, and at this point the principal cannot assign blame to the agent without blaming itself as well. The Riksdag must therefore balance two contradictory values.

When Sweden joined the EU, it was argued that the loss of formal sovereignty would be outweighed by a gain in influence within the EU. However, the loss mainly affects the Riksdag, while the gain mainly accrues to the government. Thus, the agent has strengthened its position in relation to the principal. When the government is the principal, however, conclusions are less clear. EU membership means that there is closer co-operation between the government and public authorities in policy areas that have been affected by membership. Civil servants working in public authorities act as experts in the preparatory phase of the Commission's work, and they represent the government in the Commission's commitology. The need for the comparatively small Government Office to rely on public authorities probably implies a shift in influence that favours the public authorities. Nonetheless, it is the government that formally decides policy and issues negotiating instructions to those persons who represent Sweden in the EU policy process.

The role of the Riksdag varies depending upon the parliamentary situation. Obviously, in general, majority governments have less to fear from *ex ante* or *ex post* control in parliament than do minority governments. During the period in which Sweden has been a member of the EU, it has had a fairly strong Social Democratic minority government.[33]

In addition to the parliamentary situation, cleavages in the party system also have an impact on the role of the parliament. As Henrik Oscarsson has noted, it is hardly controversial to claim that an EU dimension has emerged in the Swedish party system, and that EU membership is an issue that divides the electorate.[34] This fairly new dimension in Swedish politics affects efforts to control agents in the chain of delegation and accountability. The cleavage actually has an important impact on virtually all links. It is important for how the citizens cast their votes in the elections to both the European Parliament and the Riksdag. However, many voters probably face problems of information with regard to EU issues. There is still no common European forum for political debate. Furthermore, the Swedish debate about the EU has largely continued to focus on the question of yes or no to the EU rather than on the issues under discussion in the EU decision-making process.

It is obvious how the cleavage among voters and parties determines the party groups' actions in the Riksdag with regard to questions of accountability and access to information. Members of parliament from the Green Party are the most active in EU matters. Members of parliament from the Left Party are also active.[35] Despite this, the Green Party and the Left Party argue that the present system for controlling of Riksdag's agent is insufficient.

The new situation has been dealt with differently in different policy areas. One evaluative study shows that Sweden has had a relatively clear policy on environmental issues. It has probably been more successful in this area than most others. Sweden has traditionally pursued environmental issues in various international fora, and this tradition seems to influence Swedish work in the EU.[36] In other areas, there has been a lack of political leadership in EU matters.

Many parts of the Swedish political system have been affected by EU membership. This is true for two areas that have traditionally been a matter for domestic decision making. It is true for agriculture and communications, but also for foreign affairs. Actually, the degree of the changes in the Ministry for Foreign Affairs is surprisingly great.[37] One could almost say that most matters in foreign affairs are in one way or another discussed in the EU, for example in the General Affairs Council, yet most of the issues discussed in the EU are traditionally domestic matters.

Our interest in this article has concentrated on accountability as a process of control. We have described how membership has affected the institutions that can be used to hold agents accountable. However, there are also consequences related to outcome. Agency losses occur when agents act in ways that produce consequences that are different from those that would have occurred if the agent had been a perfect agent – that is an agent that does what the principal would have done if the principal possessed unlimited information and resources. Such losses appear to have arisen in at least two policy areas as a consequence of the membership. These areas are trade and agriculture.

As a small open economy, Sweden is heavily dependent on export. It is obviously a friend of free international trade. When it joined the EU,

Sweden had to introduce EC customs rules on goods such as bicycles, bananas and electronic equipment. Moreover, although Sweden had successfully deregulated agriculture and abolished almost all subsidies, these had to be reintroduced when the country joined the EU. These policies and regulations were imposed on Sweden by the EU and were accepted by national principals – a majority of voters, MPs and the government – as an unavoidable part of membership. Only those who benefited from the changes, for example some of the farmers, welcomed the changes.

To implement the CAP in Sweden the Swedish government had to expand the National Board of Agriculture. Its resources increased, as did the amount of red tape associated with agricultural regulation. Nevertheless, instances of misuse of resources (fraud, mistakes and other problems) were soon reported and the agents requested new resources. It appears that the position of the relevant bureaucrats was improved after membership. The reversion point might have changed to their advantage.

As for accountability in terms of the institutional aspects of the chain of delegation and accountability, it is the duty of the government to inform and deliberate with the Riksdag on EU matters as regulated in the Riksdag Act. With that exception, Swedish membership in the EU has not led to any important formal changes in the Swedish Constitution with regard to the balance of power between the Riksdag, the government and state authorities. However, in reality there have been significant changes in the relationships between these central institutions. These changes have not been one-sided, and they differ across different policy areas. Nonetheless, new conditions for the process of delegation and accountability have clearly been created.

NOTES

1. D.R. Kiewiet and M.D. McCubbins, *The Logic of Delegation. Congressional Parties and the Appropriations Process* (Chicago, IL: University of Chicago Press, 1991), p.24.
2. G. Brennan and J.M. Buchanan, *The Power to Tax: Analytical Foundations of a Fiscal Constitution* (Cambridge: Cambridge University Press, 1980).
3. F. Sterzel, *Riksdagens kontrollmakt* (Stockholm: Norstedt, 1969).
4. I. Mattson, 'Parliamentary Questions in the Swedish Riksdag', in M. Wiberg (ed.), *Parliamentary Control in the Nordic Countries. Forms of Questioning and Behavioural Trends* (Helsinki: The Finnish Political Science Association, 1994), pp.276–356.
5. Cf. Kiewiet and McCubbins, *The Logic of Delegation*, p.27.
6. Cf. B.R. Weingast, 'The Congressional-Bureaucratic System: A Principal Agent Perspective', *Public Choice*, Vol.44 (1984), pp.147–91; M.D. McCubbins, 'The Legislative Design of Regulatory Structure', *American Journal of Political Science*, Vol.29 (1985), pp.721–48; M.D. McCubbins, R.G. Noll and B.R. Weingast, 'Administrative Procedures as Instruments of Political Control', *Journal of Law Economics, and Organization*, Vol.3 (1987), pp.243–77; M.D. McCubbins, R.G. Noll and B.R. Weingast, 'Structure and Process, Politics and Policy: Administrative Arrangements and the Political Control of Agencies', *Virginia Law Review*, Vol.75 (1989), pp.431–82.

7. For an introduction and analysis of general aspects of the chain of delegation and accountability, see T. Bergman, 'Sweden: From Separation of Powers to Parliamentary Sovereignty – and Back Again', in K. Strøm, W. Müller and T. Bergman (eds.), *Delegation and Accountability in Parliamentary Democracies* (Manuscript, Umeå University).

8. Cf. K Jacobsson, *Så gott som demokrati. Om demokratifrågan i EU-debatten* (Umeå: Boréa, 1997).

9. M. Gilljam and S. Holmberg, *Ett knappt ja till EU. Väljarna och folkomröstningen 1994* (Stockholm: Norstedts juridik, 1996).

10. See, for example, R. Lindahl, 'Missnöjda EU-medlemmar', in S. Holmberg and L. Weibull (eds.), *Ett missnöjt folk* (SOM-rapport no 18, 1996), pp.163–84.

11. M. Gilljam and S. Holmberg, *Sveriges första Europaparlamentsval* (Stockholm: Norstedts juridik, 1998).

12. H. Oscarsson, *Den svenska partirymden* (Göteborg: Statsvetenskapliga institutionen, 1998), p.270 *et passim*. Cf S. Holmberg, 'The Extent of European Integration', in A. Todal Jenssen *et al.* (eds.), *To Join or Not to Join. Three Nordic Referendums on Membership in the European Union* (Oslo: Scandinavian University Press, 1998), pp.276–7.

13. S. Rokkan, 'Faser og mønstre i fremveksten av massepolitik i Norden', in *Stat, Nasjon, Klasse* (Oslo: Universitetsforlaget, 1987); Oscarsson, *Den svenska partirymden*.

14. M. Brothén, 'Svenska EU-parlamentarikers representativitet', in I. Mattson and L. Wängnerud (eds.), *Riksdagen på nära håll* (Stockholm: SNS Förlag, 1997), pp.63–85.

15. The share of the electorate who indicated that they were interested or very interested in EU-related issues decreased from 74 to 51 per cent between 1994 and 1995. Source: Gilljam and Holmberg, *Sveriges första Europaparlamentsval*.

16. A more detailed description of how the Riksdag deals with EU matters is found in H. Hegeland and I. Mattson, 'The Swedish Riksdag and the EU: Influence and Openness', in M. Wiberg (ed.), *Trying to Make Democracy Work. The Nordic Parliaments and the European Union* (Stockholm: Gidlunds, 1997), pp.70–107. This section is also based on some 20 interviews with MPs and staff members at the Riksdag, as well as on participant observation.

17. Committee report 1994/95: KU22, p.14. All political parties except the Green Party stood behind this statement.

18. For a comparison between the Swedish and Danish European Committees, see H. Hegeland and I. Mattson, 'To Have a Voice in the Matter: A Comparative Study of the Swedish and Danish European Committees', *Journal of Legislative Studies*, Vol.2, No.3 (1996), pp.198–215.

19. Committee report 1994/95: KU22, p.15.

20. See, for example, committee report 1996/97: KU2, pp.42–3. These two parties do not have identical views on these matters. The Green Party has, for example, argued more intensely for holding deliberations prior to Council meetings in the relevant standing committee rather than in the EU Advisory Committee. However, they represent, in a broad sense, a common and – compared to the majority – different view on these issues.

21. The Intergovernmental Conference in 1996–97 implied a special challenge for parliamentary control. The Swedish chief negotiator (the state secretary at the Foreign Affairs Office) met the Advisory Committee on European Affairs almost every week during the IGC. It should be noted that in the Amsterdam Treaty Bill the government consistently referred to earlier statements by the Riksdag, as well as to how well Swedish interests had been fulfilled in the treaty. Even if it was obvious that the Riksdag would ratify the treaty, there would probably have been a more intensive political debate on the government's conduct in the negotiations had there not been such close co-operation with the Riksdag before and during the IGC.

22. Cf. S. Ahlbäck, *Att kontrollera staten* (Uppsala: Statsvetenskapliga institutionen, 1999).

23. This section, as well as the following one, is based mainly on internal memoranda from the Government Office and studies conducted by the Committee on the Constitution, the Parliamentary Auditors and the Swedish Agency for Administrative Development.

24. Bergman, 'Sweden: From Separation of Powers to Parliamentary Sovereignty – and Back Again'.

25. M. Ekengren, *Time and European Governance. The Empirical Value of Three Reflective Approaches* (Stockholm: University of Stockholm, Department of Political Science, 1998).

26. M. Jerneck, 'Democracy and Interdependence', in L.-G. Stenelo and M. Jerneck (eds.), *The Bargaining Democracy* (Lund: Lund University Press, 1996), pp.147–218.
27. Bergman, 'Sweden: From Separation of Powers to Parliamentary Sovereignty – and Back Again'.
28. Instrument of Government 11:7
29. Cf. T. Larsson, 'Sweden', in J. Blondel and F. Müller-Rommel (eds.), *Cabinets in Western Europe* (London: Macmillan, 1988), pp.197–212.
30. *Autonomous EU Agencies for a more efficient Union and enhanced national influence* (Report by The Swedish Agency for Administrative Development, 1997:21A).
31. F. Sterzel, *Vilket hinder utgör EU för svensk avreglering?* (Stockholm: SAF, 1999) and *EG-regler och svensk regelkvalitet* (Report by The Swedish Agency for Administrative Development (Statskontoret) 1998:27).
32. Cf. M. Karlsson, 'Svensk och europeisk intresserepresentation i EU', in K.M. Johansson (ed.), *Sverige och EU* (Stockholm: SNS, 1999).
33. However, this position is only strong because the principal has given its support. In one sense, the agent derives its strength from the strength of the principal. For an interesting analysis of parliamentary power in multi-party systems, see M. Sjölin, *Coalition Politics and Parliamentary Power* (Lund: Lund University Press, 1993), esp. Ch.9.
34. H. Oscarsson, 'EU-dimensionen', in M. Gilljam and S. Holmberg (eds.), *Ett knappt ja till EU. Väljarna och folkomröstningen 1994*, pp.237–67.
35. Cf. D.A. Christensen, 'Europautvala i Danmark, Sverige, og Noreg: Sandpåströningorgan eller politiska muldvarpar?', *Nordisk Administrativt Tidsskrift*, No.2 (1997), pp.143–62.
36. G. Sundström, *Att tala med en röst. En studie av EU-medlemskapet påverkar samordningen inom Regeringskansliet* (unpublished paper, Department of Political Science, University of Stockholm, 1999).
37. Ekengren, *Time and European Governance*, p.57.

Delegation and Accountability in an Ambiguous System: Iceland and the European Economic Area (EEA)

SVANUR KRISTJÁNSSON and RAGNAR KRISTJÁNSSON

A prominent scholar of Icelandic law has recently observed that Iceland's membership in the European Economic Area (EEA) will most likely lead to the most profound changes in domestic law making since the thirteenth century.[1] In a similar vein, many people, including MPs, have noted that the Althing (Alþingi, the Icelandic parliament) is increasingly impotent in the legislative process. Government ministers dominate it. So does the government bureaucracy, interest groups and – last but not least – the EEA.[2] There is a general feeling that Iceland's relations with the outside world have undergone a qualitative shift, that membership in the EEA implies lasting economic, social and political change.

Therefore the authors of this paper turn to the subject of the relationship between the Icelandic political system and the EEA with a sense of excitement and urgency. We will present few, if any, final conclusions. Our goal is rather to outline the basic framework of the analysis, to review existing knowledge and to identify fields for further research. Our main focus is the impact of Iceland's EEA membership on the national chain of delegation and accountability. We start by dividing the chain into four steps: (1) Voters as principals and MPs as agents; (2) parliament as principal and cabinet as agent; (3) cabinet as principal and individual ministers as agents; and, finally, (4) cabinet ministers as principals and civil servants as agents.

The basic issue is the impact, if any, of EEA membership on democracy in Iceland. Has membership altered the relationships between principals and agents, for example by changing the flow of information or altering reversal points? If so, what is the direction of change – towards greater or lesser accountability? Our task is complicated by the fact that we must treat the fundamental and complex issues of national sovereignty and democracy under new and continuously evolving circumstances.

Svanur Kristjánsson is Professor, Department of Political Science, University of Iceland. Ragnar Kristjánsson is an official at the Ministry of Foreign Affairs.

VOTERS AS PRINCIPALS AND MPs AS AGENTS

The EEA agreement was approved by the Althing on 12 January 1993 by a vote of 33 for, 23 against and seven abstentions. Prior to the vote in favour of the EEA, a motion to dismiss the bill was narrowly defeated by a vote of 30 for, but 33 against. A proposal to put the agreement to a national referendum was also rejected. On 13 January 1993 the Althing approved, again by a narrow margin, a bilateral fisheries agreement with the EU.

The parliamentary debate on the EEA was a very long one. It started in early August 1992 and continued, with some intermissions, for five months. The process divided MPs of all parties except the Social Democratic Party, which – under the chairmanship of Jon Baldvin Hannibalsson, foreign minister 1988–95 – remained steadfast in its support for EEA membership.

The Althing vote was not the end of the decision-making process. According to the Icelandic constitution the president has the right to refuse to sign any law passed by parliament. In this case the law takes effect but must be put to a vote in a special national referendum. A negative vote in the referendum renders the law invalid. Although no president has ever refused to sign an Althing proposal, this does not alter a basic feature of the constitution. It mixes parliamentary and semi-presidential government without clearly demarcating authority. At least in principle, the popularly elected president can exercise considerable power and influence by relying on his/her constitutional status and by appealing directly to the people as guardians of the national interest and even as supreme symbol of the nation's very soul.

About 35,000 people (that is, more than ten per cent of the population) had signed petitions calling for a national referendum on EEA membership. Public opinion polls also indicated substantial majority support for a referendum.[3] In addition, 300 prominent citizens appealed to the president not to sign the agreement, thereby forcing a national referendum.

The whole experience was painful for those involved, bringing back the trauma of a euphoric newly independent nation (1944) being torn apart by the cold war, NATO membership and, especially, the stationing of American troops in Iceland. The issue of a referendum landed squarely in the hands of the president, Vigdís Finnbogadóttir. The president had three obvious options: (1) sign the agreement, thus securing its ratification; (2) refuse to sign; (3) refuse to sign and resign from office.

Iceland's ambiguous political system tended to confuse and muddle matters with regard to several contentious issues. One such issue was the question of constitutional law. Some legal scholars argued that Iceland's membership in the EEA was constitutional, others argued strongly that it was not. A constitutional court could not resolve the question, because it is simply foreign to the Icelandic political system. Another confusing issue was the demand for a national referendum. The constitution does not spell out any procedures for holding a national referendum, except when one is 'forced' by the president's refusal to sign a bill, the Althing's removal of the president or Althing action to change the status of the Lutheran state church. Finally, there was the question of the details of the EEA agreement as compared to other options, in particular a comprehensive bilateral agreement with the EU.

The president could not, by a simple decision to sign or not sign the EEA treaty, untangle this mess of procedural and substantive uncertainty. The prime minister had a firm view about the constitutional issue – namely, that the president's decision not to sign would involve only the substance of the bill, not procedure. According to him, 'the Icelandic constitution allows the president only to oppose a decision by the Althing, go into opposition against the Althing or take sides in a controversy. Thus a war between the presidency and parliament would have started.'[4]

After a great deal of deliberation, the president requested a meeting of the state council, which includes the cabinet and the president. The president issued a statement during the meeting in which she elaborated on her conception of the presidency and explained her decision to sign the EEA agreement. In the statement the president emphasised the role of the presidency in nurturing unity and national consensus and stated that 'no president has intervened against legal decisions reached by the democratically elected Althing'.[5]

In this context, one question inevitably arose. Did the president's state council declaration change the political system, turning it into an unbridled parliamentary government and wiping out the semi-presidential character of the constitution? Today the answer is quite clear: not only is the constitution unchanged, public perception continues to view the political system as a semi-presidential one. Thus in the last presidential election, in 1996, three of the four candidates asserted the president's right to refer laws passed by the Althing to a national referendum. The president, it is argued, is accountable only to the people. Should parliament take positions opposed by the people, then the president should side with the people. It is also worth noting that the current president, Ólafur Ragnar Grímsson, is an experienced politician as well as a former professor of political science. He is well aware of the fact that the semi-presidential constitution creates numerous possibilities for the president to exercise power. In fact, as an MP and chairman of the Socialist People's Alliance, Grímsson opposed the EEA agreement in 1993. He is also vehemently opposed to Iceland's membership in the EU, a view he reaffirmed during a visit to President Clinton at the White House in the summer of 1997, when he likened the fishery policy of the EU to the planned economy of the Soviet Union. The president's view undoubtedly strengthens the opponents of EU membership and keeps membership supporters isolated and largely confined to one small political party, the Social Democrats.

Iceland's political party system has consisted of four major parties since the 1930s. The Independence Party (IP) was founded in 1929 by a merger of the Conservative Party (founded 1924) and the Liberal Party (founded 1926). It usually receives about 40 per cent of the vote. The second largest party, the Progressive Party (PP), is located in the centre of the political spectrum. It was founded in 1916 and over the past 20 years has received about 20 per cent of the national vote. The Social Democratic Party (SDP) was founded in 1916 as the political arm of the labour movement. Organisationally, it was tied to the Icelandic Federation of Labour until 1942. Since that time, the SDP has most often been the smallest of the four main parties, usually receiving about 14–16 per cent of the vote. Finally, the People's Alliance (PA) is a descendant of the Communist Party and other SDP-breakaway groups. It usually gets between 15 and 18 per cent of the vote, thus making it the third largest party. Since the early 1990s one or two smaller parties have also been represented in the Althing. The Women's Alliance (WA) has held seats since 1983. In the most recent election (1995) the WA received 4.9 per cent of the vote and gained three MPs.[6]

The main parties are formally organised as mass political parties. In reality they are rather loose organisations. They do not collect membership dues, nor do they maintain reliable membership lists. Since the 1970s all four traditional parties have adopted primaries to select candidates for parliamentary elections (the WA has used selection committees for nominations). The primaries have reinforced the cadre-party characteristics of the parties, and have contributed to frequent internal disunity. Primaries have also reduced the parties' ability to formulate policy insofar as they encourage parties to settle for the lowest common denominator with regard to policy positions. At the same time, however, the established parties have been able to retain their central political role as a result of the conservative consequences of Iceland's proportional electoral system and its very strong tradition of majority coalition cabinets.

On the whole, Icelandic political parties contest elections and form governments as organised entities, while they are weak with regard to policy formulation and execution. Thus, the effects of parties are more observable in the delegation from voters to MPs and in the link between parliament and cabinet than in the delegation of authority from cabinet to individual ministers or from individual ministers to civil servants. During the cold war the four main parties generally had a rather fixed position on foreign policy issues. The right-wing Independence Party (IP) and the Social Democratic Party (SDP) strongly supported Iceland's membership in NATO and the stationing of American troops in the country. The socialist People's Alliance

(PA) strongly opposed both, while the centrist Progressive Party (PP) sought to hold a middle position. Leaders of the Independence Party, particularly Bjarni Benediktsson, then foreign minister, played a key role in formulating Iceland's post-Second World War foreign policy, emphasising NATO membership and 'the American connection'.

The parties' positions on Iceland's EEA and EU membership do not fit into the cold war pattern. The political parties' policy making with regard to Iceland's ties to Europe reveals much about Icelandic politics, especially the continuing importance of nationalism as the basic political ideology. It also illustrates the weakness of the parties as cohesive organisations and reveals their inability to implement policy.

The combination of nationalism and weak political parties has resulted in a cautious approach to policy making. A clear example of this is the Icelandic approach to European integration:

> The Icelandic government has never seriously contemplated membership of the European Union. It has emphasised favourable trade relations rather than political ties. In 1989 Iceland, along with the other EFTA [European Free Trade Association] states, began a negotiation process with the EC which led to the formation of the European Economic Area in 1994. Yet, neither the government nor most of the political parties had at that time formed any clear policy on Iceland's objectives or strategies in the negotiations. In fact, Prime Minister Hermannsson (Progressive Party) stated serious reservations at the Oslo meeting of EFTA leaders in March 1989 concerning three of the four freedoms; all except the free movement of goods.[7]

By the time of the Althing's vote on the EEA membership in 1993, three of the four major political parties had changed their positions on the issue. While they were in governmental opposition they opposed the agreement and expressed support for bilateral negotiations with the EU. When in government, however, they supported the agreement.

European issues are, in fact, potentially explosive for all political parties. The issue taps into other intra-party cleavages such as the urban–rural cleavage and the protected economy versus pro-market split. The fundamental disagreements on European co-operation and integration do not run between political parties, but between generations – with young people being much more in favour of integration than older ones.

The political parties consistently attempt to keep European issues off the domestic public agenda. The parties simply do not believe they can reap any benefits from staking out firm public positions on European questions. On the contrary, discussions of Europe only create trouble, not least internal party division and conflict. Furthermore, opponents are strong in the politically dominant regions, in the powerful organisations of agriculture and the fisheries, and among those over the age of 40 – which is the age group that holds most of the positions of influence in the political system. The numerical strength of those in favour of membership is not reflected in the political system, because these citizens are concentrated in the Reykjavik-Reykjanes area; they tend to be under 40, and they lack interest organisations to promote their cause (at least they did so up to December 1994 when the Chambers of Commerce came out in favour of membership).[8]

In analysing people's attitudes toward the European union, a distinction must be made between two issues: (a) public opinion on an application for EU membership, and (b) public opinion on EU membership itself. It used to be that, with some fluctuations, the Icelandic public was divided into three roughly equal groups with regard to these issues: for, against and undecided. More recently, a large gap has developed. On the issue of applying for membership, roughly half of the electorate is in favour, while about 20 per cent are opposed. On the other hand, the yes and no forces are almost evenly matched on the question of Iceland's immediate membership of the EU.

Current developments in the EU provide little incentive for the parties to bring up the issue of EU membership. One example is that the 1999 election to the European Parliament was met by relatively little interest from the both the public and the media. No discussion of the question of Iceland's possible EU membership was raised in the media. Instead, comments centred on three other aspects: low turnout, the influence of domestic factors on electoral results and gains made by the middle-right parties and the electoral losses of the socialist parties.

In the near future three factors might change the balance of forces in favour of membership:

(1) More pressure for membership from interest organisations. Already there are strong signs of such a trend. Labour union leaders express very positive evaluations of the impact of EU laws and regulations on workers' rights and welfare. The Chambers of Commerce and the Association of Industries are also very much in favour of the EU.

(2) Changes in the electoral system which come into force in the elections in 2003 will strengthen parliamentary representation from centre regions, which tend to be more pro-European integration than are peripheral regions.

(3) External factors, for example the proposed enlargement of the EU to include eastern European countries, or, more importantly, if Norway joins the EU. In the next few years, the development of the EMU will have a great impact on Iceland. Should the EMU founder, Iceland's

EU membership will become less attractive, while a successful EMU – especially if Denmark, Sweden and, most importantly, Britain join – will almost 'inevitably' pull Iceland into the Union. (Currently one-third of Iceland's international trade is with EMU countries, while another one-third with EU countries that remain outside the EMU).

In general, it is rather safe to predict that in the near future Iceland will stick to its traditional re-active rather than pro-active foreign policy; and external factors will therefore continue to be the most decisive ones.

PARLIAMENT AS PRINCIPAL AND CABINET AS AGENT

The Althing has a special place in the Icelandic political system. It has traditionally been *the* symbol of the Icelandic nation. Its establishment in the year 930 was the highpoint of the Commonwealth period, which started with the first settlement in 874 and ended with the loss of independence to the king of Norway in 1262. The Althing's demise in the dark ages was a manifestation of Iceland's deepest humiliation, just as the Althing's restoration in 1845 became the starting point and focus of Iceland's path to self-determination.

Moving from mythology to description of reality, however, it is difficult to define the Althing's role in the political system with precision. The Althing is a single-house legislature. Sixty-three MPs are elected in eight constituencies. The Althing is usually convened in early October and adjourns in May. In recent years, the four traditional political parties and two smaller parties have held seats in the Althing. Each party's MPs are organised into a parliamentary party that elects its own chairperson and vice-chairperson. Since 1971 each parliamentary party has received state funding to pay for specialised assistance to help it carry out legislative work. In practice the money goes into the parties' general office funds, as most parties are in poor financial shape.

The political party in government and its legislative party remain closely intertwined. Generally, only MPs become ministers. Moreover, ministers retain their parliamentary seats and receive salaries for both jobs. Neither the MPs nor the ministers are agents of strong independent party organisations outside the Althing and the cabinet. Thus, the main line of conflict between opposing interests is usually not between parliament on the one hand and the cabinet on the other, but rather between opposition MPs and government MPs, some of whom are also ministers. Both the parliament and the executive branch operate under increasingly powerful external constraints.

The committee structure of the Althing has not been affected by EEA membership, just as it was not changed as a result of European Free Trade Association (EFTA) membership. The committee system was strengthened by a reorganisation in 1991. Eleven specialised committees deal with legislation. All legislative proposals are referred to one of the committees, which examines the bill and then reports back to the general assembly. In 1993, opposition MPs were elected chairpersons of three specialised committees. This custom was maintained after the 1995 election. The size of the professional staff of the committees has increased, as has technical assistance available to committees and individual MPs. The work of the committees had become more professional as MPs increase their co-operation across party lines. MPs from each electoral district also meet regularly. Meetings of MPs from outside the capital constituency often resemble an intermediate administrative level, connecting local government within their district to central government authorities. In some cases the district MPs' groups are directly involved in administrative functions, for example the allocation of funds to various public projects.

The Foreign Affairs Committee is unusually strong, which reflects the importance attached to achieving and maintaining foreign policy consensus. The Financial Committee also has a relatively strong position. Both committees are always chaired by MPs from government parties. The nine members of the Foreign Affairs Committee of the Althing meet once every week for two hours, sometimes more frequently depending on the Committee's workload.[9] The Committee is supposed to discuss forthcoming EEA questions once every month, in advance of the EEA Joint Committee meeting. While the Committee has not always done so, it does receive detailed information from the Ministry of Foreign Affairs about current EEA matters as well as information about issues that are expected to come up in the future. On the basis of this information, it is up to the Committee to decide whether or not action is necessary. The Foreign Affairs Committee forwards relevant information on current and forthcoming EEA matters to other standing committees for specialised scrutiny. In matters of great importance the Foreign Ministry keeps the committee posted by submitting reports and, occasionally by arranging for the Minister of Foreign Affairs to deliver a report before the committee.

Four members of the EEA Parliamentary Committee are from the Althing. This committee is a co-ordinating body composed of members of the European Parliament and members of parliaments in EEA states (Iceland, Norway, Lichtenstein). The EEA Parliamentary Committee supervises the enactment and general development of the EEA agreement and issues evaluations of EEA developments. The committee meets twice a year. Between these meetings the committee's executive meets. The head of the Icelandic delegation to the EEA Parliamentary Committee is always a member of the executive.

The decreasing cohesiveness of political parties has affected the work of MPs in a number of ways. The individual MP has greater freedom of action in parliament, often as a consequence of the open primary. Each MP competes with fellow party MPs in his/her constituency. Intra-party friction and conflict in the Althing has increased. This trend towards competition and friction is, however, counterbalanced by another tendency – the growing importance of co-operation among MPs from the same party. They all run on the same ticket and they are on the same side in the Althing – either government supporters or opponents.

In sharp contrast to the other Nordic countries – chiefly Denmark, Norway and Sweden – Iceland has no tradition of minority government in the post-Second World War era.[10] The 1917–44 period was quite different in this respect – during these years majority coalition governments were in power less than half the time. The formation of coalitions has become an open game in which all combinations are possible. None of the political parties rules out the possibility of forming a government with any of the other parties, although some parties might indicate their preference for a particular coalition. The behaviour of parties in the coalition formation process is largely explained by their pragmatic, cadre-party nature. They energetically seek the spoils of office, and ideology is not a decisive factor. The question of Iceland's relations with the European Union clearly illustrates this feature of Icelandic political life. Most of the parties have shifted policy position depending upon whether or not they are in government. Nevertheless, ideology is not completely missing from Icelandic politics. While it is not particularly important as an explanation of party behaviour, it provides politicians with justifications for what is basically pragmatic and self-serving action.

Thus, European issues were used to justify remarkable events in recent Icelandic politics: the decision of the Social Democratic Party (SDP) not to continue in government after the 1991 election and an identical decision by the Independence Party (IP) after the 1995 election. In both cases, the governing coalition had survived the election by winning a minimum working parliamentary majority – that is, 32 MPs. Yet both lost office as a result of the post-election, coalition-formation game. In 1991 the SDP cited its strong commitment to Iceland's membership in the proposed EEA as the main reason for its decision to change partners. In fact, during the election campaign the SDP had been attacked by its coalition partners (the Progressive Party and the People's Alliance) for being 'soft' on Icelandic membership in the European Union. Similarly, in 1994 the SDP had adopted a resolution advocating Iceland's membership in the EU, despite the fact that the resolution was contrary to stated government policy and the SDP chairman held the post of foreign minister. The prime minister, who was from the IP, correctly viewed the SDP action as an attempt to attract young, pro-European voters from the IP. In addition, the question of EU membership is a potentially explosive issue inside the IP because the party is deeply divided on the matter.

One does not need to refer to ideology to explain the SDP decision in 1991 or the IP decision in 1995. In both instances their behaviour was clearly self-serving. The SDP, with ten MPs, wanted more ministerial posts than the three it had held previously. The IP prime minister continued in office with a majority parliamentary coalition larger than the one he had in coalition with the SDP – thus avoiding the problem of being held hostage by every unruly government MP in a minimum coalition.

Within the Althing, Iceland's membership in the EEA has clearly strengthened the tradition of building consensus in foreign policy. All parliamentary parties are involved in the Foreign Affairs Committee, and most are also represented on the EFTA Committee and the EEA Committee. In general, the Althing has sought to increase its international contacts. Furthermore, the status of those MPs specialising in foreign affairs has clearly risen. (In fact this development is an indispensable factor in explaining the election of the current president. Prior to the election campaign he was an MP for the rather small socialist party, the PA.)

As mentioned above, in Iceland the designation of the parliament as principal and the cabinet as agent is not connected to clear and specific mechanisms of delegation. The demarcation of authority and functional responsibility between the legislative and executive branches remain muddled. The Althing is heavily involved in executive administration and the cabinet often plays a dominant role in the legislative process, for example in budget decisions.

In recent years, several steps have been taken to sharpen the separation between legislative and executive power. The Althing has become more effective as an institution, while individual MPs – usually those in opposition – have increasingly turned to parliamentary questions and extraordinary debates to oversee ministers and to direct public attention toward issues they consider important. The authority of the cabinet to issue 'temporary laws' has also been restricted.

Members of the Althing can monitor individual ministers either by putting questions to them or through the standing committees. Thus, one of the motives behind parliamentary questions is for the principal (parliament) to exercise control over the agent (that is, the cabinet and/or a minister). The Althing has three kinds of questions at its disposal: written questions (*skrifleg fyrirspurn*), oral questions, (*munnleg fyrirspurn*), and topical hour questioning (*óundirbúnar fyrirspurnir*).

Table 1 shows that 'direct' EEA-related questions have not been a priority on the agenda of MPs seeking to monitor ministers via parliamentary questions. However, an analysis of all questions, and answers

TABLE 1
EEA-RELATED QUESTIONS IN ALTHING (1991–98)

Year	Written Questions – EEA related	Total	Oral questions – EEA related	Total	Topical hour questions – EEA related	Total
1991–92	8	89	4	180	5	56
1992–93	3	103	6	141	4	35
1993–94	5	97	3	132	2	42
1994–95	1	84	2	88	1	31
1995–96	1	99	3	126	0	61
1996–97	2	135	2	117	1	53
1997–98	2	178	1	137	2	52

Source: The Althing Records, various years.

to them, reveals that the EEA agreement is actually raised and referred to quite often in the question and answer procedure.

Iceland's membership in the EEA is not a decisive factor in the changing relationship between the Althing and the cabinet as the Althing attempts to assert its role as principal. Nonetheless, the Althing and cabinet are both constrained by the EEA. The role of the Althing in relation to the EEA is in fact that of an agent: the Althing is obliged to follow the decisions made by the principal (the EEA) according to the contract initially agreed upon by the Althing. As Bogason has argued,[11] after a heated Althing debate about whether or not to ratify the EEA Agreement, the functioning of the Agreement has subsequently not been much of an issue in the Althing. In his biannual report on foreign relations, the Minister of Foreign Affairs discusses the EEA. In addition to this, each member has an unrestricted right to request EEA-related information. In reality, however, the Althing – as well as the government – is kept busy just discussing and approving the many EEA-related bills that it, *de facto*, cannot amend or reject.

Interestingly, however, the EEA institutional framework is actually based on a clearer distinction between legislative and executive functions than has customarily been the case in Iceland. In this way, EEA membership has contributed to the development of a clearer separation between the cabinet and the Althing. Domestically, EEA membership is also beneficial to parliamentary government, notably because there is no role for the president in the EEA institutions. The president of Iceland has no official role to play in the making and execution of foreign policy. Extensive contacts with powerful presidents (for example, in the USA, France, Finland) might, however, strengthen the ability of a skilled president to influence Iceland's foreign relations.

In recent years the prime minister's role in foreign affairs has become more important. It has often seemed as though Iceland has two or more Ministers of Foreign Affairs – for example when ministers for fisheries or environmental issues have been dominant figures, or when another government minister enters the 'foreign policy' arena. As the line between domestic and external affairs breaks down, so does the neat separation of functions between 'domestic' departments and ministries and 'foreign' ones. This complicates the Althing's task of supervising foreign policy and foreign affairs. The Minister of Foreign Affairs is required to give the Althing a biannual report and to consult with the Foreign Affairs Committee. Other ministers do not have similar obligations. Thus, the prime minister has relative freedom in the conduct of foreign relations. This freedom is enhanced by his status and by the fact that he has his own foreign policy advisor in the prime minister's office.

CABINET AS PRINCIPAL AND INDIVIDUAL MINISTERS AS AGENTS

The cabinet in Iceland is not a collective body dominated by the prime minister, but rather a council of highly independent ministers. There is no formal rule of collective cabinet responsibility. The prevalence of coalition governments further complicates the prime minister's role, while at the same time absolving him of political responsibility for ministers from his coalition partner(s). The successful prime minister adjusts to the formal and informal rules of the game by carefully learning on the job rather than by establishing clear chains of delegation and accountability. Majority voting is not often used in cabinet decision making. Rather, consensus usually emerges before cabinet meetings. When there is serious disagreement between ministers on questions of jurisdiction, the prime minister has the final word.[12]

The Ministry for Foreign Affairs in Reykjavík – more specifically the External Trade Department – co-ordinates legislative work related to the EEA Agreement. A high-level committee with officials from all the ministries meets once a month before meetings of the EFTA Standing Committee and EEA Joint Committee. Similarly, a group of officials and experts meets in Reykjavík before the meetings of the five EFTA/EEA Working Groups charged with solving the technical problems of transforming EU legislation into EEA legislation. The EEA Joint Committee makes the final decisions on EEA legislation on the basis of proposals from the working groups.

As mentioned above, in recent years the Icelandic political system has been faced with an increase in external constraints. The EEA agreement is the most significant. The classic division between domestic affairs on the one hand and foreign affairs on the other has gradually eroded. The EEA agreement has unquestionably made the dossier of each ministry more international (that is, European). During the EEA's first years in the operation, the agreement led to an increased workload in the ministries, and EEA matters were given priority.

The EEA agreement has not led to changes in the organisational structure of the central government. It is still divided into 12 departments (ministries). In 1993 these departments employed 366 people. The largest departments were Finance (79), Education (66) and Foreign Affairs (51). Iceland's participation in the EEA has not led to a general increase in the size of the ministries.

A marked increase in the size of the Ministry for Foreign Affairs can, however, be detected. This might be partly due to EEA work. It is expected that in the coming years even more personnel will be assigned to the Ministry for Foreign Affairs. In May 1997 the minister initiated a study on ways to reinforce the Foreign Service. A committee investigating the question completed its task in March 1998. It recommended that embassies in EU Member States should focus more on observing developments within the EU and Member States. Strengthening the Foreign Service is a measure supported by all political parties, as well as the business community.

The strengthening of co-operation between EU and EFTA states with regard to the so-called 'flanking policies' – including research and development, information services, education and training and youth policy – has led to the creation of a number of agencies with authority to act as national agencies with regard to relevant EU programmes. In many cases this has involved tasks that have been delegated from the responsible ministry to agencies that existed prior to the establishment of the EEA. For example, the implementation of the SOCRATES programme (higher education) and LEONARDO (vocational training programme) are the responsibility of institutions at the University of Iceland. These institutions have been forced to increase their staff size in order to carry out their new responsibilities.

None of the ministries has established special units or other bodies to deal exclusively with EEA affairs. EEA-related work has therefore been integrated into the existing ministry structures. However, every ministry has established a point of contact for EEA matters. Similarly, the government appointed an advisor to the government in EEA matters in 1997. Interestingly, the appointment of an EEA advisor was a way to resolve a dispute that had developed between a cabinet minister and a top-level civil servant rather than a response to a sense that the government needed such an advisor.[13]

CABINET/MINISTERS AS PRINCIPALS AND CIVIL SERVANTS AS AGENTS

The executive government in Iceland is generally characterised by three main features: (1) unclear separation of power between the Althing and the executive; (2) individual ministers are highly independent; and (3) civil servants have a low degree of autonomy. Together, these characteristics produce a highly individualised style of executive government. However, as noted above, a sharper distinction between the legislature and the executive has gradually evolved during the last decade. Agencies charged with monitoring the executive have been reinforced and made more independent. The right of the public *vis-à-vis* the executive has also been increased.

The Ministry for Foreign Affairs is responsible for the functioning of the EEA agreement in Iceland. The largest Icelandic embassy is the EU mission in Brussels (17 staff members, including secretarial staff). All ministries, with the exception of the Office of the Prime Minister, are represented in Brussels. Three staff members represent two ministries each (agriculture/transport, social affairs/health, environment/industry and trade).

The EEA mechanism gives Icelandic representatives access to a large number of expert groups at the 'pre-pipeline' stage – that is, while they are under preliminary discussion. Under Article 99 of the EEA agreement the Commission is obliged to 'informally seek advice from experts from the EFTA states, in the same way as it seeks advice from experts of the EU Member States in the elaboration of its proposals'. Thus, while EFTA states did not achieve participation in the decision-*making* process, they were granted access to the decision-*shaping* process within the EU. When new legislation in a field that is governed by the EEA agreement is being discussed and drafted, the EU Commission is to discuss the matter with EEA states.

The small size of Icelandic society and administration – both in personnel terms and other resources – puts severe limits on the policy and the practice of Iceland's management of EEA membership. As a small state with an economy dominated by one sector which is not included in the EEA agreement, it has developed a rather pragmatic approach to participation in EEA co-operation, including the development of new acquis, that is, participation in the decision-shaping procedure. It is generally seen as simply too expensive to try to influence decision making in the early stages of the policy process in policy areas not considered to be of vital national interest. Pragmatism has meant that the Icelandic state follows what is happening (that is, what others are doing), but does not get actively involved as long as emerging legislation does not seem to harm the national interest. This way of operating is at least partly a result of the fact that those responsible for fields covered by the EEA agreement are overloaded with other responsibilities and must therefore limit their involvement in EEA procedures.[14]

Icelandic representatives are assigned to the EU committees on the basis of their policy responsibilities within their respective ministries or agencies. Requirements about reporting back to the ministry/agency seem to vary and there are cases in which representatives do not report back at all. The EEA agreement has led to an increased number of persons attending meetings in Brussels, and has thus increased government travel expenses.

Available evidence suggests that Iceland does take seriously the implementation of EEA policies. Support for this position comes from an examination of Iceland's record in transposing EU directives into Icelandic legislation or regulation. Table 2 illustrates the point.

By the end of 1998, the EFTA members of the EEA had fully implemented well over 90 per cent of all directives. Iceland fares well in comparison with the other EEA states (and apparently also in comparison with many of the EU Member States). Another indicator of Iceland's compliance with the EEA agreement is the number of formal infringement proceedings initiated by the EFTA Surveillance Authority. Table 3 covers the five years during which the EEA agreement has been in operation. The

TABLE 2

IMPLEMENTATION STATUS OF DIRECTIVES COMPLIANCE DATE ON OR BEFORE
31 DECEMBER 1998

In numbers	Iceland	Liechtenstein	Norway
Total numbers of directives	1290	1290	1290
Directives with effective transition periods	0	274	0
Directives where no measures are necessary	183	96	66
Applicable directives	1107	920	1224
Status:			
Full implementation notified	1050	854	1168
Partial implementation	24	47	34
Non-implementation	33	19	22

In per cent	Iceland	Liechtenstein	Norway
Full implementation notified	94.9%	92.8%	95.4%
Full or partial implementation notified	97.0%	97.9%	98.2%

Source: EFTA Surveillance Authority, 1998 Annual Report (www.efta.int).

TABLE 3
FORMAL INFRINGEMENT PROCEEDINGS INITIATED AGAINST ICELAND

Year	Letters of Formal Notices sent during 1994–98	Reasoned Opinions sent during 1994–98	Cases referred to EFTA court in 1996–98
1994	19	0	
1995	14	6	
1996	31	5	2
1997	10	5	2
1998	32	7	0
Total	104	23	2

Source: EFTA Surveillance Authority, 1998 Annual Report (www.efta.int).

table shows that the Surveillance Authority has sent a number of reprimands to the Icelandic government. But it also shows the general willingness of Iceland to comply. To illustrate, in February 1996 the ESA sent to the EFTA court two cases against Iceland. Both were about internal taxation. Since Iceland adopted the necessary measure soon thereafter, the application was withdrawn. In March 1997 two cases were referred to the Court against Iceland regarding partial implementation of Directives on genetically modified organisms. Iceland notified full implementation shortly after the decision and the cases were not actually referred to the Court.

CONCLUSION

In general it is difficult to isolate the impact on Iceland of three external developments: the globalisation process, for example, increased economic interdependence, international trade, environmental issues (the Kyoto agreement); international legal development, particularly in the field of human rights; the European Union (EU) and the European Economic Area (EEA). In this paper we have focused on one of these three factors, namely Iceland's EEA membership, and its impact on the national chain of delegation and accountability. We should, however, resist attributing the impact of globalisation and international legal development to EEA membership. For example, the landmark 1989 legislation separating local judicial and executive powers was clearly forced upon Iceland by the European Commission of Human Rights, which had ruled against Iceland in a complaint brought by an Icelandic citizen. Similarly, Iceland's EFTA membership both predated and greatly influenced Iceland's decision on EEA membership.

Nevertheless, EEA membership has deeply affected the nature of Iceland's system of delegation and accountability. To start with, almost all Icelanders view EEA membership as an irreversible decision. They are simply not willing to pay the price of exit that would result if Iceland decided to refuse to comply with EEA rules and regulations.

To assess the impact of EEA membership we first review its impact on each of the four steps in the parliamentary chain of delegation and accountability. We then turn to some final tentative conclusions.

Voters as Principals and MPs as Agents

Formally, the value to voters of being the first principal is diminished by Iceland's EEA membership. The curious EEA agreement – delegation without accountability – surely implies a loss of sovereignty. In reality, however, there is also another tendency. During the period of the EEA membership both the reversion point and the flow of information in the relationship between voters and MPs have changed in favour of the principal. If voters (individual citizens, economic firms, interest organistions) cannot make their agent (the MPs) do their bidding, or if voters and MPs do not agree on the *status quo*, then the principal can press their MPs by referring to EEA rules and directives in fields covered by the EEA agreement.[15] The voters have increased their information dramatically through various contacts with EU/EEA bodies and institutions. All instances of Iceland's non-compliance with EEA legislation are quickly and prominently reported in the Icelandic mass media.

Parliament as Principal and Cabinet as Agent

The designation of parliament as principal and cabinet as agent lies at the core of parliamentary government. In the Icelandic political system it is very difficult to identify the boundaries between these two actors. Instead, one is struck by their fusion and overlapping functions. Political parties, patronage politics and a tradition of majority government unite both institutions. They are also united in their opposition to the semi-presidentalism inherent in the constitution.

Nevertheless, the MPs have clearly lost legislative power as a result of EEA membership. One veteran MP and former party leader has estimated that 80 per cent of legislation now comes from the EEA.[16] On the other hand, it is necessary to avoid any simplistic conclusions such as 'the decline of parliament'. The Althing's 'autonomy' as law-making body was greatly restricted prior to the EEA membership as a result of the actions of cabinet ministers, the government bureaucracy and interest groups. The enforcement mechanism that the EEA agreement gives outsiders is quite tangible to MPs, but limited autonomy due to domestic factors has also been tangible.

There is an important qualitative difference in the Althing's relationship with the cabinet and other domestic forces compared to its relationship to the EEA framework. Domestically, the Althing can always assert its rights as the principal law-making institution. MPs have often asserted their primacy in relations with the cabinet, in particular on local issues vital to their electoral district. In contrast to this, the Althing does not negotiate on EEA rules and directives. In this case, its role is one of adaptation and implementation. As a result, the role of the Althing as principal *vis-à-vis* the cabinet has been irreversibly weakened. Naturally this affects its capacity to assert itself as an autonomous law-making body.

A different picture emerges when we look at the impact of EEA membership on the Althing's role as overseer of the executive branch. Within the EEA framework there is a clear division between legislative and executive institutions. The EEA Committee has responsibility for supervising and evaluating the operation of the EEA Treaty. This organisation has supported the tendency, evident in Iceland since the 1980s, towards both a clearer separation between legislative and executive powers and a strengthening of the Althing as an institution for overseeing the executive.

Cabinet as Principal and Individual Ministers as Agents

At the institutional level not much change can be detected in this relationship. The rules of coalition governments are unaltered. Each government party is responsible for its ministers, not the prime minister (except as party leader). However, globalisation in general, and the EEA treaty in particular, have strengthened the prime minister and Minister of Foreign Affairs relative to other ministers. This has not turned the Cabinet into a more cohesive body. On the contrary, there are clear signs of rivalry between the prime minister and the Minister of Foreign Affairs, both of whom are chairman of their respective political parties, concerning the role of chief spokesman in foreign affairs.

To some degree, all ministers are now ministers of foreign affairs insofar as every government department is involved in European and international relationships. This complicates the co-ordination of the work of the ministers. The Minister of Foreign Affairs has clearly become more important as a result of its role as the official link between Iceland and EEA/EU institutions. At the same time, however, he faces more competition, particularly from the prime minister, who has his own information channels and contacts in foreign affairs – not least his counterparts in the Nordic Council.

Under these new circumstances, most importantly EEA membership, the skills of individual ministers in handling foreign relations seems to affect his/her status in the Cabinet, within the boundaries established by the tradition of coalition government.

Cabinet/Ministers as Principals and Civil Servants as Agents

Since the coming into force of the EEA Treaty, the position of the cabinet minister as principal in his relationship with the civil servants is not as overwhelmingly strong as before. This is particularly noticeable in departments dealing with areas covered by the Treaty or in departments considered responsible for implementing it, notably the Department of Foreign Affairs. The individual cabinet minister has less discretion in the implementation of policy and is more dependent on the expertise of civil servants and specialists for implementing EEA rules and directives.

The change in the flow of relevant information serves to strengthen the position of competent civil servants. The need for competence has also led to some changes in the recruitment pattern of civil servants. In particular, there has been somewhat of a shift away from patronage politics in the direction of recruitment based on education and skills, particularly foreign language competence and university education.

We should be careful, however, not to exaggerate changes in the relationship between individual ministers and civil servants. Individual ministers are still very much the principal and civil servants very much the agent. Nevertheless, the trend towards a more professional civil service is unmistakable, at least in the Department of Foreign Affairs.

In summary, our analysis of the national chain of delegation and accountability reveals that EEA membership has had a complex and sometimes unexpected impact on Iceland. Developments cannot simply be characterised as having increased 'the democratic deficit' by creating new problems of instruction and monitoring for the first principal – the people – in holding agents accountable. On the contrary, the position of individual citizens and their associations has been strengthened significantly by the EEA Treaty. This fact also explains the broad public acceptance of EEA membership in Iceland.[17]

The public interest is also indirectly served by EEA membership insofar as it has made the civil service less a system of political patronage in which individual ministers serve largely as barons within their government departments. To implement EEA rules, ministers need more competent civil servants. This increases the potential for the development of a more autonomous civil service that serves the citizens rather than the whims of their political masters.

The position of the Althing is greatly affected by Iceland's EEA membership. The Althing ratified the EEA Treaty in 1993. Since then its role has been passive – it transforms EEA directives into Icelandic law, thereby ensuring that Iceland complies with EEA directives. The Althing elects members to the EEA Committee, which is an advisory body without any legislative powers. For MPs, the EEA Treaty is something they created, but do not control. From the perspective of the Althing as overseer of the executive branch, EEA membership has further strengthened the Althing's ability to act as an institution separate from individual ministers and the Cabinet.

One big loser emerges from a primary analysis of the impact of the EEA membership on domestic actors. This is the individual ministers and the cabinet, except perhaps for the prime minister in relation to the foreign minister. These actors are being squeezed more than ever from two directions. Domestically, individual citizens, economic firms and interest organisations squeeze them. From abroad they feel the deep and far-reaching impact of EEA rules and regulations, which are backed up by a comprehensive bureaucratic framework and judicial institutions.

Our conclusion is that the analysis clearly reveals the importance of distinguishing between accountability as a process of control and accountability as a type of outcome. Iceland's membership in the EEA implies less control as a result of Iceland's loss of sovereignty. When viewed as a type of outcome, however, EEA membership can be seen as having increased the accountability of rulers to the first principal – that is, the people. This means that national sovereignty and democracy can, under certain circumstances, develop as opposite tendencies.

NOTES

1. S. Líndal, 'Innreið nútímans í íslenska lagagerð', in G.J. Gudmundsson and E.K. Björnsson (eds.), *Íslenska söguþingið 28.-31. maí 1997. Ráðstefnurit II* (Reykjavík: Sagnfræðistofnun Háskóla Íslands and Sagnfræðingafélag Íslands, 1997), pp.339–44.
2. See, for example, the interview with P. Blöndal, MP, in *Nýja mánudagsblaðið* (an Icelandic weekly newspaper), Vol.1, No.1 (1997).
3. In the autumn of 1992 a poll showed 65 per cent of all respondents in favour of a national referendum on Iceland's membership in the EEA. Twenty-one per cent were opposed, while 12 per cent reported being undecided. See *DV* (an Icelandic daily newspaper), 5 Nov. 1992.
4. *Morgunblaðið* (an Icelandic daily newspaper), 14 Jan. 1993.
5. The president's statement was printed in *Morgunblaðið* on 14 Jan. 1993.
6. See A. Styrkársdóttir, 'Women's Lists in Iceland – A Response to Political Lethargy', in C. Bergqvist *et al.* (eds.), *Equal Democracies? Gender and Politics in the Nordic Countries* (Oslo: Scandinavian University Press, 1999), pp.88–96.
7. See G.H. Kristinsson, 'Iceland and the European Union: Non-Decision on Membership', in L. Miles (ed.), *The European Union and the Nordic Countries* (London: Routledge, 1996), pp.150–65, at p.150.
8. Kristinsson, 'Iceland and the European Union: Non-Decision on Membership', p.163.
9. The following information on the foreign affairs committee comes from Th. Bogason, 'Althingi and the EEA Rules in the Making', in M. Wiberg (ed.), *Trying to Make Democracy Work: The Nordic Parliaments and the European Union* (Stockholm: Gidlunds, 1997), pp.117–21.
10. See T. Bergman, *Constitutional Rules and Party Goals in Coalition Formation* (Umeå: Department of Political Science, Umeå University, 1995).
11. Bogason, 'Althingi and the EEA Rules in the Making', pp.120–21.
12. S. Kristjánsson, 'Delegation and Accountability in Parliamentary Democracies: The Case of Iceland', *Draft Chapter* prepared for the volume *Delegation and Accountability in Parliamentary Democracies* (Reykjavík: Department of Political Science, University of Iceland, 1998).
13. In 1993 the Secretary General of the Ministry of Trade and Industry, Björn Friðfinnsson, was granted a three-year leave to take a position as a one of three members of a College at the EFTA Surveillance Authority in Brussels. After three years he was expected to return to his position in Reykjavík. In December 1996, however, the Minister for Trade and Industry announced that Friðfinnsson was not to return to his earlier post as Secretary General of the Ministry of Trade and Industry, but would head a unit within the ministry or take a position as director of a non-prominent agency, The Weights and Measure Office (*Löggildingarstofan*). Friðfinnsson refused this 'offer', and in the end the parties agreed that he would return to his old job at some future time. In the meantime, he was temporarily appointed as an adviser to the government on EEA issues.
14. A. Arnórsson, 'The European Economic Area: An Appraisal from an EFTA-Perspective after Three years in Force' (unpublished thesis presented for the Degree Master of European Studies at Department of Political and Administrative Studies, College of Europe, Brugge, 1997).
15. A recent and clear example of adapting new legislation to EU directives is a government bill on gender equality introduced in the Althing in the spring of 1999. In the brief accompanying the bill it is explicitly stated that the legislation is intended to meet obligations Iceland has under the EEA Treaty.
16. Public statement by Margrét Frímannsdóttir, chairperson of the People's Alliance, 14 Oct. 1998.
17. Several polling firms operate in Iceland. None of them has bothered to ask people about their attitudes toward Iceland's membership of the EEA. It is not necessary, they say, because 'nobody is against it'.

Adaptation without EU Membership: Norway and the European Economic Area

HANNE MARTHE NARUD and KAARE STRØM

While Norway has increasingly adapted itself to the new realities of the European Union (EU), it stands alone among western European states in its rejection of formal integration. Norway has applied for European Community (EC, later EU) membership four times. First in 1962, when the application was set aside after President de Gaulle said 'no' to British membership, then again in 1967, and for a third time in 1970. The latter application led to the negotiation of a treaty between Norway and the EC, which was put to a referendum in 1972. After an intense and harsh campaign the treaty was rejected by a majority of 53.5 per cent of the voters. More than 20 years would pass before Norway, together with Finland and Sweden, applied again. In the 1994 referendum, history repeated itself, and the proportion of citizens rejecting the subsequently negotiated membership treaty was almost identical to that in 1972 – 52.2 per cent. Hence, where Austria, Finland and Sweden joined the EU on 1 January 1995, Norway stayed within the European Free Trade Association (EFTA), sticking with the European Economic Area (EEA) agreement.

Through the EEA agreement, which came into force in January 1994, Norway is part of the EU's internal market, some of whose main elements are:[1] free trade in industrial products and free movement of capital, services and persons by means of joint legislation; establishment of a joint decision-making process whereby new EEA legislation can be adopted by unanimous agreement between EFTA and the EU; assurance of joint surveillance of common legislation.

Norwegian authorities have undertaken to implement and administer Community rules, and to respect the relevant case law of the European Court of Justice. This allows Norway to reap the benefits of the internal market without being part of the EU's political system. However, as pointed out by Sejersted, there is a catch: 'Through the EEA Norway has gained not only the advantages, but also many of the disadvantages of European

Hanne Marthe Narud is Senior Researcher at the Institute for Social Research, Oslo, Norway. Kaare Strøm is Professor at the Department of Political Science, University of California, San Diego, and Adjunct Professor at the Department of Comparative Politics, University of Bergen, Norway. They would like to thank Therese Evensen for research assistance.

integration. Deparliamentarization is one of them.'[2] Sejersted's complaint may be interpreted as meaning that the directly elected representatives of the Norwegian people have lost control over the institutions that they ostensibly instruct and oversee: the domestic executive branch and, more indirectly, the relevant EEA institutions. In describing this process of deparliamentarisation, he probably has in mind something akin to agency loss.

Since 1994, Norway has thus struck out on a path that is different from that of all its Nordic neighbours except Iceland. In reorganising its political institutions to cope with the increased European integration that even EEA association implies, Norway has again opted for mechanisms that differ from those of other Nordic states. Why has this happened, and what have been the consequences? We believe that much of the answer to the former question can be found in Norway's constitutional history, specifically in the legacies of the peculiar form of parliamentary government that has evolved.

In this paper we discuss the latter question: the impact of EU integration on the chain of delegation and accountability in the Norwegian political system. We do so by pointing to the main institutional features regulating each link of the parliamentary chain, and assessing the way in which the question of EU membership/EEA agreement has influenced the relevant relationships.

Parliamentarism, Norwegian Style

In order to understand what Sejersted means by deparliamentarisation, we have to consider the chain of delegation that constitutes the Norwegian form of democracy. Although the written constitution gives no recognition to this practice, Norway has *de facto* been a parliamentary democracy since 1884, and cabinet accountability to the parliamentary majority has acquired the status of a constitutional convention (*sedvanerett*). In practice, Norway conforms to most of the key features of parliamentary government. At the time of the struggle over parliamentary government, the battle cry of the Liberal Party was 'all power in this assembly', meaning the Storting. Although the Liberals may not have realised their goal in full, they have come far in transforming Norway into a political system in which there are few and relatively weak constraints on those who constitute the parliamentary majority.

Norway is a unitary state. Under the Norwegian Constitution, all legislative authority 'is exercised by the people through Parliament' (Art. 49). Outside the parliament, there are few domestic constraints on the legislative policy process. Although local government was established as early as 1837 and enjoys broad support and participation, it is constitutionally weak, and much of its revenue comes in the form of transfers from the national government. And although some constraints (for example, a weak version of judicial review) exist on delegation and accountability through the parliamentary chain, Norway is in practice a fairly pure case of parliamentary democracy.

While the Storting has always faced the usual challenges involved in overseeing policy implementation through the executive branch, it has operated in a small and close-knit community in which preferences and expectations have been largely shared and information has been relatively inexpensive. In relating to the agencies of the European Union, the Norwegian parliament finds itself in a much more challenging situation, grappling for instruments it has only begun to develop.

VOTERS AS PRINCIPALS AND MPs AS AGENTS

In examining these challenges, let us turn to the first link in the Norwegian chain of delegation and accountability: the voter–parliament relationship. Members of the Storting are the only national agents elected by the people. The rules by which these members of parliament are selected and held accountable are embodied in various legislative instruments. Some of these rules are contained in the constitution; others are spelled out in ordinary legislation, the most important of which is the Election Law of 1 March 1985.[3] Norway applies a modified St Laguë system, in which each province, including both urban and rural areas, is a separate constituency. In 1988 (effective with the 1989 elections) eight adjustment seats were introduced. Since then, there have been 157 first-tier seats and a pool of eight national second-tier seats.[4] Unlike most parliamentary systems, legislative terms are constitutionally fixed at four years, and there is no provision for the early dissolution of parliament. This system is one in which ordinary citizens have very limited opportunities to sanction representatives effectively once they have been elected. The absence of preference voting, primary elections, or recall mechanisms contributes to this condition.

The Referenda

The referendum represents the only mechanism by which the Norwegian voter has a direct say in national policy making. It is not, however, a mechanism that is entrenched in the Norwegian Constitution. Hence, the formal status of the referendum is ambiguous and only consultative referenda can be constitutional at the national level.[5] In fact, only six national referenda have been held, four of them by the 1920s. In contrast to some of the other Nordic countries, the Norwegian Constitution does not require a referendum over EU membership. Despite this, the people have been invited to take part in two consultative referenda on membership (1972 and 1994). Popular support for EU referenda has been strong and increased strongly from 1972 to 1994.[6] While only 55 per cent of the population thought that a referendum was the best way to decide the EU membership question in 1972, this proportion had risen to 94 per cent by 1994.

There has been a debate in Norway as to whether the Storting should be free to set aside the results of a consultative referendum, specifically the1994 EU referendum. Whereas the 'yes' parties argued that the referendum must be interpreted as binding, the 'no' parties at that time argued that the pro-membership side had to win both the referendum and a three-quarters majority in a Storting election. When the membership option was first introduced during the first EC debate in 1962, legislators decided to require a three-quarters majority for such a momentous decision, and the Constitution was duly amended. At the same time it was agreed that the negotiated agreement with the EC should be subjected to a consultative referendum. This has later come to be regarded as the standard procedure concerning European integration.[7] The main argument has been that when the government has decided to 'ask the people', it should also be obliged to follow the 'people's advice'.[8] Hence, on this particular issue, the Norwegian Storting has, through the referendum, in effect returned political authority to the voters.

The Party System

The Norwegian party system has been defined around six dimensions of political cleavage determined by economic, geographical and cultural circumstances.[9] In the post-war period, the socio-economic class cleavage has been expressed through the ideological left–right dimension; the territorial and sectoral cleavages have been reflected through the centre–periphery and urban–rural dimensions, whereas the cultural cleavages can be characterised as a moral-religious dimension.

The party system that emerged around 1920 consisted of the Communists, Labour, the Liberals, the Agrarian Farmer's Party (later the Centre Party), and the Conservatives. In 1933 a religious faction broke away from the Liberal Party over the issue of prohibition and formed the Christian People's Party. Otherwise, the party system was largely 'frozen' until 1961, when internal dissension over NATO membership led a left-wing Labour splinter group to form the Socialist People's Party within a policy space largely vacated by the declining Communists. When EC membership came onto the political agenda in 1972, the Liberals were split in two, and an anti-EC faction broke out of Labour and joined the Communists and the Socialist People's Party in a Socialist Election Alliance. The latter was later renamed the Socialist Left Party. Simultaneously, a right-wing populist party emerged in 1973 – the Anders Lange's Party, named after its founder. It later changed its name to the Progress Party. Finally, a tiny left-wing Marxist–Leninist party, the Red Election Alliance, has gained representation once (in the 1993–97 parliament).

Europe and Party Policy

The question of EC/EU membership has created enormous controversy each time it has emerged on the Norwegian political agenda. The European issue has had a number of significant effects on the Norwegian party system, and most of these have come as sudden and unexpected political shocks. It has caused internal splits within several of the traditional political parties, most notably Labour and the Liberals in 1972. In addition, several other parties have experienced difficult internal EU-related divisions as well. Secondly, the EU membership issue has directly and indirectly led to the formation of several new parties. The Socialist Left Party is the most durable party that has directly resulted from this controversy, whereas the Progress Party owes its existence more indirectly to shock waves generated by the EC campaign. Thirdly, high levels of voter volatility have characterised the parliamentary elections in which EU membership has been a prominent issue (1973 and 1993 in particular). The 1973 election effectively broke the five-party mould that the Norwegian party system had had since the 1920s and reduced the Liberals to the status of a minor party. In 1993, gross electoral volatility reached 44 per cent, a record high, basically because voting was conditioned by voter attitudes towards the EU.[10] Finally, both episodes have produced challenges to the party system and the entire parliamentary arena as vehicles for popular representation. The obvious reason has been the perceived breakdown of the delegation relationship between voters and members of the Storting. Studies of mass-elite opinion patterns have clearly revealed that political elites have been out of step with their voters on European integration.[11]

To understand the background of these patterns we need to examine briefly the impact of the EU on cleavages and the party system. The struggle over EU membership has activated all the underlying cleavages in the Norwegian system, but most of all the centre–periphery conflict. The opponents of EU membership have been concerned about the partition of the country into favoured, well-developed centres, and less prosperous peripheries with fishing interests and more traditional cultural identities. In the 1972 referendum the percentage of 'yes' votes ranged from 67 in Oslo to 29 in Northern Norway. In 1994 the pattern was almost identical.[12] Table 1 shows membership support by party in 1972 and 1994. In the latter case, both pre- and post-referendum surveys are reported.

The continuity of the EU issue is demonstrated by the fact that the positions of the parties were more or less the same in 1994 as they had been in 1972.[13] The two traditional antagonists, Labour and the Conservatives, joined forces in favour of membership. On the opposite side was the 'red–green' alliance between the Socialist Left Party and the Agrarian Centre Party, the latter exhibiting the most extreme opposition (together

TABLE 1
EEC/EU VOTE AND PARTY PREFERENCE IN THE 1972 AND 1994 REFERENDA
(PERCENTAGE VOTING 'YES'; NON-VOTERS EXCLUDED)

	1972 EEC preference	1994 pre-referendum preference	1994 post-referendum preference
Communist*/ Red Election Alliance**	6	0	6
Socialist People's Party*/ Socialist Left**	2	10	6
Labour Party	65	55	72
Centre Party	5	1	0
Liberal Party	42	36	31
Christian People's Party	18	10	10
Conservatives	90	80	87
Progress Party	NA	34	63
N	1465	1893	1897

Notes:
* The relevant party in 1972.
** The relevant party in 1994.

Sources: The figures referring to the 1972 referendum are from the 1973 election study, and is reported in H. Valen, 'Norway: "No" to EEC', Scandinavian Political Studies, Vol.8, No.4 (1973), pp.214–26, at p.221. The figures referring to the 1994 referendum are from the 1994 pre- and post-referendum surveys, and are reported in O. Listhaug, S. Holmberg and R. Sänkiaho, 'Partisanship and EU Choice', in A. Todal Jenssen, P. Pesonen and M. Giljam (eds.), To Join or Not to Join: Three Nordic Referendums on Membership in the European Union (Oslo: Universitetsfrlaget, 1998), p.225.

with the fringe Red Election Alliance). The Liberals and the Christian People's Party took positions against membership in 1994, though there was some minor dissent from business-friendly circles within the Christian People's Party. The Progress Party, on the other hand, eventually came out in favour of membership, even though many of its voters were sceptical. Hence, five Norwegian parties were against membership in the European Union, while three were in favour.

Table 1 also demonstrates notable opinion shifts between the first wave of surveys in 1994 and post-referendum interviews. Except for the Reds and the Christian People's Party, the supporters of all parties reported voting more consistently with the party position than their intentions had been at the beginning of the campaign. This development is particularly noticeable for Labour Party supporters, who shifted from being fairly evenly split at the beginning of the campaign to having a majority of more than 70 per cent voting 'yes' in the actual referendum. The shifts were even more dramatic for Progress Party supporters, who went from 34 to 63 per cent favourable.

The almost identical voting patterns in the EC/EU struggles of the 1970s and the 1990s indicate that these conflicts are neither coincidental nor likely to change quickly. Instead, they reflect the importance of traditional voting cleavages. They also suggest a stable element of potential future conflicts. Moreover, the 1994 decision does not comprehensively settle Norway's future relationship to the EU. Should further integration take place through the EEA agreement or should the country reject the agreement? A 1996 comparative study of voters and MPs in the Nordic countries showed that the EEA was highly unpopular in some parties.[14] As many as 29 per cent of Norwegian MPs would like to withdraw from the EEA agreement and replace it with a trade agreement.[15] Opposition among the voters at large could be substantially higher.

Mass–Elite Divisions on European Integration

In the 1990s the question of EU membership has been one of the most important issues on the political agenda. It has raised serious questions concerning two critical aspects of the voters' delegation relationship to their elected representatives: (1) Are there substantial and systematic differences in preferences between voters (principals) and political leaders (agents)? (2) Are the voters sufficiently well informed relative to the politicians that represent them? If the answer to the first question is 'yes' and the second 'no', then serious agency problems may arise.

For the effectiveness of parliamentary representation, one of the most important issues is the extent to which voter preferences are reflected in elite opinions and behaviour. On this point, Eurobarometer data have revealed rather distressing information. Empirical evidence indicates that European elites and masses are split over the question of closer co-operation and future implementation of important EU legislation. A comparative Nordic study demonstrates that Nordic elites are much more favourable to integration than are their voters. The most striking discrepancy between the two levels was found in Sweden.[16] Discrepancies between elites and voters were generally smaller in Norway, though significant gaps existed in some parties, notably the Labour Party and the Progress Party. However, in contrast to Swedish parliamentarians, for whom the EU dimension correlates almost perfectly with the left–right dimension, the former makes up a separate and distinct conflict dimension among Norwegian elites. Hence, the perceptions of Norwegian MPs correspond fairly closely to those of the voters.[17]

From a democratic point of view, the question of voter involvement and knowledge about the EU produces responses that are not very encouraging. The ability of the principal to access information is a precondition for successful delegation to take place. Moreover, factual knowledge about political phenomena is important for the way in which voters process information.[18] Borg and Esaiasson reveal, however, that the overall level of

EU knowledge among citizens is in no way remarkable.[19] This conclusion applies even to groups of highly involved citizens. Even though the Norwegian campaign prior to the referendum was particularly intense, there was no real evidence that it had an immediate impact on the level of factual knowledge among the citizens.[20] After the second referendum, the Norwegian media have maintained only a modest interest in EU-specific matters. The 1999 European Parliament elections, for example, received relatively cursory attention, and most media commentary focused on their domestic implications for the major countries, rather than on the outlook for the EU itself. Hence, on matters that deal with the European Union, a considerable cognitive gap exists between the ordinary voters and their more specialised agents. As a result, there is reason to believe that agency losses might be particularly severe.

PARLIAMENT AS PRINCIPAL AND CABINET AS AGENT

Norwegian voters' rejection of EU membership has not, of course, removed all issues of European integration from the Norwegian political agenda. To what extent the Storting, through the EEA agreement, has been constitutionally and politically able to handle issues of European integration is our next question. In Norway, the delegation of power from parliament to cabinet is regulated more by long-standing conventions of parliamentary government than by formal constitutional provisions, which still reflect the original separation-of-powers intent of Norway's founding fathers.

Formally, the Norwegian Constitution gives the king wide discretion to appoint members of the cabinet, but in practice the king has exerted no influence on the composition of any cabinet since 1928. Because of the absence of formal rules and mechanisms, Norwegian government formation is best described as 'free-style bargaining'. As regards accountability, the most important rule is what Bergman calls 'negative parliamentarism', that is, that governments can be invested and sustained as long as there is no parliamentary majority in favour of any specific motion of no confidence.[21] The right of the parliamentary majority to dismiss the cabinet has been recognised since the constitutional crisis of 1884. No confidence motions may be brought against individual ministers or against the cabinet collectively.

Post-war Norwegian cabinet formation falls into two separate and distinct periods, separated by the watershed election of 1961. Prior to 1961, Norway experienced stable, single-party, majority governments. The 1961 election, however, deprived the Labour Party of a parliamentary majority. Labour has never again captured a legislative majority. In large part, majority building since 1961 has been informal and *ad hoc*. The entire history of the EU debate in Norway falls into the latter and more unstable period.

Norwegian cabinets since 1961 have fallen into one of two categories: (1) Labour Party minority cabinets, or (2) non-socialist governments, all but one of which has been a coalition. There have been no peacetime coalitions between socialist and non-socialist parties. In fact, the Norwegian Labour Party is the only major social democratic party in western Europe never to have entered a cabinet coalition with any bourgeois party or with any of the smaller parties to its left. Thus, a socialist government has meant a cabinet of the Labour Party alone and, since 1961, also a minority cabinet. Non-socialist cabinets, with the exception of Willoch I (1981–83), have been coalitions of at least three parties. Yet many coalitions, including all of those formed since 1985, have been minority cabinets.[22]

Norwegian EU policies have had a great impact on the viability of coalition governments, which has caused severe problems for social democratic as well as non-socialist governments. Intra-coalitional controversies over EU membership have led to the demise of two non-socialist coalitions: Borten in 1971 and Syse almost 20 years later.[23] In addition, in 1971, Kjell Bondevik of the Christian People's Party failed to get the four non-socialist parties that had constituted the Borten coalition to patch up their EC-related differences. In effect, the Centre Party's opposition to Norwegian EC membership rendered no prospect for a broad non-socialist coalition.

In 1971, the outcome was given once Bondevik's attempt had failed: a minority Labour government under Trygve Bratteli. In 1972, Bratteli himself became the next victim of the EC controversy. Despite bitter dissent within his party, the Labour prime minister staked the life of his cabinet on a popular majority in favour of membership in the 1972 referendum. Bratteli's brinkmanship failed, as 53.5 per cent of the voters rejected membership, and the prime minister promptly resigned as promised. The subsequent coalition bargaining was heavily constrained by the referendum and its aftermath. The outcome of this vote meant that the agenda of the new government would be dominated by the need to conclude a satisfactory trade agreement with the European Community. Given Bratteli's personal commitments and the Labour Party's rejection of the trade agreement alternative during the campaign, the party was effectively out of contention for cabinet participation. The Conservative Party was similarly unavailable. Hence, the new government would have to consist of parties that had been on the winning side of the EC referendum. However, these parties controlled only about a quarter of the seats in parliament. The post of prime minister went to Lars Korvald of the Christian People's Party, which had never previously enjoyed this favour.

The EU membership was dormant for most of the 1980s and thus did not constrain government formation. In 1990, however, the EU juggernaut re-emerged and brought down Conservative Jan P. Syse's fragile one-year coalition of the Conservatives, the Centre Party, and the Christian People's Party. These parties subsequently failed to revive their coalition, for much the same reason that Bondevik's efforts failed almost 20 years earlier: differences over EU membership. During the following two parliamentary terms, Labour held government office. It resigned after losing the 1997 parliamentary election. Labour's loss opened the door for a small centrist coalition headed by Kjell Magne Bondevik, a nephew of the Christian leader whose formation attempt had failed in 1971. As in the previous case, policy distance between the Conservatives and the Centre Party on the membership issue was too great, and Bondevik's cabinet came to consist of three parties with a parliamentary basis of only about 25 per cent. Hence, the very parties that voted against EU membership have recently administered the EEA agreement, whose purpose it is to accommodate EU directives and regulations in Norwegian legislation.

The European integration issue has, throughout its life, had several significant effects on Norwegian coalition politics. One such effect has been to prevent any broad non-socialist coalition, since EU membership has so deeply divided the bourgeois parties. Secondly, the issue has tended to weaken both of the two parties that have dominated Norwegian politics since the 1930s: the Labour Party and the Conservatives. The Labour Party has been weakened because of internal divisions, the Conservatives because they have been deprived of their natural allies. Finally, in part as a consequence of this, these two traditional adversaries have been brought into much closer co-operation during times when European integration has been on the political agenda.

Parliamentary Influence and Veto Power in Europe

Thus, European integration has had profound domestic consequences for Norwegian democracy, primarily by exacerbating mass–elite preference diversity and by constraining the options that have been available in coalition bargaining. On the other hand, Norwegian choices regarding European integration have also, and more directly, affected the involvement of Norwegian voters in the resolution of issues in the European arena. Through the EEA, the Norwegian parliament is involved in European legislative processes in a consultative capacity. It does not, however, have any direct influence on matters that are dealt with inside the European Union. For the Storting, access to EU institutions is, of course, more limited than for the parliaments of the Member States. First of all, Norwegian MPs have no members of the European Parliament with whom they can consult. Nor are they invited to the conferences of the parliaments of the EU Member States. The main channels open to the Storting for gathering information are the EEA Parliamentary Committee and the annual bilateral meeting between representatives from the Storting and the European Parliament. Another channel is the co-operation that takes place between political parties at the European level.[24] The best networks belong to Labour, both bilaterally and through the party of European Socialists, and the Conservatives, through the European Democrat Union. The problem is that much of the inter-party co-operation takes place within EU organs, from which Norway is largely excluded.

The most direct means the Storting has for influencing EU legislation is through Art. 103 of the EEA agreement, which gives the national parliaments veto power over the decisions of the EEA Committee.[25] This Article was introduced to accommodate constitutional requirements in the EFTA states, and reflects the fact that formally the agreement is only an ordinary international treaty. Under Art. 26 of the Norwegian Constitution, new international obligations of particular importance must be accepted by the Storting before they can be ratified.[26]

Norway has on some occasions threatened to use its veto in EEA co-operation. Two particular areas of policy have been of major concern: food and gas. On the former issue, in 1996 EU-sceptical MPs tried to mobilise a majority in the Storting to veto the EU's 'food cosmetics' directive, which would allow certain artificial sweeteners, colourants and other additives to be added to foods. The latter issue was raised in 1997 by the new Minister of Petroleum and Energy, Marit Arnstad. She hinted that she might veto the EU gas directive, which would put Norway at a competitive disadvantage compared to gas suppliers outside the EEA, such as Russia and Algeria. However, in spite of the conflicts that have troubled Norwegian MPs and members of government, the veto has never been used. Thus, Norway has without reservation accepted more than 2,000 pieces of legislation or regulation emanating from the EU.[27]

The problem with Article 103 is that, in reality, it is costly to use. First of all, on some issues, by using the veto Norway would put itself on a collision course with several of its major partners in trade. Second, national parliaments are only consulted after a decision has been made in the EEA committee, which means that consensus has already been reached between the national governments. Third, and perhaps most important, a national veto would have the effect of blocking the decision for the whole EEA, and it would give the EU the right to take counter-measures. Hence, Sejersted points out that if the Storting really wants to block a development in the agreement, it is much more likely to do so by formally or informally instructing the government at an earlier stage, thus preventing the proposal of adverse legislation in the first place.[28]

Parliamentary Organisation and Control

European integration has also led to significant changes in the ways in which the Storting exercises its oversight and control of the executive branch. As yet, many of these changes are so recent that it is difficult to track their development and implications.

The most important internal vehicle for legislative oversight in the Storting is its standing committees. All matters requiring substantive Storting decisions are referred to a standing committee for scrutiny, discussion and negotiation. Each of the 165 representatives is a member of one and only one standing committee, which has a fixed membership and jurisdiction. Under normal circumstances, members serve on the same committee during the full, four-year parliamentary term.[29] Re-elected representatives often retain their committee assignments. In general terms, the jurisdictions of parliamentary committees tend to mirror those of the ministerial departments, though exceptions have become increasingly common.[30]

Since 1922 the Storting has featured a Foreign Affairs Committee, and European issues have traditionally been the domain of this committee. The organisation of EU affairs in the Storting confirms that this is still the case. In the early 1990s, the possibility of EU membership raised the question of creating a special consultative body in the Norwegian Storting. Prior to the 1994 referendum there were plans to form a special EU committee in the event that Norway joined the Union. In May 1994 the Storting established the European Consultative Organ (ECO) – also named the EEA Commission, which consists of all the members of the Foreign Affairs Committee, supplemented by the six Norwegian representatives to the EEA Joint Parliamentary Committee. Due to some personnel overlap, the total membership of the EEA Commission may vary – it included 17 members during the 1993–97 parliamentary term. The Storting has decided that the government's consultation with the Storting on EEA matters shall take place through the EEA Commission.

Meetings in the EEA Commission are merely consultative, and government ministers have no obligation to take the opinions voiced there into consideration. Nor is there any reporting back to the Commission after the governments' meetings in Brussels.[31] Usually it is the Minister of Foreign Affairs who meets with the EEA Commission, but he may also include other ministers if the agenda warrants doing so. The meetings of the EEA Commission are not open, though minutes from the meetings are released to the public after one year. The Storting has no special staff designated to assist the 165 members on EU issues. The information asymmetries resulting from these procedures clearly create the potential for agency problems.

The Norwegian way to organise legislative oversight of EEA matters is both constitutionally rooted and consequential. It is important that all EEA matters are scrutinised in what is essentially an expanded version of the Foreign Affairs Committee. This organisation reflects a view of EEA issues as belonging to the domain of foreign relations, a view that may become increasingly obsolete and misleading. Since Norwegian parliamentarians serve on one and only one standing committee, the major domestic politics committees, and the members who serve on them, have no institutionalised access to EEA deliberations. In this respect, Norway differs from both Denmark and Sweden.[32] Finally, the conception of EEA matters as foreign affairs is important because such matters constitutionally belong to the prerogatives of the executive branch (originally the king). Though the separation-of-powers ideal that underlies this prerogative has long been eclipsed by parliamentarism, the Storting is still somewhat reluctant to instruct the cabinet in matters of foreign policy. Moreover, the Ministry of Foreign Affairs guards its autonomy with greater jealousy than any other ministerial department (with the possible exception of Finance). All of these institutional factors militate against vigorous parliamentary oversight through the EEA Commission.

The records of the EEA Commission reinforce these expectations. Absenteeism among the commission's members has been high, and a small number of representatives, mostly from the Euro-sceptical parties, dominate the deliberations. In the first year-and-a-half of the Commission's existence, the three Euro-sceptical parties on the Commission (the Centre Party, the Socialist Left Party, and the Christian People's Party) accounted for 87 per cent of all recorded interventions. The Labour Party's representatives were entirely silent, except for a single representative on a single occasion. A single Conservative member accounted for all interventions by members of that party.[33] In sum, there is no reason to believe that the EEA Commission has been a vehicle for effective legislative oversight.

Parliamentary Questions

Informing the Storting is particularly important with regard to the possibility that parliamentarians will be able to influence new EU legal acts. Information may take place through written reports or oral statements, or the Storting may put forward written questions to the government. Parliamentary questions are indeed an important means by which the members of the Storting can monitor the actions of domestic and European executives. Parliamentary questions have been asked in the Storting as far back as 1885 and have played an increasingly important role in Norwegian parliamentarism. This is less due to deliberate design than to the incentives facing individual legislators and opposition parties specifically. As Rasch notes, 'parliamentary questions are in fact used quite extensively as a means of controlling the executive. This is not because the legislators necessarily intend to control. Rather, control is realised as a by-product of behaviour motivated primarily by an attempt to reach other (less collective) aims related to – or derived from – the electoral arena'.[34]

Parliamentary questions represent a way for individual MPs to deal with concerns and problems of relevance to their parliamentary work, their party, or their home constituency. Rasch demonstrates a dramatic increase in questioning since the early 1970s.[35] However, this increase is not particularly reflected in the number of questions posed about issues concerning the EU or the EEA.[36] In the period from 1986 to 1994 a total of 272 EU-related questions were posed, with a slight increase over time. The number of questions reached a peak in the early 1990s, when it increased from 16 in 1992–93 to 40 in 1993–94.[37]

Informational Deficit

Some criticism has been directed at the government's failure to provide information on EU issues to the Storting.[38] The EU directives and regulations are most often complicated, and some MPs have requested that the government give the Storting access to more information and documents at an earlier stage. Thus, the Foreign Affairs Committee has concluded that: 'Two years experience with EEA membership has clearly revealed a democratic deficit concerning the handling of EEA matters as compared to other relevant issues the Storting is working with.'[39] The committee also pointed to the short time frames the Storting has on matters related to the EEA. Moreover, the process of handling EEA matters is rather closed to 'fire alarm' oversight by interested third parties, since the meeting documents are not immediately made public. In 1997 access to EU documents was extended to the public, but only at a late stage in the decision-making procedure. This means that the possibility of influencing the formal decision is very limited.[40] Overall, the Storting's ability to control government activities is rather limited.

Sejersted argues that the powers of the Storting have been weakened in two ways:

> First, the EEA means a massive transfer of real, if not always formal, power from the Storting to the Community institutions, through the EEA organs. Second, it has led to a shift in the balance of power on the national level, weakening parliament and strengthening the government and the administration, as well as the courts. Like their colleagues in the member states, Norwegian parliamentarians face the challenge of regaining power lost.[41]

Several observers point to what they consider to be a transfer of legislative power from parliament to the executive branch through the handling of EEA matters in the Commission.[42] Sejersted concludes that it is primarily the legislative function of the Storting that has been weakened by the Europeanisation process, whereas other functions, for example, the financial and budgetary powers, have been less affected. Unlike parliaments in the Member States, the Storting has not transferred any formal legislative powers. However, while the EEA represents an alternative of less rapid integration compared to full membership, it actually creates less favourable conditions for parliamentarism. One reason, Sejersted argues, is that 'the formal status of the Agreement camouflages the real transfer of power, and so keeps the Storting from introducing necessary reform'.[43]

Such considerations have provoked some commentators into characterising the EEA as a 'constitutional catastrophe', because it gives the impression that Norway has retained more sovereignty than is really the case.[44] The most important reforms would include better access to information and internal organisational reform. Overall, the main changes that have taken place in the parliamentary arena may be summarised as follows:[45]

- Since EU matters are cleared politically through the EEA Commission prior to negotiations, parliament has in fact transferred its legislative role to the government, which on the supranational level is responsible for the drafting of new legislative proposals.
- The distinction between domestic and foreign affairs, on which the Storting still organises its division of labour, has been rendered obsolete.
- The principle of openness (transparency) is in reality compromised, since the public has no access to the views held by the members of the EEA Commission.

CABINET AS PRINCIPAL AND INDIVIDUAL MINISTERS AS AGENTS

The next stage of delegation is from the prime minister and the party or parties forming the government to individual ministers. The Norwegian Constitution of 1814 formally recognises the cabinet as the Council of State, which is vested with extensive constitutional powers. It is the supreme, collective leadership of the central administration. The cabinet normally meets three times per week, with all formal decisions (Royal Resolutions) being made on Fridays in the largely ritualistic Council of State. The cabinet initiates and prepares most legislation, in the form of bills and white papers, that is subsequently adopted by the parliament. When parliament is not in session, the cabinet can issue decrees with the force of law. It is routinely granted broad implementation powers through regular legislation. Within certain limits, the cabinet can delegate authority, most commonly to a specific ministry.

The Prime Minister

The prime ministership is the only cabinet office established by the Constitution. Yet the Norwegian prime minister is, in the words of Johan P. Olsen, 'a political organizer but no superstar'.[46] The prime minister is the head of the cabinet, and his (or her) responsibilities include counter-signing all decisions of the Council of State, preparing the cabinet agenda, and chairing cabinet meetings. The prime minister has the right to request information from any cabinet member, but he cannot issue orders, change ministerial jurisdictions, dissolve parliament or, technically, dismiss ministers. In reality, there has been substantial variation in the discretion enjoyed by prime ministers in selecting and dismissing cabinet members. Prime ministers in coalition cabinets have been much more constrained than those in single-party governments. The Office of the Prime Minister used to be a very small operation, but has gradually grown in size and importance. It prepares the cabinet agenda and also performs co-ordination functions, such as calling meetings to which both political appointees and civil servants may be summoned.

Cabinet Members

Article 12 of the constitution states that the cabinet consists of a prime minister and at least seven other members. Since 1945 the number of cabinet members in Norway has varied between 13 and 19, gradually increasing over time. The general rule, spelled out in Article 2 of the standing orders of the cabinet (*Regjeringsinstruksen*), is that each cabinet member is the administrative head of some department (formally known as a ministry). Occasionally, however, ministers without portfolio have been appointed. Though cabinet members may have close ties to parliament, they cannot serve as representatives while they hold cabinet office. Nor are ministers expected to have served in parliament prior to being appointed to the cabinet. Between 1945 and 1978, 52 per cent of all Norwegian cabinet ministers had no prior parliamentary experience.[47] Particularly in ministries with distinctive and well-organised clienteles (for example, agriculture and fisheries), it is considered much more desirable for cabinet members to have good interest group ties than parliamentary experience.

Surveys of ministers show that most of them focus their energies on matters pertaining to their own ministries. Eriksen's survey of 35 ministers reports that, on average, they devoted almost two-thirds of their time (64 per cent) to departmental matters, while an average of 22 per cent of their time was spent in, or preparing for, cabinet meetings. Most ministers therefore choose a specialist role, though some exceptions apply. Occupants of the ministries of Finance, Municipal Affairs, and Environmental Affairs tend to spend more time on issues pertaining to other ministries. And the prime minister, of course, does not even have his (or her) own ministry. In addition, ministers from smaller parties in coalition cabinets are more likely to spend time on matters outside their own jurisdiction than are ministers in single-party governments.

The prevailing specialist orientation is reinforced by the workload cabinet ministers are under, by patterns of recruitment and experience, and by the norms of cabinet meeting deliberation. Most cabinet members feel severely overworked, and many report that they have little time to invest in matters concerning other ministries.[48] The Ministry of Foreign Affairs has traditionally been very much of a specialist ministry. Ministers of Foreign Affairs have rarely attempted to exercise much authority on domestic issues, except occasionally on defence matters. Conversely, they have been able to count on strong norms of deference in international matters. This has been particularly true under Labour governments, in part due to the personal authority that several Labour Foreign Ministers (for example, Halvard Lange 1946–65 and Johan Jørgen Holst 1993–94) have enjoyed.

European Issues

Since the late 1980s, that is, well before the second membership referendum was even scheduled, the Norwegian government has worked to create a structure in which European issues could be integrated into government decision making. The first such effort was Prime Minister Gro Harlem Brundtland's establishment of an inter-ministerial co-ordinating apparatus in 1988. This was in anticipation of the negotiations that eventually led to the EEA agreement. Before the second referendum, and especially during the interim period in 1994, Norway enjoyed two main forms of access to the European Union. One channel went through the bodies subordinated to the European Council, the second through the Commission and its associated committees and working groups. The two channels were conducive to somewhat different patterns of co-ordination, with distinctive effects on domestic policy making. The Ministry of Foreign Affairs performed a stronger co-ordinating function with respect to issues falling within the responsibility of agencies associated with the European Council than with respect to those associated with the Commission. Matters under the aegis of Commission agencies tended to lend themselves more to sectoral policy making, which reduced the effectiveness of domestic policy co-ordination and, more specifically, the power of the Ministry of Foreign Affairs. After the Norwegian electorate had rejected membership the government lost direct access to the European Council, and the agencies of the Commission became the dominant channel of policy integration. Consequently, the Ministry of Foreign Affairs has lost even more of its powers of co-ordination, and policy issues that traditionally belonged to the domain of foreign policy have become 'domesticated'.[49]

There are today three different levels of co-ordination on European issues in the Norwegian government.[50] The highest of these levels is the cabinet itself, which constitutes the supreme organ for political co-ordination in these as well as other issues. If the particular issue at hand is of relevance only to a smaller set of ministries, it is generally referred to the Cabinet Committee on Europe (*Regjeringens Europautvalg*). The Minister of Foreign Affairs exercises some agenda control with respect to the cabinet's involvement in European issues. Before any other minister can put an issue related to the EU on the cabinet agenda, he or she must brief the Minister of Foreign Affairs, who then has an opportunity to state a position before the cabinet deliberations. The second level of co-ordination is the Coordinating Committee (*Koordineringsutvalget*), administered by the Ministry of Foreign Affairs, while the third is a set of some 20 Special Committees (*spesialutvalg*) consisting of experts in different policy areas. Since both of these are essentially administrative organs composed of civil servants, they will be discussed in the next section of this paper.

Compared to traditional foreign policy decision making, the Office of the Prime Minister has played a key role in the creation of the various institutions for co-ordination of European affairs. Under Prime Minister Brundtland, this office took a leading role in the development of the new organs and procedures and kept this process under tight control. Prime Minister Brundtland had several reasons to reinforce her powers as co-ordinator of Norway's policies toward the EU. One was that she was personally strongly committed to EU membership and made it a central part of her political agenda for the 1990s. A second and related reason was her desire to contain the diversity of attitudes that existed among her cabinet members and, more generally, among the leading members of the Labour Party. Thirdly, her co-ordination function was consistent with the increasingly authoritative leadership role that she came to play within her party and government. As a consequence, European affairs decision making has become centralised, and the Office of the Prime Minister has made a practice of issuing instructions in policy areas that have previously fallen within the responsibility of the Ministry of Foreign Affairs. Thus, at the cabinet level, European affairs decision making has remained tightly controlled by the Prime Minister and seems to have strengthened his or her co-ordination role within the cabinet.[51]

Thus, European integration has, for various reasons, occasioned a weakening of the co-ordination function of the Norwegian Minister of Foreign Affairs. This has been caused in part by the sectoral decision making of agencies under the aegis of the European Commission. Secondly, the Foreign Minister's diminution has been due to a centralisation of decision making in the cabinet, whereby the prime minister has come to appropriate functions that were previously exercised by the Foreign Minister. Thus, even in non-member Norway, European issues have gradually come to be regarded at the cabinet level as domestic rather than (or at least as much as) international. This is where we find a curious asymmetry between the legislative and executive branches. Whereas the Storting persists in treating EEA issues as foreign policy, within the cabinet they increasingly fall within the purview of the prime minister and other domestic ministers. This incongruence cannot but impede the ability of the Storting to oversee the cabinet's activities in European affairs. However, even if the cabinet has strengthened its role *vis-à-vis* the parliament, it is not in a particularly favourable position relative to the institutions of the European Community. 'Downstream' delegation from the cabinet to civil servants is still an area in which the Norwegian government faces many unresolved problems, as we shall see below.

CABINET/MINISTERS AS PRINCIPALS AND CIVIL SERVANTS AS AGENTS

Under professional civil services systems, politicians have limited *ex post* control over the civil servants to whom they delegate. In Norway, as in most parliamentary democracies, civil servants cannot be hired or fired at will. *Ex ante* controls, on the other hand, are quite strong, as the credentials that are required of civil servants tend to be quite substantial. Moreover, in a traditionally transparent society, fairly effective screening is feasible. Accountability takes place in two ways: (1) civil servants have explicitly designed contracts that prevent them from taking various types of hidden or arbitrary action; and (2) all decisions taken in the executive branch explicitly carry the authorisation of the head of department. A great deal of formal authority is therefore placed in this minister's hands.

The Norwegian Civil Service

The Norwegian civil service was, in its initial form, an inheritance from Denmark through the 1814 Constitution. As one of the few social organisations with professional expertise, it played a major role in the political and economic development of Norway in the nineteenth century. Throughout the development of the Norwegian civil service, there has been an ongoing debate over the merits of a centralised and hierarchical, versus a decentralised and professional, administrative structure. In organisational terms, this has been a debate over whether the civil service should be organised around a smaller set of hierarchical departments under strong political control (traditionally known as the 'Danish model'), or as a larger set of more autonomous and professional agencies under less direct political control (traditionally, the 'Swedish model'). The former principle has been embodied in a structure of departments, the latter in a set of directorates. Gradually, a pragmatic balance has evolved that places Norway somewhere in between these two organisational models. There are currently 16 departments and approximately 70 directorates in the Norwegian central administration. Since the early 1980s, the total number of civil servants in the Norwegian central administration has hovered between 3,000 and 4,000, with a slight decline throughout the 1980s.

European Affairs

Two of the levels of co-ordination on European affairs that were mentioned in the previous section are located at the administrative level below the Cabinet. The second of these, and the highest civil service co-ordination body, is the Coordination Committee, which falls under the jurisdiction of the Ministry of Foreign Affairs. The latter provides the committee chair and runs its secretariat. The main function of the Coordination Committee is to maintain overall co-ordination of all matters related to the EU and the EEA and especially to ensure co-ordination between different government agencies. Any issue on which there is disagreement in the lower ranking special committees is referred to the Coordination Committee.[52] All ministries are represented on the committee, which includes 21 higher level civil servants up to level of the permanent undersecretary of state. Cabinet ministers are allowed to participate in the meetings of this committee whenever there is an issue that falls under their respective jurisdictions. Two department-level offices, the Ministry of Finance and the Office of the Prime Minister, are required to attend all meetings of the Coordination Committee. These meetings take place on a monthly basis.

The special committees constitute the lowest level of co-ordination on European matters in the Norwegian government. Since autumn 1997, there have been 22 of these, each of which is chaired by a particular ministry. Most members are policy experts from that ministry or other agencies of the Norwegian government. The Ministry of Finance and the Ministry of Foreign Affairs, as well as the Office of the Prime Minister, are entitled to representation on any of these experts committees. However, the vast majority of these committees are chaired by a representative from one of the domestic 'line ministries'. The activity level of the different special committees has varied greatly.

The Norwegian government also maintains a permanent staff in Brussels, the so-called EU Delegation. This office comes under the aegis of the Ministry of Foreign Affairs but is staffed in part by civil servants from other ministries as well. The EEA office within the Ministry of Foreign Affairs in Oslo has a staff of approximately 15 civil servants, plus some clerical personnel.

The Office of the Prime Minister has designed a standard procedure by which new legislation relating to the EEA is handled. These guidelines were presented in April 1995, only a few months after Norway's second 'no' to EU membership. This procedure places responsibility for the introduction of such legislation with the individual ministries. When doing so, the ministry must present a 'framework document', which accompanies the case dossier of the legislative initiative through the decision-making process in the executive branch. This enclosure is supposed to provide background information on EEA legislation in that specific area, as well as a review of existing Norwegian legislation. In addition, the document is to include a discussion of budgetary implications, the positions of the other Nordic countries, and the views of affected interest groups that have expressed themselves through the process of remiss.[53]

The Norwegian government has succeeded in implementing a large proportion of all relevant EU legislation. Through the end of 1998, Norway had fully implemented 1,168 out of 1,224 applicable directives (95.4 per cent) and partially implemented 34 others. Only 22 directives had not been implemented in any form. This puts Norway at the top of the class among the EFTA states (for further information, see the article on Iceland in this issue). On the other hand, Norway also narrowly leads the same countries in the number of infringement cases initiated by the EFTA Surveillance Authority. By the end of 1998, 105 such cases had been initiated against Norway, compared to 104 and 76 in the cases of Iceland and Liechtenstein, respectively. Table 2 provides additional information.

While Norway has apparently developed the capacity to respond to the inputs it receives under the EEA agreement, it is less clear that this legislation is subjected to the customary standards of democratic scrutiny. To date, the Norwegian mechanism of *ex ante* control of EEA legislation

TABLE 2
EEA INFRINGEMENT CASES, NORWAY, 1994–98

Year	Letters of Formal Notices sent during 1994–98	Reasoned Opinions sent during 1994–98	Cases referred to EFTA court in 1996–98
1994	14	1	NA
1995	15	1	NA
1996	32	8	0
1997	19	11	2
1998	25	10	0
Total	105	31	2

Source: EFTA Surveillance Authority, 1998 Annual Report.

does not appear to have been entirely successful. Some behavioural data is available from a survey of Danish and Norwegian policy co-ordination toward the EU during the interim period between the signing of the EEA accord in Korfu on 24 June 1994, and the Norwegian EU referendum of 28 November. Respondents in the various Norwegian ministries reported that the pace and volume of legislative initiatives to which they had to respond shocked them.[54] Civil servants reported an increased level of policy co-ordination in the relevant areas both within and across departments. Interdepartmental co-ordination was particularly prevalent with respect to issues under the jurisdiction of the European Council. The Coordination Committee and the special committees both reported a high level of activity. Among the various departments, the Ministry of Foreign Affairs played a key role in policy co-ordination, although its primacy seems to have been perceived more strongly by representatives of that ministry itself. Somewhat to their surprise, all departments reported that the European Council, rather than the Commission, was the main point of contact within the EU.[55] Norway's rejection of EU membership led to a significant shift in the pattern of administrative interaction with EU organs, as contacts with agencies under the European Commission came to predominate.

An extensive 1996 survey of 1,482 Norwegian civil servants can help illuminate patterns of European policy making after the 1994 referendum. About half of these civil servants reported that their work was affected by the EU or the EEA to some significant extent. The civil servants who reported repeated contact with agencies of the European Commission during the preceding year amounted to about half (49 per cent) of all civil servants in the Ministry of Foreign Affairs, compared to approximately one-quarter (26 per cent) of civil servants in all other ministries. As regards contact with EEA or EFTA agencies, the distinction between the Ministry of Foreign Affairs and other ministries was less pronounced, with 40 per cent of the former and 28 per cent of the latter reporting repeated contact. Foreign Affairs personnel were also more likely than other civil servants to describe agencies of the EU, the EEA, or EFTA as important to their work.[56]

CONCLUSION

Although Norway's rejection of EU membership has spared the country the complexities of integrating its system of representation within the larger European community, even the less demanding co-ordination required by Norway's entry into the EEA provides challenges for Norwegian democracy. The Norwegian version of parliamentarism has traditionally relied heavily on *ex ante* mechanisms and on a fairly singular chain of delegation. To make this system work, Norwegians have been accustomed to homogeneity of preferences (due to a population without great cultural diversity) and relatively good public information (due to social transparency, which is, itself, the consequence of a relatively small and close-knit political community).

These conditions do not apply particularly well in the European context. The European Union has much greater preference diversity than does Norway, and the transparency of the political community is much lower. The Norwegian political authorities may therefore be forced to accept some painful readjustments as regards established structure and procedure. Many of the problems that Norway is currently facing are clearly informational. The problem is less that Norwegian authorities lack power *vis-à-vis* their EU counterparts, but rather that they do not have access to the information they need to make informed and timely decisions. A longer and more complex chain of delegation increases informational demands, while the short deadlines under which EEA decisions are made exacerbate them. This is not to say that changes in rules are in themselves unimportant, however. Within the EEA, the reversion point in decision making has effectively become the EU's proposal rather than the domestic *status quo*. That change in itself could have enormous consequences for a political system accustomed to an incremental and inclusive decision-making process more akin to the ideals of consensus democracy.[57] Suddenly, affected interests must be prepared to be on a much higher level of alert.

Thus, even Norway's limited integration with Europe has already caused significant changes in domestic political institutions, and more are sure to come. Within the Norwegian political system, adaptation has been more extensive in the executive branch than in parliament, and more extensive in parliament than among the voters. In other words, the further 'downstream' in the process of delegation, the more profound have been the changes. European integration has meant two discernible shifts in power. The cabinet has been strengthened relative to the parliament. Within the cabinet, the position of the prime minister has been reinforced relative to that of the foreign minister. These developments have taken place largely during a period when Norway has had strong prime ministers, but numerically weak minority governments. Hence, the cabinet's new-found strength might be expected to be more durable than that of the prime minister. Both developments, however, seem to be consistent with trends in other countries. They may also lead to other adaptations in Norway's political, and other, institutions.

The extent to which Norway's closer relationship to Europe will fundamentally change established patterns of delegation and accountability, however, remains to be seen. So far, the democratic deficit implied by Norway's commitment to the EEA has been much more of a cause for concern among policy experts than among the general population. For the issue to reach a greater salience among the citizens, more deep-rooted values in Norwegian society would probably have to be at stake.

NOTES

1. K. Myhre-Jensen and B. Fløistad, 'The Storting and the EU/EEA', in M. Wiberg (ed.), *Trying to Make Democracy Work* (Stockholm: The Bank of Sweden Tercentenary Foundation & Gidlunds Förlag, 1997), p.108.
2. F. Sejersted, 'The Norwegian Parliament and European Integration – Reflections from Medium Speed Europe', in E. Smith (ed.), *National Parliaments as Cornerstones of European Integration* (London: Kluwer, 1996), p.125.
3. H. Valen, 'Valgsystemet', in T. Nordby (ed.), *Storting og regjering 1945–1985: Institusjoner – rekruttering* (Oslo: Kunnskapsforlaget, 1985); and H. Valen, 'Equity of Representation: Party versus Territory', in H. Valen and H.M. Narud, *Professionalization, Political Representation and Geography* (Oslo: Institutt for samfunnsforskning, Report 15, 1998), pp.41–55; and O. Overå and S. Dalbakk, *Den Norske Valgordningen* (Oslo: Sem & Stenersen, 1987); and B. Aardal, 'Electoral Systems in Norway 1814–1997' (Paper presented at the conference on the Evolution of Electoral Systems and Party Systems in the Nordic Countries, Laguna Beach, CA, 13–14 Dec. 1997).
4. Adjustment seats, allocated to parties that are underrepresented on the basis of constituency representation, are given to provinces in which the respective parties have the highest remainders (in raw numbers) of unused votes. The highest remainders tend to be found in large and underrepresented constituencies.
5. Sejersted, 'The Norwegian Parliament and European Integration – Reflections from Medium Speed Europe'.
6. A.T. Jenssen, M. Gilljam and P. Pesonen, 'The Citizens, the Referendums and the European Union', in A.T. Jenssen, P. Pesonen and M. Gilljam (eds.), *To Join or Not to Join: Three Nordic Referendums on Membership in the European Union* (Oslo: Universitetsforlaget, 1998), p.304.
7. Jenssen, Gilljam and Pesonen, 'The Citizens, the Referendums and the European Union'.
8. Myhre-Jensen and Fløistad, 'The Storting and the EU/EEA'.
9. See S. Rokkan, 'Geography, Religion and Social Class. Crosscutting Cleavages in Norwegian Politics', in S.M. Lipset and S. Rokkan (eds.), *Party Systems and Voter Alignments* (New York: Free Press, 1967); and S. Rokkan, *Citizens, Elections, Parties* (Bergen: Universitetsforlaget, 1970); and S. Rokkan and H. Valen, 'The Mobilization of the Periphery', in S. Rokkan (ed.), *Approaches to the Study of Political Participation* (Bergen: Christian Michelsens Institutt, 1962).
10. B. Aardal and H. Valen, *Konflikt og Opinion* (Oslo: NKS-forlaget, 1995); and B. Aardal and H. Valen, 'The Storting Elections of 1989 and 1993: Norwegian Politics in Perspective', in K. Strøm and L. Svåsand (eds.), *Challenges to Political Parties: The Case of Norway* (Ann Arbor, MI: University of Michigan Press, 1997).
11. T. Bjørklund, *Om Folkeavstemninger: Norge og Norden 1905–1994* (Oslo: Universitetsforlaget, 1997); and H.M. Narud and H. Valen, 'Mass and Elite Attitudes towards Future Problems', forthcoming in P. Esaiasson and K. Heidar (eds.), *Beyond Westminster and Congress. The Nordic Experience* (Columbus, OH: Ohio State University Press, 2000); and H.M. Narud and A. Skare, 'Are the Party Activists the Party Extremists? The Structure of Opinion in Political Parties', *Scandinavian Political Studies*, Vol.22, No.1 (1999), pp.45–65.
12. P. Pesonen, A.T. Jenssen and M. Gilljam, 'To Join or Not to Join', in Jenssen *et al.* (eds.), *To Join or Not to Join: Three Nordic Referendums on Membership in the European Union*, p.21.
13. O. Listhaug, S. Holmberg and R. Sänkiaho, 'Partisanship and Choice', in Jenssen *et al.* (eds.), *To Join or Not to Join: Three Nordic Referendums on Membership in the European Union*.
14. The comparative project of Nordic parliaments and parliamentarians (NORDLEG) included an elite surveys from all the five Nordic parliaments, and was designed to analyse how these democratic parliaments operate and function. The results are forthcoming in Esaiasson and Heidar (eds.), *Beyond Westminster and Congress. The Nordic Experience*.
15. T. Raunio and M. Wiberg, 'Looking after National Interests: The Nordic Parliaments' Adaption to the EU', forthcoming in Esaiasson and Heidar (eds.), *Beyond Westminster and Congress. The Nordic Experience*.

16. Narud and Valen, 'Mass and Elite Attitudes towards Future Problems'; and H. Valen, H.M. Narud and O. Hardarsson, 'Geographical Representation', forthcoming in Esaiasson and Heidar (eds.), *Beyond Westminster and Congress. The Nordic Experience.* See also H.M. Narud and H. Oscarsson, 'Mass–Elite Perceptions of the Policy Space: A Comparison between Norway and Sweden' (paper presented at the ECPR Joint Sessions of Workshops, Mannheim, 26–31 March 1999).
17. Narud and Oscarsson, 'Mass–Elite Perceptions of the Policy Space: A Comparison between Norway and Sweden'.
18. J. Zaller, *The Nature and Origins of Mass Opinions* (Cambridge: Cambridge University Press, 1992).
19. The pre-referendum waves of surveys included three questions on respondents' factual knowledge of the EU. Only one out of four respondents answered all three questions correctly. See S. Borg and P. Esaiasson, 'Exposure to the Campaign', in Jenssen *et al.* (eds.), *To Join or Not to Join: Three Nordic Referendums on Membership in the European Union.*
20. Borg and Esaiasson, 'Exposure to the Campaign', p.90.
21. T. Bergman, 'Formation Rules and Minority Governments', *European Journal of Political Research*, No.1 (1993), pp.55–66.
22. K. Strøm, *Minority Government and Majority Rule* (Cambridge: Cambridge University Press, 1990). See also H.M. Narud and K. Strøm, 'Norwegen: Eine fragile Koalitionsordnung', in W. Müller and K. Strøm (eds.), *Regierungskoalitionen in Westeuropa* (Wien: Signum, 1997).
23. See, for example, H.M. Narud, 'Coalition Termination in Norway: Models and Cases', *Scandinavian Political Studies*, Vol.18, No.1 (1995), pp.1–24.
24. K. Heidar and L. Svåsand, 'Politiske partier og europeiseringsprosesser' (Oslo: Arena. Working paper No. 8, 1995).
25. *Håndbok i EØS-arbeid* (Oslo: Statskonsult 1998), p.97.
26. Sejersted, 'The Norwegian Parliament and European Integration – Reflections from Medium Speed Europe', p.150.
27. T. Nordby and F. Veggeland, 'Lovgivningsmyndighetens Suspensjon: Stortingets rolle under EØS-avtalen', *Tidsskrift for samfunnsforskning*, Vol.40, No.1 (1990), p.90.
28. Sejersted, 'The Norwegian Parliament and European Integration – Reflections from Medium Speed Europe', p.150. It is not clear, however, what can be inferred from the failure of the Norwegian government to exercise its veto. The problem is the classical methodological issue of observational equivalence. On the one hand, Norway's failure to exercise its veto might signal that it recognises its impotence. On the other hand, it could equally well represent a situation in which no European institution makes a decision contrary to Norwegian interests because it is common knowledge that such a decision would be vetoed. If all actors derive some significant cost, and no benefit, from proposing a measure that would be vetoed by the Norwegian government, then in equilibrium (at least in the one-shot case) no such proposals should be made, and Norway should never have to exercise its veto. A more rigorous assessment of the evidence would therefore have to consider the plausibility of each of these scenarios.
29. Members of the Storting who are appointed to the cabinet must relinquish their seats to their respective deputies as long as they serve in the cabinet. If they return to the Storting before the end of the term they are not guaranteed reassignment to the same committees on which they served before their cabinet appointments.
30. H. Rommetvedt, 'Norwegian Parliamentary Committees: Performance, Structural Change and External Relations' (Paper presented at the International Conference on the Changing Roles of Parliamentary Committees, Budapest, 20–22 June 1996).
31. Myhre-Jensen and Fløistad, 'The Storting and the EU/EEA'.
32. Nordby and Veggeland, 'Lovgivningsmyndighetens Suspensjon: Stortingets rolle under EØS-avtalen'.
33. Nordby and Veggeland, 'Lovgivningsmyndighetens Suspensjon: Stortingets rolle under EØS-avtalen', p.98.
34. B. Rasch, 'Question Time in the Norwegian Storting – Theoretical and Empirical Considerations', in M. Wiberg (ed.), *Parliamentary Control in the Nordic Countries: Forms*

of Questioning and Behavioural Trends (Jyväskylä: The Finnish Political Science Association, 1996). See also S. Kuhnle and L. Svåsand, 'Spørreordningene og politiske profiler i Stortinget 1977–1981', in O. Berg and A. Underdal (eds.), *Fra valg til vedtak* (Oslo: Aschehoug, 1984).

35. Rasch, 'Question Time in the Norwegian Storting – Theoretical and Empirical Considerations'. See also B.E. Rasch, 'Electoral Incentives to Control Government Ministers: Questions from Individual Members of the Norwegian Parliament' (Paper presented at the International Conference on the Significance of the Individual Parliamentary Member in Parliamentary Politics, Budapest, 1–5 July 1998).

36. A.R. Asbjørnsen and K. Skogedal, 'EF-spørsmål i Stortingets spørretime 1986–1992' (working paper, Bergen: Institutt for administrasjon og organisasjonsvitenskap, 1992); and A. Seim, *Stortinget: En fugl Føniks på maktutredningens ruiner?* (Bergen: LOS-senteret, Report 2, 1996).

37. Seim, *Stortinget: En fugl Føniks på maktutredningens ruiner?* p.87.

38. Nordby and Veggeland, 'Lovgivningsmyndighetens Suspensjon: Stortingets rolle under EØS-avtalen'; and D.A. Christensen, 'Europautvala i Danmark, Sverige og Noreg', *Nordisk Administrativ Tidsskrift*, No.2 (1997), pp.143–62.

39. Innst. S. Nr. 252 1995–96 (Parliamentary Report no. 252 (1995–96)).

40. Nordby and Veggeland, 'Lovgivningsmyndighetens Suspensjon: Stortingets rolle under EØS-avtalen'.

41. Sejersted, 'The Norwegian Parliament and European Integration – Reflections from Medium Speed Europe', p.125.

42. Seim, *Stortinget: En fugl Føniks på maktutredningens ruiner?*; and Nordby and Veggeland, 'Lovgivningsmyndighetens Suspensjon: Stortingets rolle under EØS-avtalen'.

43. Sejersted, 'The Norwegian Parliament and European Integration – Reflections from Medium Speed Europe', p.125.

44. E. Smith. Talk given at the open hearing on the Schengen-agreement, arranged by the Foreign Affairs Committeee, 5 May 1997 (Innst. S. Nr. 229 (1996-97)) (Parliamentary Report no. 229 (1996–97), enclosure III).

45. Nordby and Veggeland, 'Lovgivningsmyndighetens Suspensjon: Stortingets rolle under EØS-avtalen', p.91.

46. J.P. Olsen, *Organized Democracy* (Oslo: Universitetsforlaget, 1983), p.81.

47. Olsen, *Organized Democracy*, p.93.

48. S.A. Eriksen, *Herskap og tjenere* (Oslo: TANO, 1988).

49. J. Trondal, 'Europeisering av sentraladministrative organer', *Norsk Statsvitenskapelig Tidsskrift*, Vol.15, No.1 (1999), pp.40–74.

50. U. Sverdrup, 'Norway: An Adaptive Non-Member', in K. Hanf and B. Soetendorp (eds.), *Adapting to European Integration: Small States and the European Union* (New York: Longman, 1997).

51. Sverdrup, 'Norway: An Adaptive Non-Member'.

52. J. Trondal, 'Tilknytningformer til EU og nasjonale samordningsprosesser: En studie av norske og danske departmenter', ARENA Working Paper No.15; Sverdrup, 'Norway: An Adaptive Non-Member'.

53. Sverdrup, 'Norway: An Adaptive Non-Member'.

54. Trondal, 'Tilknytningformer til EU og nasjonale samordningsprosesser', p.61.

55. Trondal, Tilknytningformer til EU og nasjonale samordningsprosesser'.

56. Trondal, 'Europeisering av sentraladministrative organer'.

57. A. Lijphart, *Democracies* (New Haven, CT: Yale University Press, 1984).

Conclusion: The Impact of European Integration on Nordic Parliamentary Democracies

ERIK DAMGAARD

The overall question of this volume is how the EU effects national decision-making with respect to EU/EEA issues. How is this decision-making different from other national decision-making practices?[1] To tackle this question a delegation and accountability approach was adopted. From this perspective, a chain of delegation and accountability connects a number of actors – voters, members of parliament, cabinet ministers and civil servants – in a series of principal–agent relationships. The focus is mainly on the 'processes' of delegation and accountability, in particular possible agency problems and *ex ante* and *ex post* control instruments used to prevent or solve such problems. However, some attention is also directed at accountability defined as 'outcome' (Lupia, this volume). This article compares the five Nordic countries and in particular examines similarities and differences and tries to draw some general conclusions from the evidence provided in the five country chapters.

The contributions to this volume show that the EU issue has been divisive, at times even agonising, for the Nordic countries. The question of joining or staying out of the EC/EU is one that has divided nations, parties and voters. Even when a country opted to accept membership in the supranational EU, this did not solve the problem of what position to take with regard to additional integration. Nor did it answer the question of what the relations between national institutions and the EU ought to be. Where the country decided against membership, the question of viable alternatives to membership immediately arose. These secondary questions, themselves, also generated political controversy in the five Nordic countries.

In 1972 Denmark decided to join the EC while Norwegians voted not to. Norway rejected membership again in 1994, while Finland and Sweden voted to join the EU. Iceland has never applied for membership. Thus, three of the five Nordic countries are now EU members, while Norway and

Erik Damgaard is Professor in the Department of Political Science at Aarhus University, Denmark.

Iceland are partners in the EEA (European Economic Area) agreement but outside the formal structure of the EU. The EEA brings these states into the internal market for industrial goods, services, labour and capital.

All five countries have delegated power to EU or EEA authorities. Formally, they may be able to recall this power, but presumably only at a very high cost. For this reason it can be argued that national political institutions have in fact lost some of the power they once held. On the other hand, EU members have acquired some influence in the organisation's supranational decision-making bodies, and – just like the EEA members – they retain some power over the implementation of common policies. EEA members have retained their sovereignty in matters outside the area of the internal market and other bilaterally agreed-upon areas of co-operation.

This account implies a trade-off between national gains and losses associated with different forms and levels of integration. The losses may be described as enforceable obligations to accept decisions that a national actor considers inferior to the national *status quo*. The gains refer to supranational decisions which a national actor deems superior to the national *status quo*, and which could not have been made and implemented by the national actor acting alone. From this perspective, Member States can both gain and lose from European integration. The same calculus applies to different actors and interests *within* the Member States, be they parties, interest groups or whatever. We assume that all actors would rather win than lose, and that this is reflected in their behaviour (insofar as they are able to calculate likely gains and losses). By and large the country studies confirm the fruitfulness of this approach.

ELECTORATES AND PARLIAMENTS

Referenda and Public Opinion

It is a striking fact that whenever the question of EU membership came up for decision in the Nordic countries, the voters ultimately decided the matter via referenda. This is striking because the Nordic system of government is representative democracy, and because clear parliamentary majorities were in favour of membership every time the issue arose. Why, then, did the Nordic governments and parliaments, *de facto* if not *de jure*, leave the decision in the hands of voters?

The constitutions of Norway, Sweden and Finland have no rules requiring a referendum to decide issues like EU membership. The Danish constitution requires a referendum if less than a five-sixths majority of MPs vote in favour of a delegation of power to supranational authorities. In fact, however, the 1972 Danish referendum on EC membership was announced well before a parliamentary vote was taken on the issue. Nor were subsequent referenda necessarily constitutionally mandated. Thus, constitutional requirements cannot explain the holding of referenda in the Nordic states.

The common explanation as to why referenda are held is that 'parliamentary agents' wanted to see whether 'voter principals' would support their stand on a divisive issue. However, these agents were not solely motivated by democratic principles or concern for the will of the people. More pragmatic and party strategic interests also played a role. Parties in favour of membership wanted voters to legitimise a crucial decision. Parties against membership hoped that the electorate would reject the proposal, while parties divided over membership hoped to solve their internal problems, at least temporarily, by letting the voters decide.

The record of referenda outcomes is somewhat mixed. The 1994 referenda in Finland and Sweden were positive; the two Norwegian outcomes (1972, 1994) were negative. Denmark has held five EC/EU referenda. In four of these referenda, outcomes were positive (1972, 1986, 1993, 1998), while in one case (1992) the outcome was negative. It is worth noting that, in all referenda, the electorate was less favourable toward integration than were parliamentary elites. Icelandic voters were not asked about membership in the EEA, which the Althing approved by a narrow, non-partisan majority in 1993. Today, Icelandic voters seem to favour EEA membership. In Norway, EEA membership is a 'default option' – a policy course chosen after voters rejected EC/EU membership in two referenda.

Research has shown that anti-EU attitudes in Norway, Sweden and Finland can, to a large extent, be understood as periphery protests against the more EU-friendly centres.[2] MPs from peripheral districts in Norway tend to take positions similar to their voters. Swedish MPs representing peripheral districts do not, which tends to put them on something of a collision course with their voters. This points to an interesting problem of agency loss from a delegation and accountability perspective, although Swedish voters may use elections to the European Parliament as an additional opportunity to protest against party elites and local representatives.

Voters in Denmark, Sweden and Finland are often called 'euro-sceptical' or 'reluctant Europeans' because they tend to resist political integration in many areas. They have little enthusiasm for the idea of a federal 'United States of Europe'. Eurobarometer data covering the 15 Member States show that Finnish and Swedish voters are least supportive of the EU, while Danish voters' level of support is about average.[3] Obviously, sceptical voters might constrain parliamentary agents in EU affairs. The best example of this is probably the exemptions from the Maastricht Treaty (EMU, defence, EU citizenship, justice and home affairs) granted to Denmark on the grounds that concessions were necessary in order to win voter approval for the treaty in a second referendum (1993). It is widely accepted that these opt-outs can only be repealed after a referendum in which Danish voters approve their repeal. On the whole it can be said that Nordic electorates have been called on by divided parliaments to decide the big question of EU membership. Danish voters have also been asked several times to legitimise additional integration measures.

Parties and Elections

The EU issue has had a major impact on the cohesion and electoral support of various political parties. In 1972, the EU activated all the underlying cleavages in the Norwegian party system, particularly the centre–periphery and the urban–rural dimensions. These two cleavages tend to divide the bourgeois parties, which explains why the EU has led to the breakdown of two bourgeois coalition governments in Norway (1971, 1990). In the 1993 Storting election, the anti-EU Centre Party was a big winner (although only short-term – its vote-total was cut in half in the 1997 election), while the pro-EU Conservatives lost heavily (and did not recover in the 1997 election). In 1972, the old Liberal Party split into two small parties as a result of disagreement over EU membership, while the Social Democrats had serious problems of internal opposition, something that also occurred in 1994. In contrast to the Norwegian case, the EU issue had little impact on political parties in Iceland. This is probably because membership was never seriously contemplated and could therefore be kept off the political agenda. However, if future external developments bring the issue onto the Icelandic political agenda, intra-party divisions are likely to emerge.

In Denmark, the Social Democrats and, to a lesser extent, the Radical Liberals were internally split over EU membership in the early 1970s. In fact, a main reason for promising to hold a referendum on membership in 1972 was to avoid a situation in which internal division over membership might hurt the Social Democrats in the national election of 1971. Swedish and Finnish parties did not experience much internal dissent on EU membership, although the Finnish Centre Party was divided over the issue. On the whole, the EU issue does not appear to have had much independent impact on the relative strength of parties in the national parliaments of Denmark, Sweden and Finland. However, membership did affect electoral support for several of the parties in elections to the European Parliament, most notably in Denmark.

In voter-principal terms, in EU Member States, the national channel of delegation and accountability is supplemented by a link connecting voters and members of the European Parliament (EP) in matters of European policy making. The country studies make it possible to draw at least two general conclusions on this point. First, compared to turnout in national elections and referenda (including EU-related referenda), voter turnout in EP elections is very low in all three Member States. Both national and EU elections were held in Denmark and Sweden in 1994/95, and the turnout difference was 34 and 45 per cent respectively. In Finland the turnout for the EP election 1996 was 13 per cent lower than the national election turnout in 1995. In Sweden only 42 per cent voted in the EP election, while 53 per cent voted in Denmark and 60 in Finland. Voter turnout in the 1999 EP elections was even lower. These findings, which have parallels in several other Member States, make it clear that voters do not view the EP as particularly important. There may be many possible explanations for the low turnout rates in EP elections.[4] From a rational choice perspective a good explanation is that, for voters, participation does not really involve much delegation and accountability because the EP is still seen as having rather limited power compared to national parliaments and governments. Another reason could be that many voters find themselves in a cross-pressure situation – they do not believe that their national party represents them in EU matters. In this situation, they prefer to stay at home on EP election day, while turning out for national elections.

This leads to a second general observation, which is that the party compositions of the national parliaments are not necessarily reproduced in EP elections. This is obvious in the Danish case, where quasi-parties (Euro-negative 'people's movements') are active and influential in referendum campaigns and EP elections but do not run for seats in the national parliament. At the same time, the Social Democrats have consistently been strongly 'underrepresented' in the Danish delegation to the EP. Similarly dramatic differences cannot be detected in the Finnish case, although the Greens became strongly 'overrepresented' in the EP in 1999. In Sweden, the Left Party and the Greens have consistently done better in EP elections than in national elections, here, too, at the expense of the Social Democrats. In sum, to the extent that the 'Euro-party' systems differ from national party systems, the former are more EU-negative than the latter. Thus, since the EP is not very important to voters, EP elections might be used to signal scepticism to a greater extent than is possible in national elections, in which a host of other issues – presumably issues which are more important to ordinary voters – are at stake.

In other words, the national channel of parliamentary representation is more important to the voters than the EP channel. As the transnational EP parties have so far been both 'weakly organised' and 'unstable and heterogeneous', it is understandable that rational voters behave as they do.[5]

PARLIAMENTS AND CABINETS

Considering the political controversies created by EU membership and its alternatives, it might be expected that national parliaments would resist giving governments wide freedom over EU policy making. On the contrary, having delegated powers to the EU, the parliaments of the new Member States could be expected to be very concerned about their future influence. Parliamentary government implies that a cabinet can be voted out of office (or forced to call elections) by a parliamentary majority. For a Nordic government to be formed and to stay in power, it must at least be tolerated by parliament. Herein lies a potent source of parliamentary influence.

At the cabinet formation stage, parliamentary parties can to some extent (*ex ante*) control cabinet policies by supporting the designation of one or more specific parties (and not others) to cabinet positions. In some cases coalition agreements outline the policies to be implemented by majority governments. In other cases minority cabinets may be the result. The latter governments may need the support from different parties depending on whether their own survival or their EU policy is at stake. In all cases, however, issues are bound to appear that could not possibly be handled or solved at the cabinet formation stage. Therefore, parliamentary control of government policy requires additional *ex ante* and/or *ex post* instruments of control.

Parliamentary Control Instruments

In recent decades, cabinets in Denmark, Norway and Sweden have been minority governments (single-party or coalition), whereas cabinets in Finland and Iceland have been majority coalitions.[6] In all five parliaments a variety of general control instruments is available, and in all parliaments new control structures and procedures have been introduced as a result of EU/EEA membership.

The country studies describe a number of standard control instruments. These include various forms of oral and written questions to ministers, interpellations, plenary debates, specialised committees and other bodies charged with investigating government activity.[7] Using such instruments, parliaments can request information on the intentions and plans of the government, as well as information on previous actions taken by the government. Most of the instruments can work both *ex ante* and *ex post*. If a parliamentary majority is not satisfied with the response and information provided by the government, it can invoke serious sanctions, with the no-confidence vote being the harshest. No-confidence votes are rare, but the fact that they are possible encourages governments, particularly minority governments, to anticipate parliament's reaction to government policies and actions.

As the country studies show, these well-known instruments of parliamentary control have not become obsolete, nor are they less important than they used to be. Nevertheless, they were obviously not deemed to be sufficient in an era of EU and EEA membership. To understand the nature of parliamentary adjustment to the EU it may be useful to consider briefly Philip Norton's three general stages of national parliament influence over EU policies.[8]

The first stage is one of limited or no parliamentary involvement. This was the situation that existed during the period in which the EC had only six members – that is, the six original Member States. The second stage began with the admission of new members in 1973. The parliaments of both Denmark and the United Kingdom (and especially the former – the Danish Folketing) took a position in European affairs that was different from that of the parliaments of the original members. The second phase peaked with the implementation of the Single European Act (SEA), which called for qualified majority voting in the Council of Ministers. During this period, most national parliaments adapted their procedures in order to deal more effectively with EC affairs, not least with the hundreds of directives concerning the internal market. The third stage is the current post-Maastricht (and post-Amsterdam, we may now add)[9] period. Characteristic for this period is that national parliaments, along with the EP, are seen as important means of addressing the 'democratic deficit' within the EU. This point is well illustrated by declarations on the role of national parliaments appended to the Maastrict Treaty and the protocol to the Amsterdam Treaty.

Norton concluded that the shift of political power upwards to the institutions of the European Union 'has not been matched by a shift in democratic accountability, either at the level of the EP or through national parliaments'.[10] Interestingly, David Judge has a less pessimistic view on the very same development. He claims that, if anything, national parliaments have in fact increased their powers of scrutiny over EC legislation and, furthermore, that if national parliaments do not help in solving the EU's democratic deficit it is because they exert only limited control over their own national governments.[11] The latter argument obviously refers back to the old 'decline of parliament' doctrine that, incidentally, has not received much empirical support in the Nordic countries.[12]

New Control Instruments

The evidence in the articles about the parliaments of the three Nordic Member States emphasises three new types of control instruments: a European Affairs Committee, the involvement of (other) specialised permanent committees, and new procedures and sources of information.

The most spectacular innovation in the three parliaments was obviously a European Affairs Committee (EAC).[13] The committees have different national names and varying powers, but share a common purpose – to influence national governments and national EU policy making, thus preserving or increasing parliamentary control. The main aim is to exert *ex ante* control before final decisions – both national and EU decisions – are made. However, the committees might also try to influence the behaviour of national governments through the use of *ex post* control.

MPs in all three countries consider membership on the EAC committee to be very attractive. When the Swedes and Finns established their European Affairs Committees, they could draw on the two decades of experience of the Danish EAC. The EACs are in close contact with cabinet ministers in order to ensure parliamentary influence over and support for the EU policies and strategies pursued by the government in the Council of Ministers. Regular meetings are held frequently. At the end of the meetings, the committee chairman summarises the discussion and usually concludes that there is no majority against a certain policy proposed by the government.

The three committees differ in the sense that the Danish EAC has a formal right to give ministers a bargaining mandate that must be respected, whereas the positions taken by the Swedish and Finnish committees are formally only recommendations or political advice to the government. In practice, however, this difference may not be very great because parliamentary governments ultimately need the support of their parliaments. The special role of the Danish EAC, which dates back to 1973, is probably best explained by a unique combination of strong Euro-scepticism and weak minority government.

All three EACs have instruments of (*ex post*) control of government in the form of various reporting requirements. For example, ministers are obliged to inform the committee about the results of the Council meetings. Such reports are not always followed up systematically, but if problems arise they can be important for subsequent efforts to place blame with the cabinet. It is worth noting that the model of EAC involvement in matters related to the Council of Ministers is by and large replicated with respect to EAC involvement in intergovernmental conferences and meetings in the European Council (summits).

The performance of the three EACs are evaluated in remarkably uniform ways in the country studies presented in this volume. The basic message seems to be that the systems of parliamentary control centred around the EAC work rather well and as intended – although, of course, it is acknowledged that they can always be improved (as, in fact, they have been over time).

The second major instrument of parliamentary control is the involvement of existing specialised committees that can provide substantive expertise in the various fields of public policy dealt with by the EU. While the EACs are, in principle, co-ordinating bodies for all or most policy fields, the specialised committees are repositories of detailed expertise and information. The EACs embody the idea of a general and central 'foreign policy' committee for EU affairs, while the specialised committees are 'domestic policy' bodies that might also be useful in EU affairs. In all three countries the intention was to involve the specialised committees in the processing of EU items within their 'domestic' jurisdiction. In practice, however, this has not taken place everywhere.

Only in Finland are the specialised committees fully involved at an early stage in the decision-making process. Such committee involvement is, in fact, mandatory in Finland. The EAC receives the opinions of the relevant specialised committees and usually accepts them when making recommendations to the government, although the EAC is sometimes forced to mediate between the opinions of different committees. In this way the specialised knowledge of MPs is utilised and all MPs become more or less involved in EU matters. In Denmark and Sweden the specialised committees are not obliged to participate in the EU policy process, but they have the opportunity to do so. The conclusion in the Swedish case is that the *ex ante* control envisaged for specialised committees does not function as well as intended. In the Danish case, the specialised committees have generally played an unimportant role in EU policy, although a few of them (notably the Environmental Committee) have been quite active. New rules adopted in 1999 are intended to increase input from the specialised committees. The overall impression is that the three countries may converge in the future with regard to the role of specialised committees *vis-à-vis* the EACs. In Denmark and Sweden this could create some new problems due to jurisdictional conflict.

The third major change in parliamentary control prompted by EU membership is the creation of a number of new information sources not controlled or mediated by the government, which tends to validate Lupia's argument (this issue) on the flow of information. For example, many parties in the three national parliaments also have members in the European Parliament who can provide information and evaluate emerging issues and existing problems. This source of information is, of course, available to the opposition and Euro-sceptic parties. This enables them to provide information and points of view that might not otherwise be voiced in national political debate. To date, such party-based sources of information have had only limited importance, but there are signs that they will become more significant.

In recent years all national parliaments have also received various EU documents in a more timely fashion than in the past. The Amsterdam Treaty introduced a six-week time period for national parliament scrutiny of Commission proposals before they are placed on a Council agenda for decision (with possible exceptions on grounds of urgency). Furthermore, new electronic technologies have increased the availability of information from many different sources. The main problem with information in the future does not appear to be the lack of it, except perhaps in a small number of special cases, but rather that information overload is omnipresent. In this situation, parliaments will continue to be dependent on the civil service to select and condense material into a manageable quantity. On the other hand, the larger staffs of parliaments and political parties – despite the fact that they are still relatively small – might, to some extent, counterbalance this dependency.

The EEA Members

Norway and Iceland have also adjusted their parliamentary control instruments after EEA membership, although not nearly to the extent that the three EU Member States have done. National institutions in Norway and Iceland are basically obliged – if not in law, then in practice – to adopt and implement policies already decided upon by EU institutions. Despite this, both countries have provisions for parliamentary consultation before meetings of ministers in the EEA Joint Committee, which makes the final decisions. In Norway a new body was established for this purpose. This is the European Consultative Organ (ECO), also called the EEA Commission. It consists of the members of the Foreign Affairs Committee of the Storting and the six Norwegian members of the EEA Joint Parliamentary Committee, and is thus an expanded version of the Foreign Affairs Committee. In Iceland the Foreign Affairs Committee itself plays a similar role. While the Storting's specialised committees are not formally involved in European affairs processes, the Icelandic Foreign Affairs Committee forwards documents to the relevant specialised committees for consideration. Norway appears to be a deviant case among the Nordic five insofar as European affairs are treated like foreign policy – at least with regard to the Cabinet's relations to the Storting.

The overall message is that the Storting and the Althing have lost power to the government and administration and that parliamentary control is limited. In Norway there have been complaints about lack of information, secret meetings, late involvement and short time limits. It should be remembered, however, that the parliaments of both countries are represented on the EEA Joint Parliamentary Committee, which is a co-ordinating body of the EP and the EEA countries which supervises the enactment and general development of the EEA agreement. It meets twice a year and constitutes a new source of information for parliamentarians.

INSIDE CABINETS

Not only the parliaments, but also the governments of the Nordic countries have had to find ways to integrate European matters into national decision-making systems. Thus, another important question is how the EU/EEA membership has affected the organisation, operation and internal power relations of Nordic cabinets.

First, it is worth noting that while the heads of state in the three monarchies (Denmark, Norway and Sweden) do not exert political power, the president of Iceland can potentially do so, and the Finnish president certainly does so. Directly elected presidents with more than ceremonial powers may complicate the delegation and accountability relationships. The Icelandic president decided – despite strong popular pressure – not to refer the bill passed by the Althing on EEA membership to referendum. The president has also taken the position that EEA membership has not changed the largely non-partisan role of the president. The Finnish story is different. Membership in the EU, in combination with constitutional amendments concerning the role of parliament and cabinet in the preparation of matters to be decided in international bodies, has reduced the powers of the Finnish president by limiting the area in which he has sole responsibility. The active or positive consent of the president, who is not responsible to parliament, is no longer needed to change the *status quo*. The controversial issue of Finland's representation in the European Council (PM or president) was solved by a compromise in which it was agreed that the PM would always attend summits, while the president would attend whenever he wants to do so.

The articles presented here report that the role of the PM as government leader has been expanded due to EU membership, not only in Finland but in all three Member States. This is partly due to the PM's role in summit meetings, which have become more important and frequent in recent years. It is also due to the fact that the PM co-ordinates national EU policies which do not fit the traditional international/domestic policy distinction. In Norway and Iceland, the PM has also become more powerful than s/he was in the pre-EEA area.

To some extent, this general increase in the power of the prime minister seems to have come at the expense of the minister of foreign affairs. While foreign ministers play important co-ordinating roles in all five countries – making sure that things are done correctly and properly – it appears that overall, high-level national policy-making in European affairs is increasingly a matter for prime ministerial involvement. Perhaps this is most clearly seen in the case of Sweden, where a co-ordination unit was established in the Prime Minister's Office at the expense of the Ministry of Foreign Affairs. The Norwegian PM has also been very keen on keeping

European affairs under tight control, although European policy is treated as foreign policy in relation to parliament. In general, one would expect that a strong PM role in European affairs is more likely to occur in a single-party cabinet headed by the party leader than in a coalition cabinet, where the views, interests and prestige of two or more parties are involved. At present, all Nordic states except Sweden have coalition cabinets.

While all Nordic cabinets are collectively responsible to their parliaments (even if individual ministers can be subject to a no-confidence vote), they differ in the degree to which they rely on formal collective cabinet decision-making procedures. Roughly speaking, it is fair to say that the Swedish and Finnish model rely more on collegial decision-making than does the Danish and Icelandic model. The Norwegian model is somewhere in-between. Thus, for example, the Swedish cabinet makes numerous formal (and legally binding) decisions that would be made by the individual minister in Denmark. In such cases the Danish minister (and not the cabinet) is then ultimately (legally) responsible for the decision. In reality, however, these juridical differences may not be that important for the substantive outcome of policy making and, in any case, cabinet policies and decisions have to be co-ordinated one way or another.

In all countries, membership in the EU/EEA has increased dramatically the burdens of co-ordinating the work of government departments. To maximise national influence, the ideal is thought to be that representatives of national governments speak with one voice on European affairs. Their positions are to be based, as far as possible, on national consensus or compromise worked out between interested parties. National policies in various policy areas are not supposed to contradict each other. At the top level, the Cabinet headed by the PM co-ordinates policies, but usually the Cabinet only confirms proposals that have already been prepared according to the relevant national standard procedures. In Denmark, Finland and Norway cabinet committees dealing with European affairs have been created to reduce the workload of the full cabinet. In all cases proposals must be prepared before they reach the cabinet level. The Swedish Government Office has a system for 'common deliberations' in which all relevant ministries have an opportunity to present their views. This procedure is therefore suitable for finding government positions on EU matters. The Danish, Norwegian and Icelandic solution is to rely on inputs from a committee of top civil servants chaired by the Ministry of Foreign Affairs. In Finland pre-cabinet level co-ordination appears to be less formalised and is primarily left to middle level bureaucrats.

Co-ordination in EU affairs not only involves a PM and a minister of foreign affairs, but also a number of other ministers with different 'domestic' jurisdictions. The evidence presented in the articles suggests that individual ministers in Denmark, Finland and Iceland are rather autonomous actors within their respective jurisdictions, while Swedish and Norwegian ministers seem to be somewhat more constrained by cabinets and their leaders.[14] This implies that many ministers are involved in European affairs and that some of them might exert quite strong influence over national policy positions within their sphere of responsibility *vis-à-vis* the PM and the Minister of Foreign Affairs. It also means that co-ordination might sometimes be a very serious political business.

The country studies on the three EU Member States differ in terms of their evaluation of national co-ordination procedures. The Danish system seems to work very well, perhaps reflecting many years of experience and mutual adjustment by the ministers and civil servants involved. The article on Sweden suggests a certain lack of political leadership in EU matters within the Government Office, at least in some areas. The Finnish system of decision making is described as being highly sectionalised, which leads to a lack of co-ordination among the ministries. If there are co-ordination problems at the cabinet level in some countries, they might be related to procedures in the initial stages of the EU decision-making process (see below).

Examining the articles in this volume, one might easily conclude that membership in the EU/EEA has increased the power of the PM, reduced the power of the Minister of Foreign Affairs, and increased the power of other affected ministers. In this view, the Ministry of Foreign Affairs has been squeezed between the PM, on the one hand, and the other ministers, on the other. However, this is only one possible interpretation of the articles. It is also possible to argue that the effects of membership are not a zero-sum game among the three types of ministers. According to this interpretation, all affected ministries have obtained new and important functions to perform as a result of EU/EEA membership. In the case of the PM and the ministries other than Foreign Affairs, the new tasks are just more internationally oriented than they were when the Minister of Foreign Affairs (and the president in Finland) was more clearly in charge of international relations. All ministers continue to be accountable to their parliament.

MINISTERS AND CIVIL SERVANTS

The civil servants in government departments and institutions were certainly no less affected by membership in the EU/EEA than were ministers and MPs. Nordic civil servants gained new tasks relating to the preparation and implementation of EU policies and decisions. In addition, they experienced 'culture shock' when faced with the French and Mediterranean way of conducting political and administrative businesses. In these ways, a new European dimension was added to the national bureaucracies of the Nordic countries, although the basic structure and operation of government administration remains largely unchanged despite adjustments to the EU's political and administrative system. The Danes were the first to adjust, out of a sense of necessity, and they prepared themselves carefully for the new situation. Later, the other Nordic countries could draw inspiration from the Danish model, which was designed to ensure parliamentary control, overall national policy co-ordination and utilisation of civil service expertise. It was also designed to enable the interests of organised groups to be articulated and, not least, to achieve a national consensus. With respect to the role of civil servants and experts, EU/EEA membership raises certain fundamental questions. How did the civil service adjust to the new circumstances? What effects did the EU/EEA membership have on the accountability of civil servants to their ministers?

Special Committees

The Danish solution to civil servant participation in EU policy making was to establish a number of so-called 'special committees' (currently about 30) of civil servants to prepare national positions on forthcoming EU policy proposals from the Commission. These committees have members from all ministries affected by the policies and decisions in a particular area, and they are chaired by the ministry considered to be responsible for the policy area. They are also responsible for informing their ministers about developments and for producing background notes for civil servants and ministers who will handle policy questions in later stages of the decision-making process. Many special committees include members of important interest organisations. If they do not, such groups will at least be consulted on issues under consideration. Members of special committees also participate in the numerous advisory committees of the EU Commission and working groups of the EU Council of Ministers, both when they are stationed in the national permanent representation in Brussels and when they work in a ministry in Copenhagen.

Norway, a potential EU member in 1972 and 1994, has established a similar system of specialised committees of civil servants. The Norwegian government has also issued guidelines requiring the committees to include the views of affected interest groups in the preparation process. In Finland, EU sections operating under the appropriate ministries and composed of bureaucrats from all relevant ministries and interest groups play roles similar to those of the Danish special committees. In Sweden, the competent minister and civil servants are responsible for their particular areas, but they obviously have their own ways of consulting interest groups through 'reference groups' in the various ministries. In Iceland, groups of officials and experts meet in the capital before meetings in the national and the EEA decision-making bodies.

The general impression derived from the country studies is that the Nordic countries have devised practical solutions for the inclusion of civil servants and interest organisations in policy making and policy implementation. These solutions are in keeping with their traditional national policy style. The literature on Nordic politics during the 1970s and 1980s abounded with analysis of 'corporatism' that saw bureaucrats and interest organisations as the crucial political actors and real decision makers, although – of course – ministers and parliamentary parties (usually aligned with some of the various interests in question) had to approve the deals made between those important actors. In the 1990s this general perspective has been less common in scholarly analyses, but perhaps it is again appropriate to use such an approach to answer the questions about influence in national EU policy making. If this is true, one possible answer to the specific question of the accountability of civil servants to their ministers is rather familiar. In short, the answer is that in the Nordic countries it is considered to be both fair and useful to take affected interests into account before final decisions are made. However, such a procedure might create problems with regard to the overall control and co-ordination of the results of numerous decisions made in accordance with these principles.

Civil Service Accountability

In all Nordic countries, bureaucrats in government departments continue to be responsible to their ministers, just as they were before EU/EEA membership. Nonetheless, membership has made ministers dependent on the advice and assistance of civil servants in policy areas that are new to both groups. The initial and instinctive reaction of ministers and civil servants in the new Member States appears to be fundamentally reactive. The fundamental question seems to be how can the state best safeguard its national interests, *vis-à-vis* both grandiose plans for European integration (which Nordic voters do not really like) and more mundane regulations and directives that might be welcome in a number of respects, but not in others?

A general observation is that in all countries a new class of national Euro-civil servants has emerged. Most national political issues now have an EU aspect, and professional people are needed in the public administration to attend to this. What is new about this development is that civil servants have become responsible for providing inputs to decisions that ultimately cannot be controlled by their national political institutions alone. This development also implies that civil servants can help to shape desired policies at an early stage of the decision-making process, just as they have done at the national level, albeit now in a much more complex environment. Civil servants, who are agents of ministers, have become much more important than they used to be, and this fact worries all the country authors of the present volume.

The Icelandic contribution is perhaps most outspoken on this issue. While Iceland has no right to participate in the EU decision-making process, it has obtained access to the decision-shaping process. The same, of course, applies to Norway. The three EU Member States have access to both of the decision processes, which is to say that they can, in principle, actively influence decisions at all stages of the policy process, from initiation to implementation. The real problem in the present context is whether civil servants act at an early stage to promote national interests, and whether ministers of government can control the actions of civil servants, who may be inclined or suspected to strive for national consensus and/or to hide controversial information in the early phases of the policy-making process. The answer seems to be that civil servants cannot deceive their political masters in the long run, because there are numerous new sources of information that sooner or later will be used by interested groups and political parties to reveal controversial problems publicly.

But national decision-making procedures can be designed by cabinets and ministers to facilitate the achievement of certain goals. The Swedish system of independent administrative authorities that cannot be controlled directly by ministers obviously creates some problems of democratic accountability in the phases of policy preparation and implementation, no matter how well the cabinet and the parliament are organised to deal with EU issues. In Finland, concerns are aired about the way in which responsible ministers fail to provide sufficient guidance to civil servants in EU affairs. In a delegation and accountability perspective one cannot blame agents that are not given mandates to which they should stick. It is likely that such a problem is present everywhere. However, the relationships between minister and civil servant are not based solely on written and detailed contracts, but also on tacit assumptions involving civil servants' anticipations of ministerial goals in given situations.

CONCLUSION

The transfer of national sovereignty to the supranational institutions of the EU entailed a formal loss of power, and the EEA agreement involved *de facto* loss of national power. At the same time, European integration created possibilities for desired policy outcomes that no single country (and certainly not a small one) could hope to achieve by its own efforts. It also created the risk of binding decisions imposed on an unwelcoming government. EU Member State representatives have voting rights in EU decision-making bodies. EEA Member States can only hope to influence relevant decisions more informally. In all cases, decisions to join the EU/EEA involved a trade-off between expected gains and losses in situations characterised by the fact that actors in each of the five Nordic states made very different calculations. Regardless of which solution they opted for, a general feeling in the five countries is that political power has been diffused. The well-known national models for delegation and accountability, which were close to the ideal type of parliamentary democracy, were modified by the complexities of decision making in European affairs.

As has become abundantly clear, the EU was a very divisive issue, and in many ways it still is. The EU may be considered an elite project, but the Nordic electorates were called upon to approve or reject membership when it was up for decision. In Denmark, voters were asked, several times, to decide on further developments in European integration. Voters do turn out in great numbers on such occasions (as they do in national elections), but so far they have not cared very much about EP elections. The national channel of political representation is more important to voters than is the EP channel, though the latter can be used to express varying degrees of voter scepticism or enthusiasm concerning the EU project.

How, then, did EU/EEA membership effect the normal decision-making practices of the Nordic countries once the decision to join had been made? Within our principal–agent perspective of delegation and accountability, and leaving out the many interesting and finer details of this volume, the following general conclusions may be suggested.

First, the national parliaments responded by making use of new control instruments – European Affairs Committees for consultations and agreements with the cabinet, the involvement of standing specialised legislative committees, and the development of new sources of information independent of the cabinet. These instruments of control can be used *ex ante* as well as *ex post*. They are used, in both ways and to varying degrees, especially in the three EU Member States. The procedures of the EACs can perhaps be further improved, and the specialised committees could become more involved in some countries. In the EU Member States, information overload, rather than lack of information or late incoming information, seems to be a problem for MPs.

Second, membership in the EU/EEA has apparently increased the power of the prime minister, reduced the traditional power of the Minister of Foreign Affairs, and increased the power of other affected ministries. Alternatively, one might argue that all types of affected ministries have acquired new and important internationally oriented tasks as a consequence of membership, in contrast to the days when foreign policy used to be mainly the business of the Minister of Foreign Affairs (and the president in Finland).

Third, all cabinets have some mechanisms to ensure co-ordination in European affairs. The Danish system involves what perhaps can be seen as a new type of corporatist arrangement. It apparently works well, whereas improvements might be useful in the case of Sweden and Finland. However, to understand and evaluate cabinet co-ordination instruments, one must know how inputs for cabinet-level decisions have been prepared. The Danish, Norwegian and Icelandic solution is to rely on inputs from a committee of top civil servants, representing affected ministries and chaired by the Ministry of Foreign Affairs.

Fourth, civil servants everywhere have become indispensable in European affairs. It is even possible to talk about a new EU class of national civil servants. They are needed to handle proposals at the very first stages of the EU decision-making process. In Denmark and Norway civil servant participation at the early stages of the process occurs through a number of so-called special committees consisting of bureaucrats from all affected ministries and chaired by the ministry considered to be responsible for the policy area. The committees also include the views of organised interests in their recommendations to the minister in charge. Finland has introduced a similar system. The other two countries rely on somewhat less formalised procedures, which might be problematic in terms of delegation and accountability. All country authors are, in fact, concerned about the degree to which ministers can or do control their civil servant agents in European policy making. One might actually get the impression that civil servants and interest groups are better informed, more integrated and more effective in EU/EEA affairs than are ministers, MPs and, certainly, voters. It is difficult to be certain, but if the existing control instruments are not effective, serious agency problems certainly exist.

Fifth, most, if not all, of the procedures mentioned above have an overriding goal – to create decisions and policies reflecting national consensus or broad compromises. National unity in European affairs, including during the various stages of the decision-making process, is considered vital to the achievement of the best possible policy outcomes.

The present research project was not designed to measure the ideal points of the various actors, or to compare them with the actual policy outcomes of the decisions made by EU/EEA authorities,[15] which would also be very difficult to do. But the main conclusions noted here suggest that the instruments of control in the various delegation and accountability relationships are indeed intended to promote 'good' (favourable) policy outcomes in terms of national policy positions as established through democratic processes. They also suggest that while principals in the EU Member States can suffer from agency loss, the reverse can also be true, thus confirming Lupia's main argument. However, in the cases of Norway and Iceland it is more difficult to see how the EEA might contain agency loss. In terms of the EU impact on national democracy, there is a significant difference between EU and EEA membership. The impact also seems to differ between the EEA states, with Iceland reporting more favourable consequences for the chain of delegation and accountability. In both Iceland and Norway, however, delegation to supranational institutions has created problems for the chain that is supposed to hold agents accountable.

NOTES

1. The scope is thus broader than the theme explored in P. Norton (ed.), *National Parliaments and the European Union* (London and Portland, OR: Frank Cass, 1995), while the range of countries included is smaller. Our scope is also broader than that of M. Wiberg (ed.), *Trying to Make Democracy Work. The Nordic Parliaments and the European Union* (Stockholm: Gidlunds Förlag, 1997).
2. H. Valen, H.M. Narud and Ó.T. Hardarson, 'Geography and Political Representation', in K. Heidar and P. Esaiasson (eds.), *Beyond Westminster and Congress: The Nordic Experience* (Columbus, OH: Ohio State University Press, forthcoming 2000); K. Ringdal and H. Valen, 'Structural Divisions in the EU Referendums', in A.T. Jenssen, P. Pesonen and M. Gilljam (eds.), *To Join or Not to Join. Three Nordic Referendums on Membership in the European Union* (Oslo: Scandinavian University Press, 1998), pp.168–92.
3. *Eurobarometer*, Report Number 49 (Brussels: European Commission, 1998).
4. See J. Blondel, R. Sinnot and P. Svensson, 'Representation and Voter Participation', *European Journal of Political Research*, Vol.3, No.2 (Oct. 1997), pp.243–72.
5. See the discussion in R. Andeweg, 'The Reshaping of National Party Systems', in J. Hayward (ed.), *The Crisis of Representation in Europe* (London and Portland, OR: Frank Cass, 1995), pp.58–78.
6. E. Damgaard (ed.), *Parliamentary Change in the Nordic Countries* (Oslo: Scandinavian University Press, 1992); E. Damgaard, 'Parliament and Government', in Heidar and Esaiasson (eds.), *Beyond Westminster and Congress: The Nordic Experience*.
7. For a general account of questioning activity, see M. Wiberg (ed.), *Parliamentary Control in the Nordic Countries* (Helsinki: The Finnish Political Science Association, 1994).
8. P. Norton, 'Conclusion: Addressing the Democratic Deficit', *Journal of Legislative Studies*, Vol.1, No.3 (Autumn 1995), pp.177–93.
9. See T. Raunio, 'Always One Step Behind? National Legislatures and the European Union', *Government and Opposition*, Vol.34, No.2 (1999), pp.180–202.
10. Norton, 'Conclusion', p.192.
11. D. Judge, 'The Failure of National Parliaments?', in Hayward (ed.), *The Crisis of Representation in Europe*, pp.79–100.
12. Damgaard (ed.), *Parliamentary Change in the Nordic Countries*.
13. Cf. T. Bergman, 'National Parliaments and EU Affairs Committees: Notes on Empirical Variation and Competing Explanations', *Journal of European Public Policy*, Vol.4, No.3 (Sept. 1997), pp.373–87.
14. See also the country chapters by K. Strøm (Norway), J. Nousiainen (Finland) and T. Larson (Sweden) in M. Laver and K.A. Shepsle (eds.), *Cabinet Ministers and Parliamentary Government* (Cambridge: Cambridge University Press, 1994).
15. Cf. A. Lupia's article in this volume.

Abstracts

Introduction: Delegation and Accountability in European Integration, *by Torbjörn Bergman*

The overall question of this volume is how the EU effects national decision making. We start our search for answers to this question from a principal–agent-based delegation and accountability perspective. In our search for answers, we examine the four basic steps of representative parliamentary democracy: from voters to MPs, from parliament to cabinet, from cabinet to individual ministers and from individual ministers to civil servants. Our main hypothesis is that the transfer of power from the national level to the supranational does not necessarily mean that delegation fails or that accountability is lost. Our empirical analysis examines the five Nordic countries. While Denmark, Finland, Iceland, Norway and Sweden share historical, cultural and institutional traits, they also differ from one another in important ways. Of particular relevance for this volume is the fact that three of the five are EU members (Denmark, Finland, Sweden), while two (Iceland and Norway) remain outside the EU but are closely associated with it through the European Economic Area (EEA) agreement. By combining in-depth studies of the five countries with a concluding cross-national contribution, we identify the various ways in which the EU has an impact on domestic principal–agent relationships.

The EU, the EEA, and Domestic Accountability: How Outside Forces Affect Delegation within Member States, *by Arthur Lupia*

This paper clarifies how the EU and the EEA affect delegation and accountability within Member States. Many people presume that the Member States of the EU and the EEA weakened themselves by delegating important powers to these international organisations. Such a presumption need not be true with regard to the matter of domestic accountability. This article argues that the EU and the EEA are 'outside forces' that can increase accountability among domestic political actors. To make this argument, the article focuses on what happens to domestic accountability when an outside force shifts domestic reversion points (for example, changes a domestic policy *status quo*) or affects domestic actors' information (for example, the EU leads a domestic government to be more precise about its issue positions). It is shown in both cases how the presence of outside forces allows domestic actors to make credible commitments and provide collective benefits that would not be possible in the absence of these forces. In sum, a formal model, simple graphs and tables, and a few empirical examples are used to clarify when outside forces do (and do not) affect domestic accountability.

The European Union and Danish Parliamentary Democracy, *by Erik Damgaard and Asbjørn Sonne Nørgaard*

The consequences of Danish EU membership are studied from a national delegation and accountability perspective. Investigating the chain of principal–agent relationships leads to the following conclusions: (1) Voters are highly assertive in EU matters. Voter behaviour in EU-related referenda and European Parliament elections does not strictly follow party recommendations. On the other hand, the EU dimension has little impact on national voting and party allegiances. (2) The EU has not induced changes in the general organisation of parliament–cabinet relations. However, procedural innovations have increased parliamentary control, notably through the European Affairs Committee, over the cabinet in EU matters. (3) The principle of ministerial autonomy prevails in EU affairs. Nonetheless, the Foreign Ministry assumes a co-ordinating role and the prime minister has been strengthened. (4) While ministerial autonomy is also the norm at the civil servant level, a new committee system ensures some inter-ministerial co-ordination and varying degrees of interest organisation participation in the early phases of policy preparation. In general, and in spite of tensions between national political parties and voters, Danish parliamentary democracy has adapted to the EU challenge in a pragmatic and reactive way, observing time-honoured traditions of how to organise and make accountability work.

Building Elite Consensus: Parliamentary Accountability in Finland, *by Tapio Raunio and Matti Wiberg*

Recent developments in the Finnish political system, reinforced or directly caused by EU membership, have in many respects strengthened parliamentary democracy in Finland. One positive spill-over effect of membership is that parliamentary scrutiny has improved. At the same time, however, relative to the parliament (the Eduskunta), the government and ministries have strengthened their position in EU-related policy areas due to superior organisational resources. Another trend is that civil servants are becoming more central actors in policy preparation. Nevertheless, the most important trends are that the efficient *ex ante* scrutiny by the parliament reduces conflicts and that Finnish European policy-making is characterised by a continuous dialogue between the ministries and the parliament.

Another Link in the Chain: The Effects of EU Membership on Delegation and Accountability in Sweden, *by Hans Hegeland and Ingvar Mattson*

Membership in the EU has affected the national chain of delegation and accountability in Sweden in various ways. The effects in terms of delegation and accountability have varied. Membership need not in every instance weaken domestic accountability. On the one hand, the possibility for the parliament (Riksdag) to control the government and the bureaucracy has decreased. On the other hand, the Riksdag has gained insight into areas which were previously the privilege of the government, such as foreign affairs, or state agencies, such as the details of agriculture policy and regulation. Nevertheless, the new conditions for accountability due to EU membership present challenges for the principals in the chain of delegation and accountability. In this article, we discuss some of these challenges and identify some problems the principals encounter when trying to overcome these challenges. Among the interesting dilemmas facing the Riksdag, we discuss the trade-off between parliamentary control in advance of government action and the ability to hold government accountable after the fact. The Riksdag, as a principal, must consider whether it should give an open mandate to the government to act in the Council and then call for accountability after Council meetings, or whether to issue a narrower mandate, thereby controlling the government in advance.

Delegation and Accountability in an Ambiguous System: Iceland and the European Economic Area (EEA), *by Svanur Kristjánsson and Ragnar Kristjánsson*

Because of its combination of patronage and a constitution based on parliamentary democracy and semi-presidentialism, the Icelandic political system can perhaps best be characterised as 'ambiguous'. Together with other trends, such as globalisation in general and a growing European-wide legalism, the European Economic Area (EEA) has already had a strong impact on Icelandic politics. The EEA is largely about delegation without accountability, which means that there has been a significant loss of sovereignty to EU institutions. However, the EEA has also meant a move towards a clearer demarcation of political roles, which has in fact increased the autonomy of the parliament (the Althing) *vis-à-vis* the cabinet. The separation of roles between cabinet ministers and civil servants has also become more clear-cut. In sum, while the Iceland–EU relationship tends to make national politics more diffuse, the EEA has also made some of the domestic principal–agent relationships more transparent.

Adaptation without EU Membership: Norway and The European Economic Area, *by Hanne Marthe Narud and Kaare Strøm*

Though Norway stands alone as the only country that has twice rejected EU membership in referenda, European integration affects Norwegian politics in increasingly important ways. While the membership battles have been relatively short and intense, the two referenda split the Norwegian electorate roughly evenly and in remarkably similar ways. The EU membership issue has had a more lasting impact on parliamentary and executive coalitions. Since Norway entered into the EEA agreement, European issues have increasingly become a part of the cabinet and parliamentary agenda. Even though both the legislative and the executive branches have undergone institutional change, it appears that Norwegian political institutions have not yet succeeded in facilitating effective national control over decisions within the EEA. Thus, the Norwegian government is facing serious agency problems in its relations with European institutions, though these problems have yet to become a salient issue in domestic Norwegian politics.

Conclusion: The Impact of European Integration on Nordic Parliamentary Democracies, *by Erik Damgaard*

Using a principal–agent perspective to examine possible delegation and accountability problems in the Nordic countries, the articles presented in this volume have revealed a number of similarities and differences with regard to the impact of European integration. In all the Nordic states, the calculation of benefits and costs of EU membership took place via difficult political processes, and the electorates and parliaments in the different states did not all choose the same path. Once the five states had decided on membership in either the EU or the EEA, they subsequently adopted somewhat different solutions to problems of accountability in the principal–agent chain (voters, MPs, cabinets, ministers, civil servants) that arose as a result of membership. These solutions, not necessarily effective in all cases, include variations on common themes: new instruments for parliamentary control of cabinets (that is, European Affairs Committees, specialised permanent committees, information sources); changes in the internal distribution of cabinet powers; the inclusion of civil servants and experts in early stages of the policy-making process. Preliminary evidence suggests that the overriding goal of all governments, largely independent of their partisan composition, has been to create – if possible – national consensus with regard to position taking in the EU/EEA. This is seen as both a method for legitimising decisions and as a way to promote good EU policy outcomes (ones that national democratic procedures define as favourable). In terms of democratic process, the most striking empirical finding presented in this volume is the loss of accountability experienced in EEA member states (Iceland and Norway) relative to that of the three EU Member States.

Index

Library of
Legislative Studies

Series Editor: Philip Norton, *The Lord Norton of Louth, Centre for Legislative Studies, Hull University*

The Library of Legislative Studies comprises scholarly books – including individual country studies as well as major comparative works – that advance knowledge of legislatures and legislative processes. The volumes in the Library are designed to be of value to students and scholars in legislative studies, comparative government, constitutional law, and European and regional integration.

ISSN 1460-9649

Parliaments in Contemporary Western Europe

Parliaments have become more prominent in recnt years, not least as a result of developments in Central and Eastern Europe and as a number of military or one-party regimes in different parts of the globe have given way to democratic government. Yet the attention given to new parliaments has not been matched by a study of established parliaments.

This three volume series on the role of parliaments in Western Europe fills that gap. It draws together studies of a number of West European parliaments and it provides a detailed accessible study of the relationships not previously studied in depth. Each volume is edited by Philip Norton and draws upon an international team of specialists.

Parliaments and Governments in Western Europe

Philip Norton, *The Lord Norton of Louth, Hull University* (Ed)

232 pages   1998
0 7146 4833 7 cloth
0 7146 4385 8 paper
The Library of Legislative Studies

Parliaments and Pressure Groups in Western Europe

Philip Norton, *The Lord Norton of Louth, Hull University* (Ed)

232 pages   1998
0 7146 4834 5 cloth
0 7146 4386 6 paper
The Library of Legislative Studies

Parliaments and Citizens in Western Europe

Philip Norton, *The Lord Norton of Louth, Hull University* (Ed)
200 pages   2000
0 7146 4835 3 cloth
0 7146 4387 4 paper
The Library of Legislative Studies

The New Roles of Parliamentary Committees

Lawrence D Longley, *Lawrence University, USA* and
Roger H Davidson, *University of Maryland* (Eds)

Parliaments had widely been expected to decline in significance in the later part of the twentieth century, but instead they have developed new and vital political roles and have innovated in their institutional structure – most recurrently in newly organised or invigorated parliamentary committees, not only in a few parliaments but as a global phenomenon.

Even as newly democratic parliaments throughout the world experiment with more elaborate committee structures, those with older, highly developed committee systems are reaching for more varied and flexible alternatives. In short, parliamentary committees have emerged as vibrant and central institutions of democratic parliaments of today's world and have begun to define new and changing roles for themselves.

This publication is devoted to the study and evaluation of these important and still emergent parliamentary developments – to an understanding of the new roles of parliamentary committees in the quest for effective parliamentary influence in and contribution to democratic government.

264 pages   1998
0 7146 4891 4 cloth
0 7146 4442 0 paper
A special issue of The Journal of Legislative Studies
The Library of Legislative Studies

FRANK CASS PUBLISHERS
Newbury House, 900 Eastern Avenue, Newbury Park, Ilford, Essex IG2 7HH
Tel: +44 (020) 8599 8866 Fax: +44 (020) 8599 0984 E-mail: info@frankcass.com
NORTH AMERICA
5804 NE Hassalo Street, Portland, OR 97213 3644, USA
Tel: 800 944 6190 Fax: 503 280 8832 E-mail cass@isbs.com
Website: www.frankcass.com

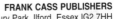

Parliaments in Asia

Philip Norton, The Lord Norton of Louth, University of Hull and Nizam Ahmed, University of Chittagong (Eds)

Legislatures span the globe. They have important consequences for their political systems. Much has been written about legislatures in Western countries, but relatively little has been written, especially in English-language literature, on legislatures in Asia. This volume provides a much-needed description and assessment of Asian parliaments. It looks in detail at the parliaments of seven cuntries – India, Bangladesh, The Republic of Korea, Japan, The People's Republic of China, Mongolia and Nepal – and assesses key variables that determine the impact of parliaments.

Contributors: Philip Norton, Nizam Ahmed, Arthur G. Rubinoff, Chan Wook Park, Akira Miyoshi, Ming Xia, Alan J.K. Sanders and Surya P. Subedi.

180 pages   1999
0 7146 4951 1 cloth
0 7146 8010 9 paper
A special issue of The Journal of Legislative Studies
The Library of Legislative Studies

Conscience and Parliament

Philip Cowley, University of Hull (Ed)

'Conscience and parliament is a timely successor to Peter Richards' seminal treatment of this subject in 1970, Parliament and Conscience. It surveys much the same battlefields but updates the account of the contests.'
Political Quarterly

This book considers how the British policy process deals with 'conscience' issues, those social issues which have strong moral overtones. Debates on these subjects have produced legislative change. Unlike in many other policy areas, this change has largely resulted from decisions made by parliament. The book describes the changes, analyses the process behind them and considers what influences MPs when the whips are removed.

224 pages   1998
0 7146 4836 1 cloth
0 7146 4388 2 paper
The Library of Legislative Studies

FRANK CASS PUBLISHERS
Newbury House, 900 Eastern Avenue, Newbury Park, Ilford, Essex IG2 7HH
Tel: +44 (020) 8599 8866 Fax: +44 (020) 8599 0984 E-mail: info@frankcass.com
NORTH AMERICA
5804 NE Hassalo Street, Portland, OR 97213 3644, USA
Tel: 800 944 6190 Fax: 503 280 8832 E-mail cass@isbs.com
Website: www.frankcass.com

National Parliaments and the European Union

Philip Norton, *The Lord Norton of Louth, University of Hull* (Ed)

'... a solid comparative collection, providing up-to-date and in-depth illustration of the potential, and problems, involved in thinking about parliamentary democracy in established EU member countries.'

International Affairs

'... To anyone seriously interested in the question of which Parliament should be legislating for Europe the book is a must.'

The European

198 pages 1996
0 7146 4691 1 cloth
0 7146 4330 0 paper
A special issue of The Journal of Legislative Studies
The Library of Legislative Studies

Members of Parliament in Western Europe: Roles and Behaviour

Wolfgang C. Müller, *University of Vienna and* Thomas Saalfeld, *University of Kent* (Eds)

Traditional comparative studies of parliaments have focused on constitutional and organisation charateristics of parliaments, or differences in the historical contexts, in which legislative assemblies have developed. The motivations of individual Members of Parliament have been neglected. This volume provides empirical work onlegislative role orientations and behaviour in six West European parliaments: Belgium, Denmark, Germany, the Netherlands, Norway and the United Kingdom. All contributions present a wealth of empirical findings on parliamentarians' role orientations in different institutional contexts.

176 pages 1997
0 7146 4821 3 cloth
0 7146 4369 6 paper
A special issue of The Journal of Legislative Studies
The Library of Legislative Studies

FRANK CASS PUBLISHERS
Newbury House, 900 Eastern Avenue, Newbury Park, Ilford, Essex IG2 7HH
Tel: +44 (020) 8599 8866 Fax: +44 (020) 8599 0984 E-mail: info@frankcass.com
NORTH AMERICA
5804 NE Hassalo Street, Portland, OR 97213 3644, USA
Tel: 800 944 6190 Fax: 503 280 8832 E-mail cass@isbs.com
Website: www.frankcass.com